Virginia W
AND THE
Fictions of Psycl

CW00922106

Women in Culture and Society
A Series Edited by Catharine R. Stimpson

Virginia Woolf
AND THE
Fictions of Psychoanalysis

Elizabeth Abel

The University of Chicago Press
Chicago and London

The University of Chicago Press, Chicago 60637
The University of Chicago Press, Ltd., London
© 1989 by The University of Chicago
All rights reserved. Published 1989
Paperback edition 1993
Printed in the United States of America

98 97 96 95 94 93   5 4 3 2

LIBRARY OF CONGRESS CATALOGING-IN-PUBLICATION DATA

Abel, Elizabeth.
  Virginia Woolf and the fictions of psychoanalysis / Elizabeth
Abel.
    p.   cm.—(Women in culture and society)
  Bibliography: p.
  Includes index.
    1. Woolf, Virginia, 1882–1941—Criticism and interpre-
tation.   2. Psychoanalysis and literature.   3. Memory in
literature.   I. Title.   II. Series.
PR6045.O72Z534   1989   89-4810
823´.912—dc19   CIP
ISBN 0-226-00079-6 (cloth)
ISBN 0-226-00081-8 (paperback)

∞ The paper used in this publication meets the minimum
requirements of the American National Standard for Information
Sciences—Permanence of Paper for Printed Library Materials,
ANSI Z39.48-1984.

For my parents
Marion Buchman Abel
Reuben Abel

and in memory of my aunt
Rebecca Bookman Weisberg

CONTENTS

FOREWORD

Spurning a single identity, postmodernism spawns contradictory images of what it might be. Often, it seems a wild young thing, at home in the carnival. From time to time, however, it seems a dour scold, at home in a bare room, stripped of the furniture and bric-a-brac of illusions. Among the most fixed if ornamental of illusions, much postmodern theory asserts, is the belief that we can seek and name our origins, no matter how hidden they might be. This belief assures geneticists that they can legitimately trace biological and biochemical lines of descent back to their beginnings. It assures genealogists that they can, as legitimately, trace lines of descent for a family, be it of blood or thought, back to their beginnings. Beware, a postmodernist might warn, one may find little that is reliable besides the fact that the names of both enterprises have a common Greek root, the verb "to engender" or "to procreate."

In 1882, the year in which Virginia Woolf was born in London, Sigmund Freud was twenty-six, learning medicine in Vienna. Each was, of course, a formidable architect and carpenter of modernity. For many who have inherited their works and deeds, they are, as well, prophets of the instabilities and discontents of postmodernity. The issue of origins—of consciousness, culture, creativity—was to compel each of them. So did the meaning and nature of sexual difference. Both Freud and Woolf conjoined the questions. They asked, for example, how a child's recognition of sexual difference arose; how forcefully that perception might then engender an individual sense of identity, a work of art, a society. The language of their answers was literary. They wrote, not equations, but narratives; not with formulae, but metaphor.

The Hogarth Press, which Virginia and Leonard Woolf began, published Freud in English. Members of her immediate family helped to found psychoanalysis in Great Britain. Nevertheless, Woolf overtly resisted it as theory and therapeutic practice. Her apparent aloofness was deceptive. In *Virginia Woolf and The Fictions of Psychoanalysis*, this polished and incisive book, Elizabeth Abel discovers and recovers the ways in which Woolf's stories "echo and rewrite the developmental fictions of psychoanalysis." So doing, Abel is a dazzling navigator among various currents of discourse that could both run with and against each other, that were both complements and competitors.

In the 1920s, Woolf offered a visionary, deep alternative to Freud's "paternal genealogies." *To the Lighthouse* plays Freud off against that alternative. Like some British anthropologists, whom Freud refused to accept, she could construe a matricentric, rather than a patricentric, commencement of human culture. Famously, she urged women writers to think back through their mothers. As Abel demonstrates, her narratives about mothers did resemble those of at least one psychoanalyst, a woman, Melanie Klein, born, like Woolf, in 1882, whose ideas were ultimately to touch such feminists as Jessica Benjamin, Nancy Chodorow and Jane Flax. In 1925, the year in which Woolf published *Mrs. Dalloway*, Klein was reconstructing the power of the mother over her children in a series of lectures to the British Psycho-Analytic Society. The mother can both feed her children and deprive them of the milk of life. Klein delivered her lectures, not at a university, nor in a hall, but at the home of Adrian and Karin Stephen, Woolf's brother and sister-in-law.

In the 1930s, however, Woolf turned from the figure of a mother's ambivalent daughter and returned to the figure of a father's ambivalent daughter. In part, she feared the Fascist celebration of "The Mother." She read Freud skeptically, but seriously. In a stunning passage, Abel compares Woolf's last novel, *Between The Acts*, to Freud's *Moses and Monotheism*. Both are "crisis texts" that tell of a world that is ending. In despair, Woolf believed that Fascism marks the triumph of patriarchy, to her the source of disorder and barbarism. As inconsolably, Freud believed that Fascism marks the decline of patriarchy, to him the containment of disorder and barbarism.

In Greek and Roman culture, Psyche, the soul, was invariably a female figure. Grammatically, her name in Greek was a noun of feminine gender. In the late seventeenth century, when English started to deploy the word "psychology," the soul had mostly metamorphosed into the mind, a psychic and mental organism, and men were more apt than women to be granted mental powers. After the late nineteenth century, when Freud gave us that word "psychoanalysis," his narratives ratified such an unhappy custom. Strong and supple, elegant and precise, *Virginia Woolf and The Fictions of Psychoanalysis* is too aware of complexity, too balanced between the riot of the carnival and the drone of the scold, to endorse any founding narrative of the origins of consciousness, culture, creativity, and sexual difference. This book does show how greatly Woolf, like Klein and her school, nurtured our understanding of women's psychologies. Such narrators also proved, since proof seemed to be necessary, how grandly women might think; how bountifully and bumptiously a revisionary Psyche might analyze love and work, their mergers and ruptures, and their rocky, fluid narratives.

Catharine R. Stimpson

ACKNOWLEDGMENTS

Four people contributed centrally to the making of this book. Carol T. Christ launched it by discerning the outlines of a book on Virginia Woolf within my inchoate early plans for a psychoanalytic reading of twentieth-century fiction by women. By commenting painstakingly on successive drafts, Michael Rogin and Alex Zwerdling helped decisively to shape both the overall argument and the readings of individual texts. Janet Adelman, to whom my debt is greatest, tirelessly discussed the manuscript with me sentence by sentence in a conversation that was woven into the substance of our friendship over many years.

Of the many other people who helped to clarify the argument pursued by this book, I want especially to thank, for their careful readings: John Bishop, Kim Chernin, Catherine Gallagher, Judith Kegan Gardiner, Marianne Hirsch, Dorothy Kaufman, Jane Marcus, and Françoise Meltzer. To W. J. T. Mitchell and Janel Mueller, my former colleagues at the University of Chicago, I owe a special debt for believing in this project from its earliest, most uncertain origins. I am also grateful to Dr. Noel Bradley for sharing with me his knowledge of British psychoanalysis in general and of Karin Stephen in particular; to Judith Hughes for guiding me through the evolution of object relations theory in England; and to Martin Friedman for checking out the resources of the British PsychoAnalytical Society in London.

By offering me a teaching position in 1982, the Department of English at the University of California, Berkeley, gave me both the time and the intellectual context that enabled the writing of this book; I am very grateful for both. I am also indebted to the University of California for granting me a Regents Junior Faculty Fellowship in 1983, and for extending to me its generous policy of maternity leave, without which the completion of this book would have been substantially delayed. I am grateful, as well, to the Rockefeller Foundation for awarding me a Humanities Fellowship in 1983–84, which enabled this book to begin to emerge from an unwieldy earlier manuscript.

Throughout my work, the staff of the University of Chicago Press has been exceptionally helpful. I want especially to thank Mary Caraway for her superlative copyediting. I am also grateful to Catherine R. Stimpson, editor of the Series on Women in Culture and Society, and to Barbara Hanrahan, former humanities editor, for their long-standing interest in this project.

Many people helped research and produce this text. Ann Kibbie and Janet Silver offered early bibliographical and editorial assistance; Judith Rosen intervened at a critical moment to untangle the mysteries of word processing; Leila May helped patiently to solve the bibliographical problems that emerged at the end; and Jane Garrity skillfully proofread and indexed the final manuscript. Tricia Moran provided indispensable scholarly and practical assistance all along the way.

My deepest gratitude is to my family: to my parents, Marion and Reuben Abel, whose support has been unwavering and unconditional; to my husband, Richard Meyer, whose affection, understanding, and faith in my work have been the ground from which this—and every—project has grown; and to my son, Benjamin Abel Meyer, whose arrival in the midst of this endeavor graced work with love.

PREFACE

We do Virginia Woolf's novels a disservice if we accept too readily her protestations about narrative: "[T]his appalling narrative business of the realist," as she called it, "getting on from lunch to dinner."[1] For much as she disdained and suspended the conventions of plotting observed by her Edwardian precursors, Woolf was obsessed with the experience of living in time. "I ask myself sometimes," she muses in the same diary entry, "whether one is not hypnotised, as a child by a silver globe, by life. . . . I should like to take the globe in my hands and feel it quietly, round, smooth, heavy, and so hold it, day after day. I will read Proust, I think. I will go backwards and forwards." Sharing Proust's conviction that the present gains depth by assimilating the past, Woolf hollows out a fictional space whose plots she invites us to discern.[2]

New modes of plotting demand new reading habits. "For the moderns," Woolf warns her readers, " 'that,' the point of interest, lies very likely in the dark places of psychology. At once, therefore, the accent falls a little differently; the emphasis is upon something hitherto ignored; at once a different outline of form becomes necessary, difficult for us to grasp, incomprehensible to our predecessors. . . . [A]nd then, as the eyes accustom themselves to twilight and discern the shapes of things in a room we see how complete the story is."[3] Woolf's own readers must learn to detect, beneath the flux of consciousness she substituted for realist narrative, fictions that tie the present to the past that slides beneath it.

Woolf's discovery of a technique for rendering the stereoscopic play of time made *Mrs. Dalloway* a breakthrough novel. Though *The Voyage Out* and *Jacob's Room* had plunged into subjectivity and radically revised closure as death, they had adapted their new conception of character to the linear structure of the Bildungsroman. In composing *Mrs. Dalloway*, Woolf discovered her famous "tunneling process," which enabled her to "tell the past by installments," as she needed them, to "dig out beautiful caves" behind her characters, to evade the tyranny of sequence by reshaping time as depth.[4] Even when her novels resume a more straightforward course from infancy to age, memory repeatedly realigns the present with the past, proliferating histories. We detect these pathways to the past by refocusing our gaze on unemphatic moments, on faint variations among recurrent metaphors, on near repetitions of sentences and scenes which gesture toward stories that are never told.

These stories echo and rewrite the developmental fictions of psychoanalysis. *Virginia Woolf and the Fictions of Psychoanalysis* examines and contextualizes this exchange within the historical moment Woolf shared with Sigmund Freud and Melanie Klein. Although Chapter 1 maps Woolf's lines of access to the psychoanalytic culture that emerged in London in the 1920s, the book is less concerned with influence than with intertextuality. Woolf, as we will see, was familiar with the debates unfolding within British psychoanalysis, but rather than addressing them specifically, she engages in her novels the set of terms that generated the debates. Reading across the discourses illuminates them both. By alerting us to certain recurrent but submerged narrative tensions in Woolf's texts, psychoanalysis helps make us the discerning readers she desired. Woolf's fiction, in turn, de-authorizes psychoanalysis, clarifying the narrative choices it makes, disclosing its fictionality.

Woolf's engagement with psychoanalysis was deeply embedded in history. Increasingly through the 1920s—the major decade of her career, and the primary focus of this study—Woolf's narratives move backward toward a maternal point of origin that Freud, in the same decade, both acknowledged and occluded and that Klein mapped with greater complexity. In the 1930s, however, Woolf swerved abruptly, although reluctantly, from Klein toward Freud as the ideologies of motherhood that flourished in the 1920s and that fostered her critique of Freud were appropriated and irretrievably contaminated for her by the fascist state. By no means a static configuration, Woolf's relationship to Klein and Freud shifts dramatically in the course of the two decades that mark her career. My project is to highlight and to explicate the signal moments that (re)define the shape of this career.

The book opens with a chapter on the gendering of narrative in psychoanalysis, anthropology, and literature in the 1920s. Freud's construction of the Oedipal narrative, Klein's excavation of the early mother-infant bond, and the rival anthropological claims for an originary matriarchy or patriarchy constitute a gender discourse of which Woolf was aware and in which her texts participate. The next three chapters focus more sharply on the multiple narratives within Woolf's two most cele-brated novels. Chapter 2 plays the submerged story of *Mrs. Dalloway* (1925), Clarissa's evolution from Bourton to London, against the Oedipal narrative Freud wrote contemporaneously. Chapters 3 and 4 move for-ward (chronologically) and backward (psychologically) to *To the Light-house* (1927), whose diverse inscriptions of the family romance make it the richest text for my inquiry. These chapters tease apart the novel's patri-centric and matricentric narratives and locate at the level of the individual sentence Woolf's dense and complex play with genealogy. Chapter 3 maps the effects of gender on the central Ramsay children, James and Cam; Chapter 4 shifts to Lily Briscoe's painting, whose spatial relations articu-late the boundary negotiations that shape the mother-infant bond.

The more deeply Woolf excavates the relation with the mother, the more intense the ambivalence she uncovers, and the greater her affinity with Klein. Her most conflicted vision finds expression not in the vulnera-ble private sphere of the autobiographically grounded *To the Lighthouse* but in the more mediated discourse of her nonfiction texts. I turn next, therefore, to *A Room of One's Own* (1929), Woolf's most explicit, ex-tended, and hostile celebration of matrilineage. *Room* marks the end of an era; in its sequel, *Three Guineas* (1938), the female subject becomes the "daughter of an educated man." Reading the discursive texts together, the project of Chapter 5, reveals the central disjunction in Woolf's career to be a shift from maternal to paternal genealogies.[5] The obsession with the father in *Three Guineas* both reflects and reinforces Woolf's new interest in Freud.

The book concludes with a reading of the final full-length works of Woolf and Freud, texts composed in the spreading shadow of fascism's victories. Woolf read Freud's *Moses and Monotheism* (1934–38) as she began to write *Between the Acts* (1939–40). In this final intersection is a final irony: the mother whose absence haunts *Between the Acts* and fuels the unwilling turn to Freud represents for Freud a catastrophic return of the repressed.

Freud, Klein, and the theorists who extend them are major figures in this book, but Woolf defines its center and shapes its plot. Her novels determine which psychoanalytic fictions will be scrutinized, and when. The scrutiny is also skewed. Dispersed through multiple discursive texts, psychoanalytic narratives are most coherently assembled at some distance from their contexts. I use the psychoanalytic essays to articulate, and to interrogate, certain narratives; but I read the literary narratives as texts.

The question of Woolf's relation to psychoanalysis has usually been posed as either a question of her response to Freud or of her anticipation of a mother-based theory. I try in this book to resist such a simple opposition by tracing the trajectory of Woolf's engagement with the developmental narratives of both Klein and Freud. By playing these narratives against each other, I seek to dislodge the binary construction of the encounter not only between Woolf and psychoanalysis but also between literature and psychoanalysis as criticism habitually couples them.[6] Woolf encourages the practice of triangulation: the differences within her texts invite a heterogeneous psychoanalytic reading; and the differences among her texts, the reversal in the hierarchy of narratives in the course of her career, solicits an account of the ways that history mediates literature's negotiations with psychoanalysis.

1

(EN)GENDERING HISTORY

The past only comes back when the present runs so smoothly that it is like the sliding surface of a deep river. Then one sees through the surface to the depths. In those moments I find one of my greatest satisfactions, not that I am thinking of the past; but that it is then that I am living most fully in the present. For the present when backed by the past is a thousand times deeper . . .

Virginia Woolf, "A Sketch of the Past"

Psychoanalysis, after all, is primarily a narrative art, concerned with the recovery of memory and desire.

Peter Brooks, *Reading for the Plot*

Woolf's novels are thick with a variety of pasts. Each character cherishes a different history, and different fictions connect these pasts to the present. By rendering the past primarily through memory, Woolf diversifies it: the pasts reconstructed in part 3 of *To the Lighthouse,* for example, differ from one another and from part 1. Evading the grip of a unitary fiction, analogous in her eyes to the ego's tyranny, Woolf generates heterogeneity not only by shifting narrative perspective but also by pluralizing history.

Each character, nevertheless, reverts to certain privileged memories that Woolf marks formally in ways she suggests in her own autobiographical essay, significantly entitled "A Sketch of the Past": "I find that scene making is my natural way of marking the past. Always a scene has arranged itself: representative; enduring. . . . Is this liability to scenes the origin of my writing impulse? . . . [I]n all the writing I have done, I have almost always had to make a scene."[1] In her fiction, Woolf transmits this strategy for marking the past to her characters. Constituted by a minisequence of self-contained actions within a constant visual space, the fictional scenes create a sense of closure, temporal and spatial, enabled by the work of memory. Against the flux of the present, these scenes, "representative; enduring," yet not accentuated, provide backdrops whose distance from the present the characters' baffled backward gaze solicits us to bridge.

Although Woolf's scenes are typically fashioned unselfconsciously, the narrative positions them deliberately. Lily Briscoe, Woolf's closest fictional representative, wonders in part 3 of *To the Lighthouse* why a scene of herself, Mrs. Ramsay, and Charles Tansley on the beach ten years earlier has "survived, ringed round, lit up, visible to the last detail, with all before it blank and all after it blank, for miles and miles."[2] Never represented in the present, the scene is tangential to the central narratives. Yet despite her bewilderment at its arbitrariness, Lily suggests why this scene is encircled and preserved: in this moment of uncharacteristic harmony between herself and Charles Tansley (the only scene in which she calls him Charles), she perceives Mrs. Ramsay's capacity to resolve "everything into simplicity," to make "of the moment something permanent (as in another sphere Lily herself tried to make of the moment something permanent)" (239, 241). The moment's distillation from the blur of memory launches Lily's revision of her relationship with Mrs. Ramsay, a relationship whose history is rendered only through discontinuous scenes.

Woolf also voices through Lily the anxieties of scene making. To enclose moments and endow them with (in Lily's words) "a wholeness not theirs in life" (286) is to tamper with the reality of change and veer dangerously close to the "nuggets of pure truth" whose abstraction from history Woolf satirizes in *A Room of One's Own*.[3] The necessity of making scenes to hold the past, one's own or others', renders the products no less fictive: "[T]his making up scenes about them, is what we call 'knowing' people, 'thinking' of them, 'being fond' of them!" Lily scoffs as she half recalls and half creates the marriage of Paul and Minta Rayley. "Not a word of it was true; she had made it up; but it was what she knew them by all the same" (258). Intimating the theater and the performance of roles more crisply outlined than the heterogeneous psyche, the distillation of experience to scenes is as suspect as it is gratifying. Hence Woolf plays the clarity of scenes against their dissolution into consciousness. Scenes narrate in her fiction by their failures to encapsulate history, by the discrepancies within them and among them. Rather than arresting narrative, they are vehicles of stories that hover in a potential literary space which the reader articulates within Woolf's texts.

Attending to stories unrecounted in Woolf's texts honors her own insistence on the places of silence in literary discourse. Woolf calls attention to the "sidelong" ways, the strategies of evasion, the tactics for provoking us "to supply what is not there" that contribute to her assessment of Jane Austen as the "most perfect artist among women." Had Austen lived, Woolf speculates, "she would have devised a method . . . for conveying not only what people say, but what they leave unsaid. . . . She would have been the forerunner of Henry James and of Proust—but enough."[4] The silence following Proust's name coyly marks Woolf's own place in this lineage. From her first fictional portrait of a novelist, Terence Hewet, who wants to write "a novel about Silence; the things people don't say," to her final novel, in which shreds of conversation dangle on the page and "silence add[s] its unmistakable contribution to talk," Woolf conforms to the aesthetic she attributes to Austen, who "by not saying something . . . says it."[5]

By requiring her reader to fabricate the links among scenes, Woolf adapts a modernist strategy she projects retrospectively on a female precursor. Of the modernists, she is as always closest to Proust. Yet if Proust translates his obsession with fragments of "pure time," apprehended in the difference between past and present moments, into a narrative technique that stimulates the reader to generate characters from discontinuous stills, Woolf juxtaposes scenes to produce not synchronic understandings of character but fictions that join a moment in the present to its antecedent.[6] It is no accident that Austen is constructed as Proust's precursor, for Woolf qualifies her alliance with literary modernism by allegiances to narrative and to matrilineage.

Woolf's interest in the fictional shapes of private history peaked in the mid-1920s, when her narrative breakthroughs freed her from a predetermined chronology and allowed her to explore the multiple links that join the present to the past. As she tunneled backward, she encountered the points of origin marked by mother and father. Powerful private sources fed her representation of origins: until her death Woolf preserved what she called her "child's vision" of "those old people—I mean father & mother—how simple, how clear, how untroubled."[7] Magnified, and in Woolf's case quintessentially gendered, the parents seen from childhood stand as untroubled—yet troubling—figures of origin. "Until I was in the forties . . . the presence of my mother obsessed me. I could hear her voice, see her, imagine what she would do or say as I went about my day's doings," Woolf insists. "Yet he [her father] too obsessed me for years. Until I wrote it out, I would find my lips moving; I would be arguing with him; raging against him; saying to myself all that I never said to him." "I was obsessed by them both unhealthily; and writing of them was a necessary act."[8] Woolf's discourse elevates this private necessity to an axiom of subjectivity: the mind, she explains in *A Room of One's Own*, "can think back through its fathers or through its mothers" (101).

By exploring the consequences of this choice, Woolf joins in the narrative project on which psychoanalysis was embarking concurrently. In the central decade of her career, Woolf's narratives interrogate Freud's. "A woman writing," the sentence from *Room* concludes, "thinks back through her mothers." By questioning the paternal genealogies prescribed by nineteenth-century fictional conventions and reinscribed by Freud, Woolf's novels of the 1920s parallel the narratives Melanie Klein was formulating simultaneously and anticipate the more radical revisions that emerged in psychoanalysis over the next half century.[9]

The challenge Woolf's fiction poses to Freud was bolstered by the discourse on gender and history that flourished in London in the 1920s. During this decade the developmental narratives emerging within psychoanalysis intersected the evolutionary narratives receding from anthropology. Gender was a constitutive feature of both genres. The patricentric and matricentric narratives launched by Freud and Klein, respectively, recapitulate in a different register the narrative contest that since 1861 had divided British social anthropologists into patriarchalists and matriarchalists.[10] Klein's move to London in 1926 and the increasingly explicit matricentric orientations of British anthropology made London the site of a heated debate about the gender of personal and social origins. One textual focus of the debate was *Totem and Taboo:* Freud's use of British anthropology to argue that "the relation to the father" is the "single concrete instance" that can solve "the problems of racial psychology" engaged, and inflamed, discussions within anthropology.[11] Reconstructing Freud's argument in the light of recent anthropological claims for "mother-right," Ernest Jones, president of the British Psycho-Analytical Society, cautioned that "few themes, if any . . . arouse more emotional prejudice than the comparison of male and female, particularly if it includes the question of the respective parts played in life by the father and the mother."[12] This question spanned literature, psychoanalysis, and anthropology. To map precisely the discursive field of Woolf's developmental narratives, we must outline the composition of their psychoanalytic counterparts, chart the routes through which the psychoanalytic narratives circulated in Woolf's environment, and identify the points at which they intersected, and were disseminated by, anthropological constructions of history.

I

Gender and narrative emerge together at the center of psychoanalysis in the mid-1920s. The critical Freudian texts contemporary with *Mrs. Dalloway* assimilate gender to history by presenting as a narrative the "complex" of feelings whose discovery in 1897 transformed, or perhaps inaugurated, psychoanalysis. Freud's letter to Wilhelm Fliess describing the "one idea of general value" that had emerged from his self-analysis emphasizes conflicting emotions, "love of the mother and jealousy of the father . . . a general phenomenon of early childhood"—an emphasis repeated in his interpretation of the emotional power of Sophocles' play, whose action, of course, diverges from the erotic itinerary Freud would grant the child.[13] Freud's early unconcern with narrative is consistent with the indifference to gender that enabled his unhesitating passage from the young girl's alleged desire for her father to his own childhood love of his mother, for it was the "universal validity" of certain feelings rather than their differentiated course that initially captured his attention.[14] Only when it was narrativized in the mid-1920s did the Oedipal story become

Freud's preeminent fiction of engendering—one Woolf (re)wrote contemporaneously.

Initially, Freud's discovery of childhood sexuality had produced an ungendered narrative. *Three Essays on the Theory of Sexuality* (1905), his major text on sexuality, examines primarily the discontinuities between infantile and adult sexuality. The text traces the course of the component sexual instincts, pleasure-seeking and autoerotic, split in childhood (and in neurotic adulthood) from one another and from the object world. In this pregenital history, the recognition of sexual difference is deferred until puberty. The Oedipus complex, submerged in this other story, is located indeterminately between childhood, to which it belongs and from which it is excluded by the polymorphousness of childhood sexuality, and the onset of puberty. It was in part to clarify the chronological and theoretical place of the Oedipus complex that Freud kept returning to the *Three Essays,* which he revised and reprinted every five years until 1924. That year, in "The Dissolution of the Oedipus Complex," he outlined a coherent Oedipal narrative that took precedence over the prior history with which it had shared pride of place uneasily.[15]

In a footnote he added to the *Three Essays* in 1920, Freud insists on an evolution: "With the progress of psycho-analytic studies the importance of the Oedipus complex has become more and more clearly evident."[16] Four years later, in the opening sentence of "The Dissolution of the Oedipus Complex," he reiterates that position, with a difference: "The significance of the Oedipus complex as the central phenomenon of the sexual period in early childhood reveals itself more and more."[17] The parallel claims and phrasing underscore the shift in emphasis from an evaluation, implicitly grounded in clinical evidence, of the psychological power of the Oedipus complex to an assertion of its centrality within a particular narrative frame. In the few years that separate these remarks, a critical advance in theory enabled the rewriting of the Oedipus complex as a story that, however endlessly replayed, assumes its coherent narrative shape in, and as the climax of, childhood sexuality.

In *The Ego and the Id* (1923) Freud offers one of his fullest expositions of the Oedipus complex as part of his account of the new structural model that maps the psyche topographically as ego, id, and superego. The Oedipal configuration is now a key to explaining the complex relations among these divisions. Focusing for the first time on the dissolution of the complex, Freud argues that the (male) child succeeds in repressing his incestuous desire by strengthening his identification with his father. This identification proceeds through a curious form of internalization, for rather than internalizing the object of unlicensed desire (the mechanism of melancholia), the boy gains the strength to renounce his mother by internalizing the law that demands renunciation. As the residue of the father's prohibition and the agency of cultural law, the superego is "the heir of the Oedipus complex."[18] Through its new role in the constitution of the psyche, the resolution of the Oedipus complex has become the story of a critical rite of passage, the story of acculturation. Developmental history now is gendered, for the (law of the) father both succeeds and supersedes the mother. If in his turn-of-the-century texts Freud emphasizes the discovery of childhood sexuality, he now stresses the accession to culture achieved by renouncing the eventual object of that sexuality. Writing the conclusion of the Oedipal story—that is, writing it as a story—also fixed its temporal boundaries. Beginning in childhood, the Oedipal narrative finds closure in the latency period enjoined by the superego.

An inconsistency nevertheless persists between the insistence in *Three Essays* that childhood sexuality is pregenital and the location of the Oedipal narrative in childhood. In another essay published in 1923 Freud wrote what he subtitled "An Interpolation into the Theory of Sexuality," in which he adds a third, genital stage to childhood sexuality, the "phallic" stage, whose name reflects the perception of sexual difference the child achieves during its reign: "The antithesis runs: a male genital organ or a castrated condition. Not until completion of development at the time of puberty does the polarity of sexuality coincide with *male* and *female*."[19] Since Freud's discourse never transcends the phallic version of sexual difference, his attempt to locate the boundaries of the phallic stage is unconvincing; yet it is important, for by coinciding with the Oedipus complex, the phallic stage joins the question of castration, posed during this stage by the child's sight of the female genitals, to the dynamics of the Oedipal narrative.

In "The Dissolution of the Oedipus Complex" Freud integrates the two theoretical moves in a definitive closure that links the paternal prohibition to the threat of castration in a full account of what he called "the temporal and causal relations . . . between Oedipus-complex, sexual intimidation (the threat of castration), formation of the super-ego and advent of the latency period": in other words, a narrative.[20] The description of conflicting but static love and hate has become a conventional Aristotelian plot with a beginning, middle, and end. The visual moment whose consequences Freud began to ponder in the essay on the phallic stage has evolved into a peripeteia: "Some day or other it happens that the child whose own penis is such a proud possession obtains a sight of the genital parts of a little girl; he must then become convinced of the absence of a penis in a creature so like himself. With this, however, the loss of his own penis becomes imaginable, and the threat of castration achieves its delayed effect."[21] However insistently the sight is disavowed (the penis will grow; it is really there; etc.), it is the pivotal experience that convinces the boy to heed the father's prohibition. The very hinging of the plot on a single moment of vision (even one whose consequences are deferred) reveals the degree of emplottedness: from the background story of multiple glimpses and disavowals, of many rescinded and renewed renunciations, emerge the distilled and elegant outlines of a motivated sequence.[22]

Coexisting with this sequence (in which the rise of tension toward a visual climax that enables resolution is isomorphic with the "part of the body, so easily excitable and changeable, and so rich in sensation" which "occupies the boy's interest to a high degree, and never ceases to provide new problems for his epistemophilic impulse") is the female Oedipal story, "far more shadowy and full of gaps."[23] The new centrality of the castration threat disrupts the "precisely analogous" course Freud had hypothesized for the girl only one year before.[24] When the Oedipal story evolves into a full and fully gendered plot, it generates a feminine variant whose outlines (like those of the female genitals?) are seemingly harder to discern.

In 1925, the year *Mrs. Dalloway* presented Woolf's version of the daughter's Oedipal narrative, Freud turned his attention to the feminine plot. In "Some Psychical Consequences of the Anatomical Distinction between the Sexes," he articulates for the first time the inverted sequence of this plot: the knowledge of "castration" that propels the boy toward the conclusion of his Oedipal narrative inaugurates the girl's by initiating her turn from her mother, the initial object of all children's attachment, to her father, the object of her Oedipal love. In both narratives, the critical event is the sight of the other sex; but the boy sees a horrifying absence, and the girl an enviable presence. In a single moment of searing clarity, "[s]he makes her judgement and her decision. . . . She has seen it and knows that she is without it and wants to have it."[25] With desire comes the knowledge of her own inferiority, and her mother's. In his further studies of female sexuality in two subsequent essays (to which I will return in Chapter 2), Freud examines how the girl negotiates the turn from mother to father. In this initial formulation, he is primarily concerned with "the different paths along which sexual life develops": the narrative consequences of the anatomical distinction between the sexes.[26]

These consequences are most clearly marked in the double origins of the female narrative, for the female Oedipal story itself is weakly plotted by Freud. Ideally, he claims, the girl succeeds in shifting her attachment from mother to father by slipping "into a new position along the line— there is no other way of putting it—of the equation 'penis = child'. She gives up her wish for a penis and puts in place of it a wish for a child: and *with that purpose on view* she takes her father as a love-object. Her mother becomes the object of her jealousy. The girl has turned into a little woman."[27] Yet if Freud sees a clear, albeit costly, entry into the triangular configuration that bestows adult femininity, he is far more uncertain about the exit. Lacking a penis, and thus not subject to castration, the girl need never renounce her father, who, moreover, dovetails psychically with his

eventual substitutes—typically, older and more powerful men who preserve central features of his role. The Oedipal plot, deprived of closure, is
coextensive with the daughter's life. If she is fortunate enough to give
birth to the son that compensates for womanhood, however, the outlines
of her narrative are further complicated. Presumed to be totally fulfilling,
yet nevertheless a substitute, the son transforms her from the subject of
desire in one narrative to its object in another. Simultaneously the gratified, undesiring mother and the endlessly desiring daughter, woman is
granted a plot whose increasing incoherence anticipates Freud's confes-
sion that "[t]he great question that has never been answered and which
[he] has not yet been able to answer despite [his] thirty years of research
into the feminine soul, is 'What does a woman want?' "28

Freud did, however, answer the question of narrative difference by
focusing attention on the female Oedipal plot's "prehistory." In realizing
that the girl's Oedipus complex is a "secondary formation," built on an
earlier layer of exclusive and powerful love for the mother, Freud radically
gendered developmental narrative, decisively split between a maternal
prehistory and a paternal history. For the boy this prehistory, always
already tempered by his identification with his father, is continuous with,
and assimilated to, the Oedipal relation to the mother; for the girl it is
uniquely feminine, dyadic (since the father plays no role), and discontinuous with "history."29 As the metaphors of strata suggest, moreover,
writing the feminine narrative reshaped Freud's composition of history.

Narrative order is now reversed. Rather than proceeding from oral
to anal to phallic stages, for example, or sketching the "temporal and
causal relations" of the Oedipal narrative—as he did with the male, Freud
reads from the onset of "history" backward to remote, scarcely visible
antecedents. Instead of being the end point of a clearly delineated evolution, the Oedipus complex becomes a point of origin before which
everything recedes into the indistinction of prehistory. As the ungendered
pregenital terrain of the *Three Essays* is gendered in terms of object choice,
and the contrast between mother and father replaces the sequence of
libidinal stages, the relations of background and foreground supersede
those of chronology. Accordingly, as Freud continued to explore these
relations, his metaphors became more overtly spatial. In "Female Sexuality" (1931), where he devises the term "pre-Oedipus," he immediately
endows it with a spatial resonance in his famous archaeological metaphor:
"Our insight into this early, pre-Oedipus, phase in girls comes to us as a
surprise, like the discovery, in another field, of the Minoan-Mycenean
civilization behind the civilization of Greece."30 In a new construction of
anteriority, the matriarchal past is placed "behind" patriarchal history. In
the years that Woolf was digging beautiful caves behind her characters to
reconstruct the past as a backdrop to the present, Freud was writing a
female developmental narrative that spatializes history.

Freud launches the project of writing this female prehistory into the discourse of psychoanalysis. Although he projects onto this terrain the metaphors of obscurity which consistently characterize his rhetoric on femininity, he nevertheless tries to articulate a narrative for the pre-Oedipal. Yet the retrospective vision, the predetermined outcome of the turn from mother to father, clearly shapes this narrative. Prehistory is written from the vantage point of history. What Freud sees as predominant in this stage, consequently, is an ambivalence galvanized retroactively by the realization of the mother's "castration." Some sources of the daughter's grievances, Freud speculates, are oral: complaints of being inadequately suckled or of being denied nurturance because of the birth of a sibling, or, conversely, fears of being devoured by the mother, which he interprets as projections of the daughter's aggression. Yet these distinctively mother-infant issues are overshadowed by "the reproach that her mother did not give her a proper penis—that is to say, brought her into the world as a female."[31] The mother who presides over the Minoan-Mycenean stage is implicitly the phallic mother; with the discovery of her "castration" the stage comes to an end. As the Oedipal narrative shapes its prehistory, the phallus colonizes the mother's body, and the prospect of a distinctively mother-based plot is simultaneously opened and closed.

II

Melanie Klein devoted her career to writing the mother-infant plot. From the early 1920s, when she developed a mode of play therapy which she believed afforded access to the unconscious of young children in a manner analogous to Freud's verbal techniques, she began mapping the earliest stages of infantile subjectivity, transformed in her account from an indistinct prehistory to a passionate preverbal drama made articulate through play.[32] Klein's reconstruction of the developmental narrative made a dramatic entry into England with her lectures on child analysis at the British Psycho-Analytical Society in July 1925. "Melanie Klein has just given a course of six lectures in English before our Society on 'Frühanalyse'. She made an extraordinarily deep impression on all of us and won the highest praise both by her personality and her work," Ernest Jones wrote to Freud at the lectures' conclusion.[33] Klein's enthusiastic reception had been prepared by the reports sent by Alix Strachey, captivated by Kleinian theory during her year-long analysis with Karl Abraham in Berlin, to James Strachey, who relayed them to the British Society. "Jones, of course, is an absolutely heart-and-soul whole-hogging pro-Melanie," James wrote to his wife after presenting the British Society with Alix's abstract of Klein's 1924 lecture to the Berlin Society; "Melanie . . . bids fair to becoming a succès fou," he reassured her again after the British Society voted unanimously to invite Klein to lecture that summer in London.[34] These lectures were a turning point in the evolution of the British Society; and, whether it was because Klein engaged the society's already strong interest in child psychology (due, Jones speculates, to the society's unusually large number of women analysts) or because she alleviated the "inferiority feelings" plaguing a society that had not produced a distinctive theoretical perspective since its founding by Jones in 1919 (in Edward Glover's subsequent and more cynical account), her permanent move from Berlin to London in 1926 and her increasingly pronounced deviation from Freud shaped the course of British psychoanalysis.[35] Although Klein continued to modify her position over the next thirty years, her 1925 lectures, published in an altered form by the Hogarth Press as *The Psycho-Analysis of Children* (1932) and hailed by Jones as "a momentous event in the history of psycho-analysis," represent the nucleus of her revision.[36]

Klein's narrative begins with the newborn's first feeding, the originary moment in her account of an intense and phantasmatic relation to the mother. In this early stage the infant knows the mother only as a breast, the earliest object of an infantile desire that Klein (unlike Freud) depicts as object-seeking from its inception. The Kleinian infant, engaged from birth in phantasy (distinguished, by its origin in the unconscious, from "fantasy"), invests the mother's breast "from which all goodness flows" with magical powers imbibed with the milk in a partial restoration of prenatal unity: "In phantasy the child sucks the breast into himself, chews it up and swallows it; thus he feels that he has actually got it there, that he possesses the mother's breast within himself."[37] The intense gratification reinforces an idealization that experience frustrates, for the craved reunion is never achieved, the unlimited desire never fulfilled—and the resulting rage generates a complementary phantasy of a "bad," withholding breast. Moreover, Klein draws from Freud's later works to posit a death instinct the infant converts to aggression and projects onto the mother, transforming its fear of annihilation into fear of maternal persecution. The pleasure of eating thus encounters internal as well as external interference that, in a vicious circle, intensifies greed, generates new frustration, and compounds the aggression, which projection reconstructs in the image of a retaliatory breast threatening to devour the infant. As anger evolves into a desire to penetrate the mother's body and take possession of its contents, the infant imagines a world populated by objects ready to "devour it, scoop out the inside of its body, cut it to pieces, poison it—in short, compassing its destruction by all the means which sadism can devise."[38] Hence Klein designates the first three months of life the "paranoid position" (the choice of "position" emphasizing a psychological mode not confined to the era in which it originates); she later appends "schizoid" to "paranoid," to underline the splitting of the world into gratifying and hostile objects modeled on the breast.

The persecutory breast is internalized in the infant's psyche as the nucleus of a punitive superego (subsequently compounded by phantasies of the father); the phrase "gnawing of conscience" (*Gewissenbisse*), Klein proposes, testifies to the superego's origin in the reintrojection of projected oral rage.[39] In a crucial deviation from Freud, Klein transfers the formation of the superego from the paternal prohibition that resolves the Oedipal situation to the earliest relation to the nursing mother's body. As the focus of the developmental narrative recedes from sexuality and repression to hunger and oral pleasure and anger, the superego is divorced from any notion of acculturation as the passage through the castration complex into a symbolic register, and the father is displaced from his critical position as the cultural origin of the human subject. The place of the Oedipal resolution is held in Klein's narrative by the successor to the early relation to the mother's breast: a more complex relation to the mother.

The second three months of life, the critical era in the Kleinian narrative, are marked by a shift from the paranoid to the "depressive" position produced by the infant's growing ability to integrate contradictory perceptions. This shift "is of the most crucial importance in development[,] . . . a crossroads from which the ways determining the whole mental make-up radiate in different directions."[40] As the split phantasies of the breast begin to coalesce into a single ambivalent image of the mother, the infant experiences anxiety and grief produced by the realization that the object of its rage is the suddenly endangered object of its love. At risk in the infant's phantasy is not only the external mother but also her newly integrated inner counterpart. Paranoia gives way to fear for the mother's survival and to grief over a loss that devastates the child's internal world. Coinciding (in England) with the period of weaning, the depressive period is the prototype of mourning: "The object that is being mourned is . . . all that the breast and the milk have come to stand for in the infant's mind: namely, love, goodness and security[,] . . . felt by the baby to be lost, and lost as a result of his own uncontrollable greedy and destructive phantasies and impulses against his mother's breasts."[41] From the new experience of loss and guilt, the obverse of paranoia, emerges the desire to make reparation to the mother, to reconstruct the damaged object psychically, to heal, to make whole, to revive a "good" internal object. Reparative desires are "the driving forces in all constructive activities and interests" and the motivation for rebuilding a secure internal world.[42] At the "crossroads" of the Kleinian narrative is not a renunciation of the mother but her imaginary regeneration. Integral to the Kleinian framework is a notion of art as a simultaneously formal and therapeutic project of reconstructing and externalizing a fragmented inner world.[43] For Kleinians, culture, opposed not as (paternal) law to instinct but as creativity to inner chaos, emerges from the impulse to make reparation to the mother.

In the Kleinian narrative the Oedipus complex, relocated in the first year of life, is shaped by its prehistory. "Heavily shrouded" by the early relation to the mother—Klein transposes Freud's metaphors of obscurity—the Oedipus complex dovetails with the depressive position.[44] The boy's libidinal development is stimulated and reinforced by the dynamics of reparation as genital desire becomes a means of phantasmatically repairing the damage wrought by oral aggression, "of giving gratification and children to his mother and of making reparation."[45] Reparative desires likewise shape the resolution of the Oedipus complex. Supplementing the boy's castration anxiety, itself derived from early fears of maternal retaliation, are guilt over aggression toward the father, fear that the damage wished on him will cause the mother pain, and a desire to make reparation to him by renouncing the contested object of desire: the operations of the depressive position now encompass the father. No longer the turning point of the developmental narrative, the Oedipal resolution is now embedded in the psychic mechanisms emerging from the early relation to the mother.

These mechanisms are even more enduring for the girl, diverted by the frustrations of weaning from the breast to the father's penis, initially imagined as a source of "tremendous and never-ending oral gratification."[46] The critical turn from the mother to the father, precipitated for Freud by the sight of the penis the daughter knows instantly she lacks and desires, is reconceived as an evolution that requires no perception of inferiority. Downplayed for the boy, the castration complex disappears altogether from the narrative of the girl. "Freud has come to the conclusion that it is the castration complex that introduces the girl's Oedipus complex, and that what makes her turn away from her mother is the grudge she bears her for not having given her a penis of her own. . . . But, according to my view," Klein explains, "what she primarily wants is not to possess a penis of her own as an attribute of masculinity, but to incorporate her father's penis as an object of oral gratification."[47] The vaginal sensations Klein posits from early infancy, and the girl's unconscious knowledge of the penis as "the giver of children," transform oral into genital desire.[48] Klein surreptitiously rewrites Freud's equation "child = penis," according to which the girl turns to the father to compensate for her own deficiency, as "penis = child," which recasts the penis as an instrument of the daughter's desire.[49] According to the sexual phantasies of Kleinian infants, however, the father's penis resides, as a consequence of intercourse, with the babies, milk, and feces that inhabit the mother's body. This notion of the incorporative body, Klein proposes, is the real meaning of the "'woman with a penis'"—transformed in this reading from a defense against the knowledge of castration to a (frightening) image of maternal capaciousness.[50] Maternal plenitude, rather than lack, incites the daughter's anger. The newly perceived inclusiveness of the mother's body, now seen to contain and withhold not only milk but also the father's penis and the children it bestows, compounds the daughter's early rage and intensifies her phantasied attacks. Oedipal rivalry strengthens the ambivalent tie to the mother. The more aggressively the daughter imagines plundering her mother's body, the more she fears both a maternal retaliation that will rob her of her own childbearing capacity (the counterpart, in Klein's account, to the boy's castration anxiety) and her own Pyrrhic victory in mangling the body that furnishes the objects of her own desire. Increasingly violent phantasies generate increasingly powerful reparative desires. By turning to the father, the daughter ironically resituates herself in her early relation to her mother.

III

Klein delivered her 1925 lectures at 50 Gordon Square, the home of Woolf's brother and sister-in-law, Adrian and Karin Stephen, who were both approaching the completion of their psychoanalytic training. The Stephens' drawing room was an appropriate site for the lectures, not only because it was spacious enough to accommodate the society's twenty-seven members, twenty-seven associates, and their guests but also because it dramatized the intellectual home psychoanalysis had found in Bloomsbury.[51] The site of the lectures, which were organized and translated by the Stracheys, also signaled the intimacy between James Strachey and Adrian Stephen, who boarded with James at 41 Gordon Square between 1923 and 1926 during the rift in the Stephens' marriage, a separation that also heightened Adrian's intimacy with his sister. "Next door" (by her own account) in Tavistock Square, Virginia was "making up" *To the Lighthouse*.[52] Three days after the conclusion of the lectures, Adrian visited his sister. Her diary entry for that day proceeds from a speculation on "father & mother & child in the garden," her current plan for the autobiographically grounded *To the Lighthouse*, to a note on Adrian's visit: "[We] talked of cancer," she comments laconically.[53] Did they also discuss the "momentous event" that had transpired at Adrian's home during the preceding three weeks?[54] Given that Adrian and Karin had hosted the event, that the Stracheys had arranged it, and that Woolf had known James Strachey for fifteen years through his brother Lytton, perhaps her closest friend, it seems extremely likely that the lectures were discussed. Woolf's knowledge of psychoanalysis, she repeatedly declared, came not from "study" but from "superficial talk" such as that we might imagine to have taken place with Adrian after the event that captured the attention of the British psychoanalytic world.[55]

Woolf's reticence about psychoanalysis is both characteristic and complex; interpreting it requires that we heed her own insistence on authorial silences, on what is left unsaid. Six weeks before Klein's lectures, and the night before the Hogarth Press published both *Mrs. Dalloway* and the third volume of Freud's *Collected Papers* (the five case histories that James and Alix Strachey had devoted nearly four years to translating), James Strachey dined with Virginia and Leonard Woolf. "Last night I dined with the Wolves, the other guest being Dadie [George Rylands]. Virginia made a more than usually ferocious onslaught upon psychoanalysis and psychoanalysts, more particularly the latter," James wrote to Alix in Berlin.[56] The simultaneous publication of the different and definitive projects must have primed the occasion for discursive rivalry, and the scathing critique of psychiatrists in *Mrs. Dalloway* makes Woolf's "onslaught" no surprise. More surprising is her own representation of the conversation. "Yesterday was a terrific chatter day . . . James & Dadie to finish off with. . . . Dadie & James very easy & affable," Woolf notes in her diary before recounting in some detail her conversation with Dadie about how poets "fix on to a word & fill it out with meaning & make it symbolic."[57] The ferocious onslaught is unrecorded; psychoanalysis is displaced by literary criticism, discord by affability; and Woolf's literary terrain is fortified against a rival discourse. We must read between the lines of James's account to infer from his comparatives both the frequency of Woolf's comments about psychoanalysis and the distinction she drew between the theory and its practitioners, and we must read Woolf's silences for signs of the anxiety provoked by the authoritative discourse on "the dark places of psychology" to which she also staked a claim. Psychoanalysis (in Alix Strachey's account) was rejected as a treatment for Woolf's breakdowns because of the fear that it might endanger her creativity; psychoanalytic theory posed an analogous threat to her discursive primacy.[58]

Woolf's aversion to writing about psychoanalysis is matched by her resistance to reading about it. She claims to have avoided reading Freud until 1939, a deferral that must have required some effort, since from 1924, when Leonard Woolf agreed to James Strachey's request to take over publication of the International Psycho-Analytical Library, the Woolfs' own Hogarth Press published the English translation of every text Freud wrote, as well as nearly seventy additional volumes of the International Psycho-Analytical Library. The Hogarth Press publication of four volumes of Freud's *Collected Papers* in 1924–25 was the first systematic English version of the Freudian corpus (superseding A. A. Brill's earlier translations of individual texts) and the turning point in the dissemination of psychoanalytic theory in England.[59] Woolf's letters and diaries make it clear that she was involved in the publication process, but with one exception (to which I shall return) she appears to have avoided opening the books, which she consistently represents as objects to be handled rather than as texts. Her earliest reference sets the tone: "[A]ll the psycho-analytic books have been dumped in a fortress the size of Windsor castle in ruins upon the floor."[60] The next reference, days before the publication of the first volume of the *Collected Papers*, repeats the maneuver displayed in her account of the evening with James Strachey: "Dadie came back yesterday & we had a jolly afternoon . . . doing up Freud. I in two jackets, for it is freezing, & hair down; he in shirtsleeves. Thus one gets to know people; sucks the marrow out."[61] The strikingly uncharacteristic figure of predation, which for Woolf would typically condemn a relationship (it anticipates, for example, her hostile portrait of her analyst brother brooding "like a vulture" over a woman in despair), hints that a displacement from text to person defends against an interdicted curiosity.[62]

Woolf's anxiety may have been heightened by the distinctive cast psychoanalysis assumed in England in general and within her immediate Bloomsbury world in particular. Paradoxically, Bloomsbury contributed to constructing a singularly literary version of psychoanalytic discourse, which intensified both its appeal and its potential threat to writers of imaginative texts. In the first nontechnical essay on Freud in English, a review of Brill's 1914 translation of *The Psychopathology of Everyday Life*, Leonard Woolf promoted a reading of the Freudian text as literature: "Whether one believes in [Freud's] theories or not, one is forced to admit that he writes with great subtlety of mind, a broad and sweeping imagination more characteristic of the poet than the scientist or medical practitioner. . . . [H]is works are often a series of brilliant and suggestive hints."[63] The characterization of psychoanalysis as a literary rather than a scientific discourse became a leitmotiv in England; radically divided between medical and humanist sectors in their evaluation of Freudian theory, British reviewers reached consensus on the imaginative status of the Freudian text. "Imagination" is the recurrent term in the fierce debate that the publication of the *Collected Papers* provoked in the letters section of the *Nation and Athenaeum* (of which Leonard Woolf was literary editor) from June 1925 until October 1925, when an exasperated editor decreed, "This correspondence must now cease."[64] Unsympathetic correspondents decried the high ratio of psychoanalytic theory to evidence, the reliance on analogy rather than induction, the lack of controlled tests or verifiable data, in short, "the flagrant and persistent disregard of scientific method."[65] The only defense of psychoanalysis on scientific grounds depended on a reinterpretation of those grounds: critics who call Freud "unscientific," argued A. G. Tansley, whose reviews had launched the debate, forget that such unverifiable entities as libido or the unconscious are "constructs— fictions as Vaihinger calls such aids to thought—of the same logical status as innumerable others which are the everyday tools of science".[66] The fictionality of psychoanalytic texts was widely conceded: "[A]t the present stage," wrote a nonaligned contributor to the debate, "the argument in favour of Freudian theories would be very little weakened if it were to be admitted that every case published hitherto had been wholly invented by

Professor Freud in order to illustrate his ideas and to make them more vivid to the minds of his readers."[67] Commentators elsewhere underscored that psychoanalysis found confirmation not through scientific methodology but through "its close correspondence with the taboos and rituals of primitive peoples[,] . . . the forms of all great human myths, and all dramatic poems which approach to mythical significance."[68]

The emphasis on the humanistic cast of psychoanalysis was strongly endorsed within the psychoanalytic community. "Psycho-analysis is both science and art," insisted Ella Freeman Sharpe, a member of the British Society, a former literature teacher, and Adrian Stephen's analyst from 1926 to 1927; psychoanalysts "lay bare in their own minds and the minds of others the dramas that the great poets project on to the world's stage."[69] The British Society, which had the highest percentage of nonmedical analysts anywhere in the world (40 percent by late 1920s), attracted members of the British intelligentsia with extensive training in the humanities. The society established especially strong ties to Cambridge, the university that also served as Bloomsbury's feeding ground. "By the early twenties," according to Edward Glover, "few Cambridge undergraduates having any pretensions to advanced thought failed to profess an interest in Freudian psychology."[70] Even for Cambridge graduates psychoanalysis served, as it did for the Stracheys and the Stephens, as a magnet for disaffected intellectuals. Leonard Woolf describes his brother-in-law's dramatic conversion: Adrian Stephen, a former student of medieval law at Cambridge, "suddenly threw the Middle Ages and law out of the window, and, with his wife Karin, became a qualified doctor and professional psychoanalyst."[71] Karin threw over philosophy; Alix, modern languages; and James, the lethargy of his university years.

Psychoanalysis in England most nearly realized Freud's desire for an autonomous movement divorced from psychiatry and working "to affirm itself in the entire cultural field."[72] The cultural emphasis of British psychoanalysis, apparent in Ernest Jones's *Essays in Applied Psycho-Analysis* (1923), which spans anthropology, literature, folklore, and painting, made psychoanalytic discourse an especially attractive and accessible cultural idiom. Bronislaw Malinowski opens his anthropological critique of psychoanalysis by noting (disapprovingly) that "psycho-analysis has had within the last ten years [1917–1927] a truly meteoric rise in popular favour. It has exercised a growing influence over contemporary literature, science, and art. It has in fact been for some time the popular craze of the day."[73] Other observers similarly attest to the status of psychoanalysis as a "popular craze": "Freud's theories infiltrated in an expurgated form from the gardens of Hampstead to the squares of Bloomsbury and salons of Kensington. In the bus, the newspapers, and underground a new vocabulary appeared."[74] A more serious rendition of psychoanalysis infiltrated literary circles. According to the poet Bryher, "You could not have escaped

Freud in the literary world of the early twenties. Freud! All literary London discovered Freud about 1920[;] . ... the theories were the great subject of conversation wherever one went at that date. To me Freud is literary England . . . after the first war. People did not always agree but he was always taken in the utmost seriousness."[75]

The literary coloration that gave British psychoanalysis a distinctively seductive and invasive cast was only one likely cause of anxiety for Woolf, however. Another was the opposite guise of psychoanalysis, which might resemble fiction in comparison to science but nevertheless resembles science in comparison to fiction, as Woolf argues in a review, "Freudian Fiction" (1920), that casts fiction as a victim, rather than an attribute, of psychoanalytic discourse. Woolf structures her critique of J. D. Beresford's *An Imperfect Mother* as an opposition between science and fiction: "The triumphs of science are beautifully positive. But for novelists the matter is much more complex. . . . Yes, says the scientific side of the brain, that is interesting; that explains a great deal. No, says the artistic side of the brain, that is dull." Woolf insists that she disputes not psychoanalytic interpretations of infantile experience but a colonization of the literary field that transforms "characters" into "cases" through the application of a doctrinal "key" that "simplifies rather than complicates."[76] In Beresford's case the "key" is Oedipal.

Woolf's uneasiness about the psychoanalytic simplification of character recurs in her response to Lytton Strachey's psychobiographical *Elizabeth and Essex* (1928). Lytton had dedicated the book (appropriately) to James and Alix and had mailed a copy of it to Freud as a gift. In his response, Freud praises the text's profundity: "I am acquainted with all your earlier publications, and have read them with great enjoyment. But the enjoyment was essentially an aesthetic one. This time you have moved me more deeply, for you yourself have reached greater depths. You are aware of what other historians so easily overlook. . . . [Y]ou show that you are steeped in the spirit of psychoanalysis."[77] "[T]hat lively superficial meretricious book[,] . . . so feeble, so shallow," Woolf wrote in dismay about Lytton's latest work.[78] By deploring the damage psychoanalysis could inflict on aesthetic values, Woolf set herself apart from Bloomsbury's discursive writers, in particular Leonard Woolf and Lytton Strachey, both early advocates of Freud, and allied herself with the art critics, Roger Fry and Clive Bell. Leonard Woolf's universalizing claim that "in the decade before 1924 in the so-called Bloomsbury circle there was great interest in Freud and psycho-analysis, and the interest was extremely serious" fails to do justice to a division in the Bloomsbury circle.[79]

"I have just finished your pamphlet," Virginia Woolf wrote to Roger Fry in September 1924, after reading the proofs of *The Artist and Psycho-Analysis,* soon to be published by the Hogarth Press, "so I must write off at once and say how it fills me with admiration and stirs up in me, as you alone do, all sorts of bats and tadpoles—ideas, I mean, which have clung to my roof and lodged in my mind, and now I'm all alive with pleasure."[80] Fry's essay, originally delivered to the British Psychological Society, attacks Freud's claims in "Creative Writers and Daydreaming" that art is produced to gratify desires into which we are enticed through the "bribe" of form. Reversing these priorities, Fry argues that the distinctive aesthetic activity is the disinterested creation or contemplation of formal relations detached from the emotions evoked by representation. Woolf's pleasure in Fry's essay centers on this foregrounding of form: "I'm puzzling, in my weak witted way, over some of your problems: about 'form' in literature," she continues. She also makes it clear that she prefers Fry's argument to Clive Bell's rehearsal of it in "Dr. Freud on Art," which had just appeared, and would launch a debate, in the *Nation and Athenaeum*.[81] What both essays clarify, however, is that certain of Woolf's objections to psychoanalysis are specific to Freud, for the aesthetic is not devalued by Klein or her followers.

Another specifically Freudian and troubling feature of psychoanalytic theory is suggested in a letter Woolf wrote a few days later, which contains her only comments on reading the Hogarth edition of Freud: "[W]e are publishing all Dr. Freud, and I glance at the proof and read how Mr. A. B. threw a bottle of red ink on to the sheets of his marriage bed to excuse his impotence to the housemaid, but threw it in the wrong place, which unhinged his wife's mind,—and to this day she pours claret on the dinner table. We could all go on like that for hours; and yet these Germans think it proves something—besides their own gull-like imbecility."[82] Woolf was reading "The Sense of Symptoms," Lecture 17 of the *Introductory Lectures*, in which Freud recounts the case of a woman whose obsessional habit of running into the dining room, summoning the housemaid, and standing by a table with a big stain on its tablecloth corrects, rather than repeats, the behavior of her impotent husband, who on their wedding night poured red ink on the sheets to protect himself from the housemaid's scorn. In Freud's interpretation, the wife's behavior undoes her husband's shame (since she proudly displays the stain) and thus his impotence; she exculpates him in order to deny her own sexuality, a denial that constitutes the "inmost core" of her illness. Woolf's caricature, replete with a national stereotype ("these Germans") she criticizes in the novel she was writing concurrently, does not differ greatly from a psychoanalytic reduction of a literary text. Her transformation of the wife's highly motivated complicity into meaningless repetition derives from anger triggered not, presumably, by Freud's basic point, that symptoms have meaning, but by his insistence on the centrality of (hetero)sexuality and by the prurient interest and sense of conquest his rhetorical questions display: "Were you not struck by the way in which this unobtrusive obsessional action has led us into the intimacies of the patient's life? A woman cannot have anything much more intimate to tell than the story of her wedding-night. Is it a matter of chance and of no further significance that we have arrived precisely at the intimacies of sexual life?"[83] The thrice-repeated "intimacies" (once as "intimate") suggests a delectation in the discovery of (women's) secrets. If the "key" in Beresford's novel is Oedipal, here it is sexual (and phallic), the key to the bedroom door: a key possessed by Freud exclusively.

Woolf's relationship to psychoanalysis was not monolithic: many of her objections to Freudian theory do not apply to the discourse launched by Klein, which de-emphasizes sexuality, values the aesthetic, and, perhaps most importantly, calls into question the prevailing hierarchy of gender. There was, furthermore, some mutual recognition of the new discursive ties that a feminine revision of psychoanalysis enables. Two women analysts who were influenced by Klein explicitly acknowledge Woolf as a feminist theorist. In "Variations of Technique in Different Neuroses" (1931) Ella Freeman Sharpe quotes the passage from *A Room of One's Own* in which the narrator's speculation on the Manx cat—"was he born so, or had he lost his tail in an accident?"—parodies the Freudian construction of sexual difference as a question of castration. Through its title, *A Life of One's Own* (1936), Marion Milner's journal about the discovery of femininity also pays tribute to *A Room of One's Own*.[84] Woolf's divided attitude toward psychoanalysis appears in her accounts of her encounters with Freud and Klein, both of whom she met in the early months of 1939. "We [were] like patients in chairs," she notes of her visit to Freud at 22 Maresfield Gardens, where the Woolfs were entertained in "a great library" by a "screwed up shrunk very old man[,] . . . an old fire now flickering."[85] Woolf met Klein at the Twenty-fifth Anniversary Dinner of the British Psycho-Analytical Society, to which she was invited by Adrian. Amidst "food profuse, snatched, uncharacteristic," she "set upon & committed to ask to dinner Mrs. Klein."[86] Such a deliberate invitation suggests some awareness of Klein's stature and her theory; the portrait Woolf subsequently drew of Klein hints at a link between the person and the theory. "A woman of character & force & some submerged—how shall I say—not craft, but subtlety: something working underground. A pull, a twist, like an undertow: menacing. A bluff grey haired lady, with large bright imaginative eyes."[87] Klein's psyche, in this rendition, is isomorphic with her representation of the psyche; primitive forces work underground; a Minoan-Mycenean civilization, more tumultuous than Freud's, threatens to engulf a superstructure (and perhaps the viewer as well). The progress from land to water, from "underground" to "undertow," is gendered in Woolf's lexicon: Lily Briscoe's longing to become "like waters poured into one jar, inextricably the same, one with the [maternal] object one adored" is only Woolf's most celebrated figure of the daughter's desire to dissolve into the mother (79). Klein's mother-based discourse, whose difference from the discourse of libido may echo in the contrast between the "undertow" and the "old fire now flickering," enabled Woolf's closest link to the fictions of psychoanalysis.

Woolf's preoccupation with maternal origins was echoed in the psychoanalytic culture with which she was most immediately affiliated. Although the Stracheys and the Stephens eventually joined the non-aligned Middle Group when the 1942–44 Controversial Discussions split the British Psycho-Analytical Society, they were Klein enthusiasts in the 1920s.[88] The best sample of the discourse to which Woolf had informal access is provided by Karin Stephen, the most prolific writer of the group and a well-established popularizer; in Ernest Jones's preface to the published version of Karin's lectures on psychoanalysis (the first public lecture series on psychoanalysis ever given at Cambridge), he praises her ability to communicate with people trained in other fields.[89] In these lectures and in *On Human Misery,* an unpublished manuscript which Leonard Woolf commissioned for the Hogarth Press as a general introduction to psycho-analysis, Karin repeatedly qualifies the prevailing Freudian framework with Kleinian examples of oral desire, rage, and fear, whose neglect by Freud she deems *"a very important omission indeed"* (her emphasis). She also underscores the mother's imaginative primacy: "Mother then, now satisfying, now unsatisfying, is the first outside reality (the first 'not-me') on which the fantastic image of the Great Omnipotent Being, conjured up by the baby's imagination, is based." "Why," she asks, "does our civiliza-tion worship God in a male form when the baby's cry for its mother is the same uttered later in the turn to God?"[90]

Clear analogies link the tensions that Klein introduced into psycho-analytic discourse and those that fracture Woolf's major narratives. The challenge *To the Lighthouse* poses to the Oedipal story of James Ramsay (who is modeled on Adrian Stephen), for example, is echoed two years later in a piece of literary criticism written by Adrian's analyst: "The Impatience of Hamlet" revises Ernest Jones's Oedipal reading of *Hamlet* by locating the causes of Hamlet's procrastination in an antecedent rela-tion to his mother.[91] These echoes, furthermore, are embedded in a larger discursive context, especially that of social anthropology. Klein undercut Freud's effort to place the Oedipus complex at the center of *personal* history, but social anthropology destabilized the Oedipal construction of *social* history. And the anxieties that the field of psychoanalysis evoked for Woolf, which distanced her even from Klein, did not extend to a discourse that sought to retrieve the matriarchal bias of Freud's anthropological sources. The contest over the gender of history was not confined to psy-choanalysis: reading Freud's reading of British anthropology, and British anthropologists' reading of Freud, reveals a struggle to repress, and to restore, the issues that, in a different register, Klein and her followers were foregrounding.

IV

Freud represents his relation to anthropology as a gendered contest for priority. "I am reading thick books [in preparation for *Totem and Taboo*] without being really interested in them since I already know the results; my instinct tells me that. But they [*sic*] have to slither their way through all the material on the subject. In that process one's insight gets clouded, there are many things that don't fit and yet mustn't be forced. . . . With all that I feel as if I had intended only to start a little liaison and then discovered that at my time of life I have to marry a new wife."[92] Anthropology is figured as a woman whose stubborn materiality threatens to deplete the inseminating power of the psychoanalytic instinct that would infuse matter with form. The metaphorization of the disciplinary contest registers a substantive dispute, for among the "many things that don't fit" the psychoanalytic instinct are a range of anthropological claims for the mother's primacy in the transformation of nature into culture. To compose a narrative justifying the conclusion that "the beginnings of religion, ethics, society, and art meet in the Oedipus complex," Freud must assimilate dissonant voices to a univocal discourse on the "same great event with which culture began."[93]

The point of departure for Freud's narrative history of exogamy, in his own assessment "the interesting part" of *Totem and Taboo*, appears to derive straightforwardly from Darwin's theory of the primal social state as a horde governed by a single adult male who guards the females for himself and expels the sons when they reach sexual maturity.[94] Freud's tasks are to correct Darwin's naturalization of the incest prohibition; to establish a transition (which Darwin fails to make) between the primal horde and the brother clan, the most primitive social organization ever observed; and to integrate the narrative of exogamy with an account of the origins of totemism. He manages these tasks through the story of a patricide that becomes a totem feast:

> One day the expelled brothers joined forces, slew and ate the father, and thus put an end to the father horde. . . . Of course these cannibalistic savages ate their victim. . . . Now they accomplished their identification with him by devouring him and each acquired a part of his strength. The totem feast, which is perhaps mankind's first celebration, would be the repetition and commemoration of this memorable, criminal act with which so many things began, social organization, moral restrictions and religion. (141–42)

After the patricide the young males, faced with a potential struggle for power among themselves and moved by tenderness toward the father whose murder has satisfied their aggression, repent the murder, forswear its repetition, and renounce the father's women. The renunciation of the

Oedipal desires institutes the two central tenets of totemism: the prohibition against eating the totem animal (except under carefully determined
circumstances) and against having sexual relations with the women in the
totem. The narrative thus establishes the desired "unity among a series of
hitherto separated phenomena" whose relationship has vexed anthropologists (141).

This story, however, is written against a different one. J. J. Atkinson's
Primal Law (1903) opens with the identical passage from *The Descent of
Man* that Freud cites to launch his story of the primal horde. That Freud's
elaboration of Darwin bears a special relation to Atkinson's is suggested by
Freud's discussion of *Primal Law* immediately after the quotation from
Darwin and again after his own evolutionary narrative.[95] With a critical
difference, the projects have much in common. Like Freud, Atkinson
posits the rebellion of the sons expelled from the primal horde and transforms the incest prohibition from an artifact of this expulsion to the
"primal law" dividing culture from nature. But Atkinson's story has a
different turning point. Rather than constituting the single "great event
with which culture began," the murder of the father is a recurrent moment
in a vicious circle of banishment and patricide. The cycle is broken by the
mother, who intervenes to protect her sons. "Pure maternal love," produced by the increased length of human infancy, engineers the distinctively human compromise that substitutes exogamy for exile, enabling
father and sons to live in peace by prohibiting the father's women to the
sons. "In the dawn of peace between this father and son we shall find the
signpost to the new highway. . . . So portentous an alliance might well
bring the world to their feet."[96] By signaling a highway that departs from
the crossroads where the father is murdered by the son, maternal love
enables an alternative juncture out of which culture could emerge. Freud's
response to Atkinson constitutes an analogous crossroads in the production of evolutionary narrative: "So much for the very remarkable theory
of Atkinson, its essential correspondence with the theory here expounded,
and its point of departure [maternal love] which makes it necessary to
relinquish so much else" (142). Atkinson, in Freud's formulation, departs
from Freudian theory; but of course it is Freud who departs from Atkinson, in whose text the Darwinian narrative is embedded. What Freud veers
away from in Atkinson, and represents as Atkinson's swerve away from
him, is the claim for maternal primacy.

The mother's primacy is differently at stake in the reconstruction of
totemism required for Freud's other task: to assimilate the totemic prohi-
bitions to the Oedipal taboos. Freud dismisses (and subsequently
reinvokes) the account of totemism offered by his major source, J. G.
Frazer's *Totemism and Exogamy* (1910), which bases its conclusions on
contemporaneous investigations into the theories of conception held by
the Aruntas of central Australia. According to these theories, impregna-

tion occurs "without the help of men" by the totem animal's entry into the womb, from which it reemerges in the form of a human being who both belongs to that totemic group and "is" the totem, which consequently may not be eaten. "The ultimate source of totemism," Frazer concludes, is "an ignorance of the part played by the male in the generation of off-spring."[97] Resisting anthropology's acquiescence to this erasure of the father, Freud "translates" the data of anthropology into the language of psychoanalysis: a detour through a case history, the psychoanalytic narrative par excellence, opens (unsuccessfully) the way to the substitution of the father for the totem and the substitution of a law forbidding murder for an eating taboo.

Freud represents psychoanalytic experience as "one single ray of light" cast into the darkness of anthropology (126); but this singularity, privileged in a text that regularly associates singleness with truth, is fractured by the clinical material summoned to evince it. The clinical interpretation of animal phobias, Freud explains, demonstrates that "in every case" animal phobias are "at bottom" a displaced fear of the castrating father (126–28). Through his discussion of Ferenczi's case of the "little Chanticleer" Arpad—who began imititating poultry, while at the same time expressing hostility toward them, after a chicken snapped at his penis—Freud educes a more ambivalent relation to an animal, the relation characteristic of totemism, in which the totem animal is both revered and (on specific occasions) murdered and devoured. Freud's interpretation highlights a castration complex negotiated between the little boy and the chicken who stands in for his father. The case, however, equally suggests that the threat posed by the chicken is embedded in a prior dynamic of eating and being eaten and that the gender of the chicken is ambiguous. Freud interprets Arpad's avowed desire "to eat some 'fricassee of mother' (on the analogy of fricassee of chicken)" as evidence of his wish to castrate his father (131). As reported by Ferenczi, Arpad's comment continues: "'My mother must be put in a pot and cooked, then there would be a potted mother and I could eat her.'" Arpad's aggressive and protective fantasies are primarily oral and point as directly to the mother's belly as to the father's phallus: "'I'll cut your middle out'"; "'I'll cut your head off, lay it on your belly, and eat it up'"; "'I'll cut my head off. I should like to cut my mouth up so that I didn't have any.'"[98] The text of psychoanalysis points no more univocally toward the identification of the totem with the father than does the anthropological data that the single beam should illuminate.

Freud argues, however, that the substitution of the father for the totem entails "no new or especially daring step. For primitive men say it themselves and, as far as the totemic system is still in effect to-day, the totem is called ancestor and primal father. We have only taken literally an expression of these races which ethnologists did not know what to do with and were therefore inclined to put into the background" (131). That Freud himself has refrained from calling the totem "father" until this point casts some doubt on his ethnographic evidence, as does his subsequent slip in characterizing the language of "the faithful, who call god *father* just as they called the totem *ancestor*" (147; emphasis added). Indeed, he cites no anthropological text to substantiate his claim about the linguistic habits of "primitive men" but instead refers us, self-referentially, to another case history. In this critical moment of suturing the discourses, however, the seams emerge. For although the story of a dog phobia, induced by a young man who heard that his mother had been frightened by a dog during her pregnancy, may sound "remarkably like the totem theory of the Aruntas," the similarity is undone by the psychoanalytic requirement that the dog represent the father, to whom the Aruntas grant no procreative role (132).

If the totem can be made to represent the father, however, the totem feast can reenact and commemorate the primal father's murder. In the second of the sections dividing Darwin's narrative from his own, Freud turns to William Robertson Smith's *Lectures on the Religion of the Semites* (1889), a gripping account of the totem feast as the original form of animal sacrifice and a means of confirming kinship through the shared consumption of the flesh of the totem animal, eaten in no other circumstances. Smith offers Freud a means of integrating into the narrative of the primal horde the food taboos and ceremonials that, together with the incest prohibition, are the defining features of totemism; but Freud assimilates Smith at some cost, for Smith's language of common physical substance does not fully serve Freud's purposes. The "thoroughly realist conception of consanguinity as an identity of substance" that empowers food to confer or to confirm kinship is tied to a matrilineal social structure in which, as Freud himself acknowledges, "there was no kinship between the man and the rest of the members of the family" (137–38, 135). Paraphrasing Smith, Freud explains that kinship "is based not only upon the fact that we are part of the substance of our mother who has borne us, and whose milk nourished us, but also that the food eaten later through which the body is renewed, can acquire and strengthen kinship" (135).

Universalizing the properties of the mother's body, Freud prepares for the substitution of food-as-father. Smith, by contrast, specifies a *maternal* chain:

> Now, if kinship means participation in a common mass of flesh, blood, and bones, it is natural that it should be regarded as dependent, not merely on the fact that a man was born of his mother's body, and so was from his birth a part of her flesh, but also on the not less significant fact that he was nourished by her milk. And so we find that among the Arabs there is a tie of milk, as well as of blood, which unites the foster-child to his foster-*mother* and *her* kin. Again, after the child

is weaned, his flesh and blood continue to be nourished and renewed by the food which he shares with his commensals, so that commensality can be thought of (1) as confirming or even (2) as constituting kinship in a very real sense.[99]

Chronology, moreover, invalidates Freud's adaptation of Smith, for in *Totem and Taboo* the primal horde precedes matrilineage; Freud argues backward, unjustifiably, from the symbolic value of the mother's body in a matrilineal society to the significance of eating the body of the father (or its surrogate) in a prior social context. In Freud's version of the totem feast, furthermore, eating is simply an effect of murder ("Of course these cannibalistic savages ate their victim") or its commemoration; in Smith, as in most accounts of totemism, eating is primary, murder merely its precondition. By applying Smith's account of the totem feast retroactively to the primal horde, Freud both preserves a narrative of eating whose meaning is grounded in the mother's body and converts it to the story of an Oedipal patricide remembered through a feast whose symbolic content is the usurpation of the father's properties, not the confirmation of consanguinity. The various elisions—of eating and killing, mother and father, anthropology and psychoanalysis—do not quite obliterate the traces of the terms Freud assimilates.

Perhaps in part to compensate for this imperfect mastery, Freud's insistence on paternal origins is exaggerated in the final section of the text, which derives all religion from the relation to the father, represented first by the totem, later by a deity. This doubling reflects the ambivalence the father generates: the murdered totem is reinstated as an honored deity. Freud concludes his argument proper by speculating that ambivalence might not be intrinsic to subjectivity but might instead have been acquired "by the human race in connection with their father-complex." Yet this final tribute to a single origin provokes a return of the repressed. A footnote to the "father-complex" equivocates: "Or, more correctly, their parental complex" (157).

V

It is the content of this footnote that Freud would explore in the gender essays of the 1920s and early 1930s, but even that accommodation of a double origin fell short of the discussions unfolding within anthropology. A variety of factors shaped the gender bias of early twentieth-century British anthropology: the turn-of-the-century excavations of the Minoan-Mycenean civilization of Crete; Frazer's compilation of fertility myths and rituals in the twelve-volume *Golden Bough* (1907–15), which included documentation of the transcultural worship of the great mother goddess; and fieldwork in the contemporary matrilineal societies of the Pacific.

Ethnographies of tribes in Australia, New Guinea, Melanesia, and Poly-
nesia offered support for Frazer's theory of totemism. "Children, in native
belief, are inserted into the mother's womb as tiny spirits, generally by the
agency of the spirit of a deceased kinswoman of the mother," Malinowski
concludes from his research in the Trobriand Islands. "Thus instead of the
creative force of a father, the myths reveal the spontaneous procreative
powers of the ancestral mother. Nor is there any other role in which the
father appears. In fact, he is never mentioned, and doesn't exist in any part
of the mythological world. . . . There is not a single myth of origins in
which a husband or a father plays any part, or even makes his appearance."[100] Evolutionary narratives grounded in the study of animal
societies also (although differently) privileged the maternal role. Among
our anthropoid precursors, Robert Briffault argues in *The Mothers: The
Matriarchal Theory of Social Origins* (1927)—which follows Atkinson in
deriving all social organization from the prolonged need for maternal care
among the higher mammals—"paternity does not exist"; the male role,
exclusively sexual, is tangential to the animal brood; there are no patriarchal families among the animal species.[101] Despite their methodological
quarrels, diverse schools of archaeology, anthropology, and animal eth-
nology contributed to producing what Sandra M. Gilbert has described
as "a cultural context that defined motherhood as the ontological fact from
which all other facts, fictions, and myths arise."[102]

A reading of *Totem and Taboo* that was faithful to Freud was difficult
in this context, as the contradictory rhetoric of Freud's British representa-
tive reveals. Ernest Jones's strategy in "Mother-Right and the Sexual
Ignorance of Savages," delivered at a 1924 meeting of the British Psycho-
Analytical Society attended by the eminent anthropologists Charles
Seligman and Bronislaw Malinowski ("quite an historic occasion," in
James Strachey's assessment), was to explain matrilineage psycho-
analytically in ways that preserved the father's primacy. Only "primordial
Oedipus tendencies" could account, Jones insists, for the denial of paternity that enables matrilineage, restored in this way to an effect of the
ambivalence the primal father generates.[103] Within this framework Jones
could make some significant concessions, such as his opening assertion
that recent research has "amply confirmed" many of Bachofen's claims, or
his acknowledgment that "perhaps the majority of anthropologists to-day
are inclined to support" the position that the original form of society was
matrilineal.[104] But the complementary paper, "Psycho-Analysis and
Anthropology," delivered earlier that year at the Royal Anthropological
Institute, more clearly shows the traces of his balancing act. Jones's
attempt to straddle Freud's insistence on the father in *Totem and Taboo* and
the diverse privileging of the mother by anthropologists produces such
moments of discursive schizophrenia as the invocation of *Totem and Taboo*
to criticize Elliot Smith for dealing "only with the individual's relation to

the Mother" and omitting the *"almost equally* important relation to the Father."[105]

Totem and Taboo was a pivotal text in the dissemination of psycho-analytic theory in England. A wide range of nonspecialist readers were attracted to Freud's bold account of social evolution. Lytton Strachey's curiosity prompted James (who deplored the 1918 Brill translation) to produce a new translation of the critical fourth essay in 1925; Virginia Woolf's curiosity is reflected in her 1939 reading notes on Freud's *Group Psychology and the Analysis of the Ego* (1922). "End w/ the deification of the primal father of the horde," she wrote, calling attention to the text's brief summary of the phylogenetic narrative of *Totem and Taboo*.[106] Woolf's interest in this narrative was shaped most directly by the work of Jane Harrison, one of the central popularizers of Freudian theory in England, a founding member of the Cambridge school of cultural anthropology, and a longtime friend of Woolf's.[107] It was Freud's anthropology that enabled Harrison to overcome her repulsion at what she termed his "sexual mud" and become an advocate of psychoanalytic theory. In her autobiographical *Reminiscences of a Student's Life,* published by the Hogarth Press in 1925, she records the transforming impact of reading *Totem and Taboo:* "[A]t once the light broke and I felt again the sense of release. Here was a big constructive imagination; here was a mere doctor laying bare the origins of Greek drama as no classical scholar had ever done. . . . I have no confidence in psycho-analysis as a method of therapeutics. I am sure that Mr. Roger Fry is right and Freud quite wrong as to the psychology of art, but I am equally sure that for generations almost every branch of human knowledge will be enriched and illumined by the imagination of Freud."[108]

Harrison's tribute to *Totem and Taboo* was enabled by her misreading of it. Her own scholarship was dedicated to recovering the ritual origins of classical religion and tragedy and to demonstrating the matriarchal substratum of the Olympian religion, renowned for its anthropomorphic and patriarchal deities. Woolf commemorates this project in *A Room of One's Own,* among other things an elegy for the "famous scholar . . . J——H—— herself," who had died the preceding spring (17).[109] She acknowledges her debt to Harrison through the figure of the aunt whose legacy "unveiled the sky to me, and substituted for the large and imposing figure of a gentleman, which Milton recomended for my perpetual adoration, a view of the open sky" (39). Woolf's other debt to Harrison is a reading of Freud that restores the maternal narrative *Totem and Taboo* repressed.

"Here he leapt on to my bed, directly I left it, & lay reading Jane's pamphlet," Woolf comments about James Strachey while the Stracheys, "fresh from Freud," were visiting at Monk's House during the summer break in their analysis in 1921.[110] The familiar reference to "Jane's pamphlet," *Epilegomena to the Study of Greek Religion* (1921), implicitly positioned by Woolf's bed, suggests that Woolf also knew Harrison's summation and reconstruction of her archaeological scholarship in the light of recent psychoanalytic and cultural theory, preeminently Freud's. The reconstruction extends to Freud; in a section entitled "Totem, Tabu, and Exogamy," Harrison rewrites *Totem and Taboo*. After following Freud's narrative through the patricide in the primal horde, Harrison restores the story Freud repudiated. Instead of precipitating the origins of culture through the guilt of the sons, the murder of the father in her narrative perpetuates the cycle of violence as the young males "retell the old hideous story of sexual jealousy. Advance in civilization is forbidden for cooperation is impossible. But there were other forces at work. The mother counted for something, the young males were to her not merely as to their father, young males, they were sons. . . . The next step, *the* crucial step, the beginning of all our morality was taken—man began to impose tabus, and thereby arrived at a sort of social contract." To underscore the mother's pivotal role in the origins of culture, Harrison turns to her own terrain, finding an "echo of the old savage primal family" in Rhea's intervention in the struggle for power between Kronos and Zeus, her youngest son.[111]

Harrison practically quotes Atkinson, but she never mentions his name, as if the narrative against which Freud wrote *Totem and Taboo* had become indistinguishable from *Totem and Taboo*. However, some current anthropological works resisted assimilation to the Freudian account. In particular, two texts which elaborate other dissonant voices in *Totem and Taboo* explicitly challenge Freud's assumptions: Malinowski's *Sex and Repression in Savage Society* (1927) and Audrey I. Richards's *Hunger and Work in a Savage Tribe* (1932), whose title reflects both its debt to Malinowski and its more extreme revaluation of Freud. In Malinowski's text, primarily concerned with the psychoanalytic colonization of anthropology, the gendering of the disciplinary contest now takes the form of examining the expression of the "essentially patriarchal" Oedipus complex in matrilinear societies.[112] The answer is shaped by the conception of kinship as identity of substance transmitted through the mother, the conception introduced into anthropology by Smith and elaborated by Frazer. Since the father in matrilineal societies is not the same kin as his children, Malinowski argues, he has no authority over them but functions instead as a nurse or companion. The Oedipus complex thus assumes a different form: authority is vested in the mother's brother, toward whom the son feels the characteristic filial ambivalence; desire is focused on the sister rather than the mother, whom no erotic interdiction alienates from the son.

Richards's more radical revision of Freud decenters not the father but sexuality. In his preface to *Hunger and Work in a Savage Tribe*, which he proclaims "a landmark in the history of anthropology," Malinowski praises his former student's correction of the "exclusive, one-sided and unsound interest in sex" that had dominated a "modern psychology" marked by the "extraordinary" inequality in the attention it accords "the twin impulses of sex and hunger respectively."[113] Reorienting anthropological interpretation along the axis of food, Richards argues that nutrition is "more fundamental than sex. . . . [I]t is the more primary and recurrent physical want" and that "it determines, more largely than any other physiological function, the nature of social groupings."[114] Her study calls into question some axioms of *Totem and Taboo*. For example, the first taboo experienced in primitive societies in her account is the prohibition on eating the mother, the taboo enforced through weaning, a deferred and traumatic division of mother and child that affects all family relationships. Richards documents the systems of taboos, magic beliefs, and social rituals surrounding food in general and milk in particular. Citing Smith as her primary precursor, although choosing to emphasize daily eating rather than the sacrificial meal, Richards insists on the emotional intensity and centrality of food in primitive societies, the ambivalence eating evokes, the rituals designed to make food safe to eat, and the familial roles and distinctions that food preparation and consumption define. Freud's account of the totemic meal, she comments in passing, is "hardly likely to commend itself to the sociologist."[115] Extending the initiative taken by Smith—as Malinowski elaborates on Frazer, and Harrison resuscitates Atkinson—Richards contributes to the anthropological revision, among Woolf's contemporaries, of Freud's revisionist anthropology.

Woolf probably did not read Malinowski or Richards, although she did read Harrison; and such entries as "Habits in the Fiji Islands of," "Worshipped as goddesses by," and "South Sea Islanders, age of puberty among," in *Room*'s catalog of research at the British Museum, as well as the allusions to the great mother goddess in the solitary traveler's vision in *Mrs. Dalloway*, indicate her recognition of anthropology's centrality to the current discussions of gender. But intentionally or not, Woolf participated in a discourse that foregrounded and replayed certain related oppositions: father/mother, sexuality/hunger, Oedipal/pre-Oedipal. Her novels chart her changing contributions to this discourse. Let us turn now to an early instance, *Mrs. Dalloway*, concerned not with hunger for the mother, which surfaces only through the fuller exploration of the past, but with a lost pre-Oedipal world and the costs of its relinquishment.

2

BETWEEN THE ACTS OF *MRS. DALLOWAY*

Between the sentences, apart from the story, a little shape of some
kind builds itself up.
    Virginia Woolf, "The Anatomy of Fiction"

Everything in the sphere of this first attachment to the mother seemed
to me so difficult to grasp in analysis—so grey with age and shadowy
and almost impossible to revivify—that it was as if it had succumbed
to an especially inexorable repression.
    Sigmund Freud, "Female Sexuality"

The developmental story in *Mrs. Dalloway* is intrinsically disjointed and
textually dispersed and disguised. The narrative present is scaled to a single
day, both recalling the structure of *Ulysses,* which Woolf finished reading as
she began *Mrs. Dalloway,* and offering a female counterpart to Joyce's
adaptation of an epic plot. The dominant narrative of Clarissa Dalloway's
past is a strategically revised courtship narrative, dissolved into a retrospective oscillation between two alluring possibilities as the fifty-two-year-
old Clarissa continues to replay the choice she made thirty years before.
Clarissa's enduring uncertainty about the correctness of her marriage
choice sustains the courtship plot as a narrative strand which cloaks a less
orthodox emotional history.[1]

Woolf selects with precision the consciousness through which to
reveal specific segments of this history. Although Clarissa vacillates emo-
tionally between the allure of Peter Walsh and that of her husband,
Richard, she remembers Peter's courtship only glancingly; the burden of
that plot is carried by Peter, through whose memories Woolf relates the
slow and tortured end of that relationship. Clarissa's memories, by contrast, focus more exclusively on the general ambiance of Bourton, the
home of her adolescent years, and on her love for Sally Seton. Significantly absent from these memories is Richard Dalloway, whose courtship
of Clarissa is presented exclusively through Peter's painful recollections.
Clarissa thinks of Richard only in the present. Through this narrative
distribution, Woolf constructs two poles structuring the flow of Clarissa's

consciousness. Bourton to Clarissa is a pastoral female world spatially and temporally disjunct from marriage and the sociopolitical world of (Richard's) London.

Although the Bourton scenes Clarissa remembers span a period of several years, they partake of a single emotional climate that absorbs them into a homogeneous backdrop for the present day in June. Woolf excises all narrative connections between these contrasting extended moments. She provides no account of intervening events: Clarissa's marriage, childbirth, the move and adjustment to London. And she indicates the disjunction in Clarissa's experience by noting that the London hostess never returns to Bourton—which has been inherited, significantly, by a male relative—and almost never sees Sally Seton, now the unfamiliar Lady Rosseter. Clarissa's life in London is devoid of intimate female bonds: she is excluded from lunch at Lady Bruton's, she vies with Miss Kilman for her own daughter's allegiance. Clarissa's recollected history proceeds from a female-centered natural world to the heterosexual and androcentric social world. Woolf structures this progression as a binary opposition between past and present, nature and culture, feminine and masculine dispensations. Versions of this opposition reverberate through the novel in rhetorical and narrative juxtapositions. The developmental plot, which slides beneath the more familiar courtship plot through the gap between Peter's and Clarissa's memories, exists as two contrasting moments and the silence adjoining and dividing them.

Woolf endows these moments with symbolic resonance by a strategy of narrative exclusions: she juxtaposes eras split by thirty years and omits Clarissa's childhood from the novel's temporal frame. There is no past in *Mrs. Dalloway* anterior to Clarissa's adolescence at Bourton. Within this selective scheme, the earliest remembered scenes become homologous to a conventional narrative point of departure: the description of formative childhood years. The emotional tenor of these scenes, moreover, suggests deferred childhood desire. Clarissa's earliest narrated memories focus on Sally's arrival at Bourton, an arrival which infuses the formal, repressive atmosphere with a vibrant female energy. The only picture of Clarissa's early childhood sketched in the novel, by contrast, suggests a tableau of female loss: a dead mother, a dead sister, and a stern maiden aunt, the father's sister, whose hobby of pressing flowers beneath Littre's dictionary suggests to Peter Walsh the cultural oppression of women. In this barren atmosphere, Sally's uninhibited warmth and sensuality immediately spark love in the eighteen-year-old Clarissa. Sally replaces Clarissa's dead mother and sister, her name even echoing the sister's name, Sylvia. She nurtures Clarissa's intellect and passions, introducing her to the works of William Morris, Shelley, and Plato and inspiring a love equal to Othello's: "If it were now to die, 'twere now to be most happy," Clarissa feels coming down to dinner to meet Sally. Sally's kiss creates the most exquisite moment in Clarissa's life: "The whole world might have turned upside down! The others disappeared; there she was alone with Sally. And she felt she had been given a present, wrapped up, and told just to keep it, not to look at it—a diamond, something infinitely precious, wrapped up, which, as they walked (up and down, up and down), she uncovered, or the radiance burnt through, the revelation, the religious feeling!—when old Joseph and Peter faced them." Within the sequence established by the novel, this adolescent love assumes the place of the early female bond unrepresented within the narrative.[2]

The moment Woolf selects to represent Clarissa's past carries the full weight of the pre-Oedipal experience—the phase that Freud discovered to his surprise substantially predates and shapes the female version of the Oedipus complex, which, in turn, "initiates all the processes that are designed to make the individual find a place in the cultural community."[3] According to the Freudian narrative, acculturation exacts renunciation from both women and men. The loss for women, however, is less well compensated, since the boy's rewards will include a woman like the mother and full paternal privileges, whereas the girl will be requited with at best a child but no renewed access to the lost maternal body and no acquisition of paternal power. Encapsulating an image of the turn from mother to father that, whenever it occurs, terminates the earliest stage of female development, *Mrs. Dalloway* defines the moment of acculturation as a moment of obstruction. Masculine intervention, not penis envy, produces this moment in Woolf's account. In contrast to Freud, who locates violence only in the castration threat that terminates the Oedipus complex for the son, Woolf suggests that violence initiates the daughter's Oedipal relation to the father.[4]

Woolf organizes the developmental plot so that Clarissa's love for Sally precedes her alliances with men; the two young women "spoke of marriage always as a catastrophe" (50). The notion of catastrophe repeats the adolescent Clarissa's earlier premonition that "something awful was about to happen," a thought immediately followed by Peter Walsh's appearance on the terrace at Bourton (3). The eighteen-year-old Clarissa perceives Peter primarily as an irritating intruder; the scene she most vividly remembers, Sally Seton's kiss, is rudely interrupted by Peter's appearance.[5] Both the action and the language of this scene hint at psychological allegory. The moment of exclusive female connection is shattered by masculine intervention, a rupture signaled typographically by Woolf's characteristic dash. Clarissa responds to Peter's intrusion as an absolute and arbitrary termination: "It was like running one's face against a granite wall in the darkness! It was shocking; it was horrible!" (53). Her perception of Peter's motives—"she felt his hostility; his jealousy; his determination to break into their comradeship"—suggests a revised Oedipal configuration: the jealous male attempting to rupture the exclusive female bond, insisting on the transference of attachment to the man, demanding heterosexuality.[6] For women this configuration institutes a break as decisive and unyielding as a granite wall. Clarissa's revenge is to refuse to marry Peter, to select instead the less demanding Richard Dalloway, who allows "a solitude . . . a gulf" between husband and wife, a space that can incorporate the memory of Sally (181). Woolf herself exacts poetic justice by subjecting Peter to an inverted replay of this crucial scene when, thirty years later, Clarissa's daughter Elizabeth unexpectedly interrupts his emotional reunion with her mother by opening a door (in the granite wall?), asserting by her presence at that moment the primacy of female bonds (despite the actual attenuation of these bonds between Clarissa and Elizabeth). "Here is my Elizabeth," Clarissa announces to the disconcerted Peter, the possessive pronoun he finds so annoying self-consciously insisting on the mother's privileged relation to her daughter (71).

Clarissa suppresses recognition of the cost exacted by the shift from Sally and Bourton to Richard and London. Woolf reveals the disjunction in Clarissa's life obliquely through the bifurcated settings of Clarissa's history, the images that reiterate radical divides, and the gaps that are inserted in the narrative. The most striking of these gaps concerns Clarissa's sister Sylvia, a shadowy and seemingly gratuitous figure, apparently created just to be destroyed. Sylvia's death, her only action in the novel, is recalled by Peter rather than Clarissa and related in two sentences. This offhand presentation both implants and conceals an exaggerated echo of Clarissa's own split experience. As a young woman "on the verge of life," Sylvia is abruptly killed by a falling tree, a dramatically imposed barrier to life, mysteriously associated with her father: "[A]ll Justin Parry's fault— all his carelessness)" (118–19). The story echoes and revises D. H. Lawrence's novella *The Fox*, which recounts the destruction of a bond between two women by a man's quasi-intentional felling of a tree that kills his female rival, enabling him to marry the other woman.[7] Woolf's deliberate indictment of the father (the psychological analogue in Sylvia's life to Peter in Clarissa's) is suggested by the contrast with her earlier story, "Mrs. Dalloway in Bond Street," where Sylvia's death is depicted as a tranquil, vague event absorbed into nature's cyclical benevolence: "It used, thought Clarissa, to be so simple. . . . When Sylvia died, hundreds of years ago, the yew hedges looked so lovely with the diamond webs in the mist before early church."[8] The violence of Sylvia's death in the novel and the very incongruity between the magnitude of the charge against her father and its parenthetical presentation suggest a story intentionally withheld, forcibly deprived of its legitimate proportions, written both into and out of the text. This self-consciously inscribed narrative gap echoes the thirty-year gap in Clarissa's history, as the dramatic severance of Sylvia's life at the moment of maturity echoes Clarissa's painful encounter with the granite wall, a scene that may itself have been inspired by Woolf's reading of *The Fox*. The pastoral resonance of Sylvia's name also implies a larger female story of natural existence abruptly curtailed.[9] A related narrative exclusion is the crucial tale of Clarissa's relation to her mother, remarkably unmourned and unmentioned until the novel's end, when a casual party guest's brief comparison of Clarissa to her mother "walking in a garden" brings sudden tears to Clarissa's eyes (267). The story of Clarissa's resemblance to her mother, and of the pain inflicted by the mother's death, is signaled but placed outside the narrative by the double gesture of inclusion and exclusion that structures Woolf's presentation of Clarissa's history.

This history is similarly adumbrated through another inconspicuous character, Lucrezia Warren Smith, whose mirroring function is overshadowed by that of her husband, Septimus, Clarissa's more obvious double. The parallel between Clarissa and Lucrezia is implied by their roles in a network of Shakespearean allusions that ally Clarissa with Imogen through the refrain from *Cymbeline* and Lucrezia with the heroine of *The Rape of Lucrece:* in both works women are the victims of male rivalry and lust, which Shakespeare explicitly presents as a link between his texts.[10] In *Mrs. Dalloway* Rezia's history, like her name, is abbreviated, yet the course of her "development" suggestively reflects that of the heroine. Like Clarissa, Rezia finds herself plucked by marriage from an Edenic female world with which she retains no contact. Her memories highlight the exclusively female community of sisters collaboratively making hats in an Italian setting that is pastoral despite the surrounding urban context: "For you should see the Milan gardens!" she later exclaims, when confronted with London's "few ugly flowers stuck in pots!" (34). The cultural shift from Italy to England, like the shift from Bourton to London, locates this idyllic female life in a distant, prelapsarian era—before the war, before industrialization, before marriage. Marriage and war explicitly coalesce for Rezia as agents of expulsion from this female paradise: Septimus comes to Milan as a British soldier and proposes marriage to Rezia in the hope of alleviating his war-induced emotional anesthesia. Rezia's memories of Italy, a radiant temporal backdrop to her painful alienation in marriage and a foreign culture, provide a pointed parallel to Clarissa's memories of Bourton. And Rezia's final pastoral vision, inspired by the drug administered after Septimus's suicide, significantly begins with her sense of "opening long windows, stepping out into some garden," echoing Clarissa's first recollection of Bourton, where she had "burst open the French windows and plunged . . . into the open air" (227, 3). The death of her husband releases Rezia to return imaginatively to a past she implicitly shares with Clarissa: the female-centered world anterior to heterosexual bonds. After this moment of imaginative release and return,

Rezia disappears from the novel, having accomplished the function of delicately echoing Clarissa's divided history.

II

In his three essays on female sexuality, written between 1925 and 1933, Freud obsessively details the structure and costs of women's bifurcated history. Femininity, he argues in the wake of his discovery of the daughter's Minoan-Mycenean prehistory, is achieved by specific repressions from which the male child is exempt. The girl's developmental course, in contrast to the boy's, requires a reversal: she must replace her intimate attachment to her mother with a heterosexual attraction to her father; she must alter the nature of her desire (and then renounce its object). Her entire sexuality, Freud asserts, is defined in the shift from pre-Oedipal mother to Oedipal father. She switches not only the object of her erotic interest but also her erotic zone and mode, relinquishing the active, "masculine," clitoral sexuality focused on her mother for the passive, "feminine," vaginal sexuality focused on her father. Freud calls this "a change in her own sex," for prior to this crucial shift "the little girl is a little man."[11] The comprehensive change in sexual object, organ, and attitude inserts a profound discontinuity into female development, which contrasts with that of "the more fortunate man [who] has only to continue at the time of his sexual maturity the activity that he has previously carried out at the period of the early efflorescence of his sexuality."[12] The psychosexual shift that occurs in early childhood, moreover, is often reenacted in early adulthood, for marriage typically reinstates a disruption in women's experience, confined until recently to a largely female sphere prior to the heterosexual contract of marriage.

The circuitous route to female identity, Freud insists, is uniquely demanding and debilitating: "[A] comparison with what happens with boys tells us that the development of a little girl into a normal woman is more difficult and more complicated, since it includes two extra tasks [the change both of sexual object and of organ], to which there is nothing corresponding in the development of a man."[13] No woman completes this difficult process unscathed. Freud outlines three developmental paths for women; all exact a substantial toll. If she follows the first, the girl negotiates the shift from mother to father by accepting the unwelcome "fact" of her castration, detected in comparison between herself and little boys. Mortified by this discovery of inferiority, aware she can no longer compete for her mother with her better-endowed brother, she renounces her active sexual orientation toward her mother and accepts a passive orientation toward the superior father. Unfortunately, the girl's renunciation of active sexuality normally entails repressing "a good part of her sexual trends in general," and this route leads to sexual inhibition or neurosis, to "a general revulsion from sexuality."[14] If she follows the second path, the girl simply refuses this renunciation, clings to her "threatened masculinity," struggles to preserve her active orientation toward her mother, and develops what Freud calls a "masculinity complex," which often finds expression in homosexuality.[15] Only the third "very circuitous" path leads to the "normal female attitude," in which the girl takes her father as the object of her passive eroticism and enters the female Oedipus complex. Curiously, however, Freud never describes this route, which turns out to be only a less damaging version of the first path toward inhibition and neurosis.[16] To the extent that her sexuality survives her "catastrophic" repression of her "masculine" desire for her mother, the girl will be able to complete her turn to her father and seal her femininity by desiring his baby. "Normal" femininity is thus a fragile, tenuous proposition; no unique course is prescribed for its achievement. Freud's most optimistic prognosis assumes a doubly hypothetical, negative form: "If too much is not lost in the course of it [development] through repression, this femininity may turn out to be normal."[17] The achievement of this femininity, moreover, is only the first stage, for the female Oedipus complex, like the male, must itself be overcome, and the hard-won desire for the father renounced and transferred to other men. Female development thus entails a double disappointment, in contrast to the single renunciation required of men. No wonder Freud concludes the last of his essays on femininity by contrasting the youthful flexibility of a thirty-year-old male with the psychical rigidity of a woman the same age: "Her libido has taken up final positions and seems incapable of exchanging them for others. There are no paths open to further development; it is as though the whole process had already run its course and remains thenceforward insusceptible to influence—as though, indeed, the difficult development to femininity had exhausted the possibilities of the person concerned."[18]

III

Mrs. Dalloway outlines the developmental sequence Freud was plotting simultaneously. Both narratives share a radically foreshortened notion of development, condensed for Freud into a few childhood years, focused for Woolf in a single emotional shift. Both narratives eschew the developmental scope traditionally assumed by fiction and psychology (that committed to detailing the steady unfolding of a life), and both stress the discontinuities specific to female development. Woolf, moreover, portrays the sexual and emotional calcification that Freud suggests is the toll of "normal" development; but she expressly challenges his normative categories of women's sexuality.

Clarissa is explicit about her unimpassioned response to men, a response she perceives as a failure and a lack, a guarding of virginity through marriage and motherhood. Her emotional and physical self-containment are represented by her narrow attic bed, where she reads Baron Marbot's *Memoirs* of the Russian retreat from Moscow, a victory achieved by icy withdrawal.[19] The association of her bed with a grave— "Narrower and narrower would her bed be"—links her adult sexuality with death (45–46). Yet in a passage of extraordinary erotic writing, Woolf juxtaposes the narrow bed with Clarissa's passionate responses to women; the contrast implies, more powerfully than Freud, the cost of the pivotal developmental choice:

> [Y]et she could not resist sometimes yielding to the charm of a woman, not a girl, of a woman confessing, as to her they often did, some scrape, some folly. . . . [S]he did undoubtedly then feel what men felt. Only for a moment; but it was enough. It was a sudden revelation, a tinge like a blush which one tried to check and then, as it spread, one yielded to its expansion, and rushed to the farthest verge and there quivered and felt the world come closer, swollen with some astonishing rapture, which split its thin skin and gushed and poured with an extraordinary alleviation over the cracks and sores! Then, for that moment, she had seen an illumination; a match burning in a crocus; an inner meaning almost expressed. But the close withdrew; the hard softened. It was over—the moment. Against such moments (with women too) there contrasted (as she laid her hat down) the bed and Baron Marbot and the candle half-burnt. (46–47)

Woolf's language renders a passion that is actively directed toward women, and "masculine" in attitude and character, yet also receptive and "feminine"; the description of the match in the crocus, an image of active female desire, conflates Freud's sexual dichotomies. The power of the passage derives in part from the intermeshed male and female imagery, and the interwoven language of sex and mysticism, a mélange that recurs in Clarissa's memory of Sally's kiss. Fusion—of male and female, active and passive, sacred and profane—is at the heart of this erotic experience. Freud's opposition of active, "masculine," pre-Oedipal sexuality to the passive, "feminine," Oedipal norm denies the basis for this integration. Clarissa's momentary illumination, moreover, is made possible only by the sexual orientation Freud devalues as (initially) immature and (subsequently) deviant. Woolf's passage suggests the completeness Freud denies the pre-Oedipal realm and calls into question the differentiation of normal from aberrant sexuality. The stark contrast between the passionate moment and the narrow bed, a juxtaposition that (like the structure of the girl's developmental plot) conceals a schism between two radically different sexual worlds, subverts the opposition between the normal and abnormal. Woolf implicitly elevates Freud's second developmental path over the costly route toward "normal femininity," as she valorizes homo-sexuality over the inhibitions of imposed heterosexuality.

As the passage continues, the gap between the sexual options emblematized by the moment and the bed evolves into the familiar split between Sally Seton and Richard Dalloway, the split that structures the developmental plot as Richard replaces Peter. The allegorical image of the bed leads to a more concrete description of Clarissa's reaction to her husband's return: "[I]f she raised her head she could just hear the click of the handle released as gently as possible by Richard, who slipped upstairs in his socks and then, as often as not, dropped his hot-water bottle and swore! How she laughed!" (47). The contrast between the passionate moment with women and the narrow bed to which marriage paradoxically leads becomes a leap from the sublime to the (affectionately) ridiculous. Opening with the conjunction "But," the next paragraph signals a turn away from mundanity back to "this question of love . . . , this falling in love with women," inaugurating Clarissa's lengthy and lyrical reminis-cence of Sally Seton (48). The opposition between Clarissa's relation-ships with men and her relationships with women modulates to the split between her present and her past, her orientation and emotional capacities on both sides of the Oedipal divide. Woolf, like Freud, reveals the cost of female development, but she creates a far more graphic image of the loss entailed, questions its necessity, and indicates the price of equating female development with acculturation through the rites of passage established by the Oedipus complex.

In the end, however, Woolf qualifies these questions by subtly revis-ing the terms of the opposition. Her agent for this shift is Septimus Warren Smith, who serves as Clarissa's double, opposing the "insane" truth to the "sane" and the desire for death to the choice of life, while mirroring the unresolved homoerotic bond.[20] It is a critical commonplace that Clarissa receives from Septimus a cathartic, vicarious experience of death that releases her to experience life's pleasures more intensely. Less apparent is that Woolf not only transfers to Septimus the death she had originally planned for Clarissa but also uses Septimus to complete the developmental plot by transforming the choice of sexuality into the choice between life and death—an easier choice to make unequivocally. The passage describing Clarissa's reaction to Septimus's suicide reveals that he plays a specific role in resolving the developmental impasse that appears to be one cause of Clarissa's weakened heart, her constricted vitality. Woolf composes this passage as a subtle but extended parallel to Clarissa's earlier reminiscence of her love for Sally and Bourton. The interplay between these two meditative interludes, the primary sites of the developmental plot, encodes Clarissa's exploration of a conflict long suppressed. By in-terpreting Septimus's suicide in her private language of passion and integrity, Clarissa uses the shock of death to probe and resolve her relation to her past, becoming able at last both to admit and to renounce its hold. On the day in June that contains the action of *Mrs. Dalloway*, Clarissa completes the developmental turn initiated thirty years before.

Woolf prepares the parallels between the two passages by beginning them both with Clarissa's withdrawal from her customary social milieu. The emotions prompting Clarissa's first meditation on Sally and the past are initially triggered by her exclusion from Lady Bruton's lunch. Woolf then describes Clarissa's noontime retreat to her solitary attic room as a metaphoric departure from a party: "She began to go slowly upstairs . . . as if she had left a party, . . . had shut the door and gone out and stood alone, a single figure against the appalling night"; Clarissa is "like a nun withdrawing" (45). Later that night, when Clarissa hears the news of Septimus's suicide, she does leave her party and retreats to an empty little room where "[t]he party's splendor fell to the floor" (279–80). The first passage concludes with her preparations for the party, the second with her deliberate return to that party. Within these enclosed narrative and domestic spaces, Clarissa relives through memory the passionate scene with Sally on the terrace at Bourton. The second passage replays in its bifurcated structure the male intervention that curtails the original scene. In this final version of the male/female juxtaposition, however, the emotional balance is reversed.

Clarissa's meditation on Septimus's death modulates, through her association of passion with death, to a meditation on her relation to her past. Woolf orchestrates the verbal echoes of this passage to evoke with increasing clarity the scene with Sally Seton. To Clarissa, Septimus's choice of a violent early death elicits the notion of a central self preserved: "A thing there was that mattered; a thing, wreathed about with chatter, defaced, obscured in her own life. . . . This he had preserved" (280); earlier Clarissa had described passion as "something central which permeated" (46). The echoes between these passages develop through their similar representations of passion's ebb: "[C]loseness drew apart; rapture faded, one was alone" (281); "But the close withdrew; the hard softened. It was over—the moment" (47). Clarissa's sense that only death preserves the fading moment of passion prepares for her repetition of the line from *Othello* that has signified her love for Sally Seton (281, 51). The metaphor of treasure which precedes this explicit allusion to the scene with Sally further connects Clarissa's response to Septimus ("had he plunged holding his treasure?" she wonders [281]) with her memory of Sally's kiss as "a present, . . . a diamond, something infinitely precious" (52–53). Septimus's death evokes in Clarissa the knowledge of what death saves and what she has lost; her grief is not for Septimus but for herself. The verbal web Woolf weaves between the two passages summons once again the crucial scene with Sally on the terrace at Bourton, enabling Clarissa to confront her loss. Her appreciation of this loss, at last fully present to her consciousness, crystallizes in the contrast that concludes this segment of the passage: "She had schemed; she had pilfered. She was never wholly admirable. . . . And once she had walked on the terrace at Bourton" (282).

With this naming of the original scene, Woolf abruptly terminates Clarissa's recollection, replaying with a brilliant stroke Peter Walsh's interruption, the sudden imposition of the granite wall. This time, however, the masculine intervention is enacted not by Peter but by Richard, and not as external imposition but as choice. Clarissa's unexpected thought of Richard abruptly and definitively terminates the memory of Sally, pivoting the scene from past to present, the mood from grief to joy: "It was due to Richard; she had never been so happy" (282). The dramatic and unexplained juxtaposition encapsulates the developmental plot and the dynamics of its central scenes. However, this final replay of the developmental turn—the final microcosm of Woolf's narrative method—represents the abrupt transition positively. The joy inspired by Clarissa's thought of Richard persists as she celebrates "this having done with the triumphs of youth" (282). Woolf does not fill in the gap splitting past from present, grief from joy. We can only speculate that Septimus's sacrificial gift includes a demonstration of Clarissa's alternatives: to preserve the intensity of passion through death or to accept the changing offerings of life. Through Septimus, Woolf recasts the developmental impasse as a choice between development or death. By recalling to Clarissa the power of her past *and* the only method of eternalizing it, Septimus enables Clarissa to acknowledge and renounce its hold, to embrace the imperfect pleasures of adulthood more completely.

Woolf signals the shift in Clarissa's orientation by concluding the interlude with Clarissa's reaction to the old lady across the way, an unnamed character who only functions in the novel as an object of Clarissa's awareness. As the earlier meditative passage concludes with Clarissa's reflection in the looking glass, this one ends with an analogous reflection: as Clarissa's thoughts shift from Sally and the past to Richard and the present, Woolf turns the angle of vision one notch further to open a perspective on the future. The old lady solemnly prepares for bed, but this intimation of a final repose, recalling Clarissa's earlier ruminations on her narrowing bed, carries no onus for the heroine, excited by the unexpected animation of the sky, the news of Septimus's suicide, and the noise from the party in the adjacent room. Release, anticipation, pleasure in change regardless of its consequences, these are Clarissa's dominant emotions. The gulf between Clarissa and the unknown lady discloses the female intimacy forfeited to growth, yet Clarissa's willingness to contemplate an emblem of age instead of savoring a memory of youth suggests a positive commitment to development—not to any particular course but to the process of change itself. The vision of the old lady simultaneously con-

cludes the developmental plot and the depiction of Clarissa's consciousness; the rest of the narrative turns to Peter and Sally.

By turning from Clarissa at this moment in the narrative, Woolf
evades the question of the depth and endurance of Clarissa's change, as she
had evaded Clarissa's impasse by recasting her options in less evenly
weighted terms. In retreating from her most radical position, Woolf produces a less than perfectly convincing resolution. To bolster her final
perspective in the novel, she embeds Clarissa's history in a larger historical
context that allows for no alternative solutions. By contrasting Clarissa's
story to that of her daughter, Woolf suggests that the progress of society
precludes any personal or cultural return to the pastoral pre-Oedipal
world.

The action in *Mrs. Dalloway* unfolds in 1923, shortly after the war
which casts its shadow through the novel. Through the experience of
Septimus Warren Smith and the description of soldiers marching "as if
one will worked legs and arms uniformly, and life, with its varieties, its
irreticences, had been laid under a pavement of monuments and wreaths
and drugged into a stiff yet staring corpse by discipline," Woolf suggests
that the military discipline intended both to manifest and cultivate man-
liness instills rigor mortis in the living (76–77). For women, the
masculine war is disruptive in a different way. Woolf represents the world
war as a vast historical counterpart to male intervention in women's lives.
In one pointed metaphor, the "fingers" of the European war are so "pry-
ing and insidious" that they smash a "plaster cast of Ceres," goddess of
fertility and mother love, reminder of the force and fragility of the primary
female bond (129). Rezia's female world is shattered by the conjunction of
marriage and war. The symbolic association of war with the developmental turn from feminine to masculine dispensations will be more clearly
marked in *To the Lighthouse,* whose divisive central section conflates Mrs.
Ramsay's death with the violence of world war, splitting the novel into
disjunct portions presided over separately by mother and by father.

In *Mrs. Dalloway* Woolf more subtly indicates the masculine tenor of
postwar society. The youngest generation in this novel is almost exclusively, and boastfully, male: Sally Seton repeatedly announces her pride in
her "five great boys"; the Bradshaws have a son at Eton, in fact "everyone . . . has six sons at Eton"; Rezia mourns the loss of closeness with her
sisters but craves a son who would resemble his father (289). Elizabeth
Dalloway is the sole daughter, and she identifies more closely with her
father than her mother (the plaster cast of Ceres has been shattered in the
war). Male authority, partially incarnate in the relentless chiming of Big
Ben ("striking the half-hour . . . with extraordinary vigour, as if a young
man, strong, indifferent, inconsiderate, were swinging dumb-bells this
way and that"), is more ominously embodied in the medical professionals,
Holmes and Bradshaw, the modern officers of coercion (71). Septimus is

41

the dramatic victim of this authority, but Lady Bradshaw's feminine concession is equally significant: "Fifteen years ago she had gone under. . . . There had been no scene, no snap; only the slow sinking, water-logged, of her will into his. Sweet was her smile, swift her submission" (152). The loose connections Woolf suggests between World War I and a bolstered male authority have no basis in actual social change, but within the mythology created by the novel the war assumes a symbolic function dividing a pervasively masculine present from a mythically feminine past.

Critics frequently note the elegiac tone which allies *Mrs. Dalloway* with the modernist lament for a lost plenitude,[21] but nostalgia in this text is for a specifically female presence absent from contemporary life. Woolf characteristically suggests this loss primarily in interludes that interrupt the narrative. The solitary traveler's vision, for example, loosely attached to Peter Walsh's dream but transcending through its generic formulation the limits of private consciousness, is hardly, as Reuben Brower asserts, a "beautiful passage . . . which could be detached with little loss," for the dream vision of a cosmic maternal presence that might "shower down from her magnificent hands compassion, comprehension, absolution" names the absence that haunts *Mrs. Dalloway* (86).[22] In the present of the novel, the comprehensive, seductive, generative powers of the goddess shrink to the elderly nurse sleeping next to Peter Walsh, and the "visions which proffer great cornucopias full of fruit to the solitary traveller, or murmur in his ear like sirens lolloping away on the green sea waves" split into Sally Seton's exaggerated maternity and the social graces of Clarissa, clad as a hostess in a "silver-green mermaid's dress" (86, 264). In a similarly self-contained narrative interlude, the mythic figure of woman voicing nature's eternal, wordless rhythms dwindles, in urban London, to a battered old beggar woman singing for coppers. Loss is finally represented in the lecture on "Proportion" and "Conversion" (150–54), where Woolf appears to denounce in her own voice the twin evils of contemporary civilization, a narrative intrusion that calls attention to itself as a rhetorical as well as ideological antithesis to the solitary traveler's vision. Sir William Bradshaw's goddesses of Proportion and Conversion, who serve the ideals of imperialism and patriarchy and renounce their status as creative female powers, are the contemporary counterpart to the ancient maternal deity, now accessible only in dream. The historical vista intermittently inserted in *Mrs. Dalloway* echoes the protagonist's progression from a pastoral female world to an urban culture governed by men.

A last reverberation of the developmental plot takes as its subject the daughter in the altered contemporary world. Through the enigmatic figure of Elizabeth, Woolf quietly closes the door on a return to the pre-Oedipal world. Although the same age as Clarissa in the earliest recollected scenes at Bourton, Elizabeth has always lived in London; the country to her is an occasional treat she associates specifically with her

father. Elizabeth feels a special closeness to her father, a noticeable alienation from her mother. The transition implicitly so traumatic for Clarissa
has already been accomplished by her daughter. Woolf structures the
adolescence of mother and daughter as inverse emotional configurations:
as Clarissa vacillates between two men, while tacitly guarding her special
bond with Sally, Elizabeth vacillates between two women, her mother and
Miss Kilman, while preserving her special connection with her father.
Elizabeth's presence at the final party manifests her independence from
Miss Kilman; her impatience for the party to end reveals her differences
from her mother. The last scene of the novel highlights Elizabeth's closeness with her father, whose sudden response to his daughter's beauty has
drawn her instinctively to his side.

The opposing allegiances of daughter and mother reflect in part the
kinds of female nurturance available to each. Elizabeth's relationship with
the grasping Miss Kilman is the modern counterpart to Clarissa's love for
Sally Seton. Specific parallels mark the generational differences. Miss
Kilman's possessive desire for Elizabeth parodies the lines that emblazon
Clarissa's love for Sally: "If it were now to die, 'twere now to be most
happy" becomes, for Elizabeth's devouring tutor, "If she could grasp her,
if she could clasp her, if she could make her hers absolutely and forever and
then die; that was all she wanted" (199–200). Sally walks with Clarissa on
the terrace at Bourton; Miss Kilman takes Elizabeth to the Army and
Navy Stores. As her name implies, Miss Kilman provides no asylum from
the patriarchal world. Instead, in a way that anticipates the thwarted
maternal nurture represented in *A Room of One's Own*, that world saps
Miss Kilman, whose consequent hunger for Elizabeth replaces Sally's
nurturant kiss. Elizabeth's loss of the female sanctuary, however, brings
certain compensations: Elizabeth assumes she will have a profession, will
play some active role in society. Woolf does not evaluate this new developmental course, does not tally the losses and gains induced by a changing
social world. If she surrounds the past with an aureole, she points to the
future in silence. She offers little access to Elizabeth's consciousness, insisting instead on her status as enigma—her Chinese eyes, "blank, bright,
with the staring incredible innocence of sculpture," her Oriental bearing,
her "inscrutable mystery" (206, 199). Undecipherable, Elizabeth is "like a
hyacinth, sheathed in glossy green, with buds just tinted, a hyacinth which
has had no sun"; her unfolding is unknown, unknowable (186). Through
the figure of Elizabeth as unopened bud, Woolf encloses in her text the
unwritten text of the next developmental narrative.

In fact, however, Woolf deferred until *Three Guineas* and *The Years*
the narrative of women's routes through a newly available professional
world. In *To the Lighthouse* she returns to the pastoral childhood domain.
Some features of Elizabeth recur in Lily Briscoe: the name, even, as the
flowering of the bud; the Oriental eyes; the independence; and the self-

definition through work rather than marriage. But Lily serves as a vehicle for reopening the mother-daughter narrative occluded in the earlier text. The father-daughter story presaged by Elizabeth is given, instead, to Cam. *To the Lighthouse* fractures developmental narrative as the focus on an individual protagonist yields to the wider scope of a family romance.

3

TO THE LIGHTHOUSE:
JAMES AND CAM

But the centre is father's character, sitting in a boat, reciting, We
perished, each alone, while he crushes a dying mackerel. However, I
must refrain. I must write a few little stories first and let the *Lighthouse*
simmer, adding to it between tea and dinner till it is complete for
writing out.
                    Virginia Woolf, *Dairy,* 14 May 1925

But I wrote the book [*To the Lighthouse*] very quickly; and when it was
written, I ceased to be obsessed by my mother. I no longer hear her
voice; I do not see her. . . .
Certainly, there she was, in the very centre of that great Cathedral
space which was childhood; there she was from the very first.
                    Virginia Woolf, "A Sketch of the Past" (1939)

If *Mrs. Dalloway* is constructed so that "every scene would build up the
idea" of its central character, *To the Lighthouse* is in doubt about its center.[1]
The later novel dramatizes the contradictions between Woolf's prospec-
tive and retrospective definitions of its center, between "father's character,
sitting in a boat" and mother "there . . . in the very centre." In this autobiographical fiction, Woolf explores the complexities of narrating family
history. The lacuna that "Time Passes" offers as a textual center is only the
most striking manifestation of a discontinuity sustained more discreetly
through the multiple histories she hoped would counteract her theme's
potential sentimentality: "The word 'sentimental' sticks in my gizzard.
. . . But this theme may be sentimental; father and mother and child in the
garden; the death; the sail to the Lighthouse. I think, though, that when I
begin it I shall enrich it in all sorts of ways; thicken it; give it branches—
roots—which I do not perceive now."[2] Woolf's metaphors of textual
enrichment have changed since *Mrs. Dalloway:* the "beautiful caves" that
were to deepen private history have been exchanged for metaphors drawn
from the interdependent parts of a tree—a family tree, whose "branches"
and "roots" will ironize the family romance by refracting a plural subject
through a plural narrative.

   Woolf's two versions of the genesis of her text depict different parental inspirations and distinct compositional processes that reproduce the
psychoanalytic disputes over the narrative priority of each parent. As
Woolf worked on *To the Lighthouse,* she retreated psychically to an image of

her mother at the origin of her fictional and autobiographical texts, uncovering terrain *Mrs. Dalloway* occludes: "Certainly, there she was, in the very centre of that great Cathedral space which was childhood; there she was from the very first. My first memory is of her lap." Woolf's insistence matches Klein's; it is as if a curtain has been lifted and a prior image of origin has been revealed. *To the Lighthouse* appears increasingly to articulate an obsession emerging into consciousness:

> Blowing bubbles out of a pipe gives the feeling of the rapid crowd of ideas and scenes which blew out of my mind, so that my lips seemed syllabling of their own accord as I walked. What blew the bubbles? Why then? I have no notion. But I wrote the book very quickly; and when it was written, I ceased to be obsessed by my mother. I no longer hear her voice; I do not see her.
>
> I suppose that I did for myself what psycho-analysts do for their patients. I expressed some very long felt and deeply felt emotion. And in expressing it I explained it and then laid it out to rest.[3]

Comparing the production of her text to a psychoanalytic catharsis, Woolf insists that what has been released is the mother of infancy—central, majestic, "there . . . *from the very first*" (emphasis added). When she envisions her father as the center of her text, by contrast, conscious restraint replaces the imperative she represents as her maternal source. No unconscious syllabling engenders the paternal text, which is to be constructed incrementally "between tea and dinner till it is complete for writing out." Rather than selecting between the narratives determined by these images of origin, Woolf distributes them among the second generation of characters, inscribing through the different tales of James, Cam, and Lily a literary version of the psychoanalytic intersection drawn by Freud and Klein.[4]

James and Cam, the Ramsay children who reconstruct the past from the perspective of "The Lighthouse," compose their retrospective narratives under the aegis of their father "sitting in a boat." Both children construct stories that hinge on a renunciation of (the memory of) their mother. The Oedipal structure that dominates James's childhood in "The Window" is completed during his voyage to the lighthouse: in the motionless "middle of the bay"—which mirrors the empty middle of the text, in which Mrs. Ramsay vanishes—James submits to his father's will and "cease[s] to think" about his mother.[5] Woolf glosses James's alignment with his father as a (costly) accession to a symbolic order that both seduces and silences his enigmatic sister Cam. Through Cam, Woolf dramatizes the narrative dilemma of the daughter who thinks back through her father. Cam's story recalls and complicates the normative Freudian route toward femininity by emphasizing the daughter's eroticized relation to the body of the father's texts. Brother and sister both (although differently) substitute paternal texts for the (remembered) body of their mother, and both inadvertently disclose the substitution's insufficiency. Through their narratives of growth and loss, Woolf anticipates and interrogates Lacan's reading of the Oedipal structure as a gateway to the symbolic register.[6]

Lily Briscoe is Woolf's vehicle for posing a Kleinian challenge to the Freudian/Lacanian narrative. Lily's sustained and recuperative matricentric story offers a powerful alternative to James's and Cam's Oedipal fictions. Lily's statement of her painting's, and the novel's, three-part form—"It was a question, she remembered, how to connect this mass on the right hand with that on the left"—counterposes the narrative design presented through the consciousness of the six-year-old James: "[T]he wonder to which he had looked forward, for years and years, it seemed, was, after a night's darkness and a day's sail, within touch" (82–83, 9). Whereas James's account highlights the narrative thrust of the text, the journey *to* the lighthouse, and renders the novel's problematic textual center as an empty space that will incorporate maternal death, Lily's emphasizes mediation rather than progression and refigures time as space, and absence as connection. Through the parallel narratives that constitute "The Lighthouse," Woolf plays Lily's recovery of Mrs. Ramsay's image, preserved as a line drawn "there, in the centre" of Lily's painting, against James's repression of his mother's image at the center of the bay (310). The ongoing negotiation of mother-child boundaries also differentiates Lily from Cam. The place of the daughter that was occupied by Elizabeth Dalloway splits in this text between the literal daughter, Woolf's biographical counterpart within the Ramsay family, and the figurative daughter, freed by her distance from both Ramsays to think back through her (surrogate) mother.[7]

To underscore the distinctiveness of Lily's narrative, Woolf shifts the thematic focus of her story from linguistic to visual representation. Rather than pivoting on a climactic fall into language, the story disclosed through Lily's paintings highlights prelinguistic experience of the mother. In painting, Lily seeks a mode of representation outside the father's symbolic universe. Her use of spatial relations to articulate the earliest human relation looks forward to the development of Klein's perspective within object relations theory from the 1950s through the 1980s. By linking narrative, gender, and representation, *To the Lighthouse* anticipates contemporary psychoanalytic controversies in the encounter it stages between Freud and Klein.

Mapping this encounter requires a focus on "The Lighthouse," the structurally richest, if affectively starkest, portion of Woolf's text. To clarify the problems (especially for daughters) of the patricentric story as Woolf tells it in the 1920s, this chapter pairs the narratives of James and Cam; Lily's more important and intricate story requires a chapter of its own. Together, the two chapters explode the familiar shape of *To the Lighthouse* to make audible a dialogue among discrepant narratives that juxtapose, interpret, and evaluate the discourses of psychoanalysis.

I

Woolf opens *To the Lighthouse* by restaging the scene of interruption in *Mrs. Dalloway*. Mrs. Ramsay and James in the window replace Sally and Clarissa on the terrace; the bond to be broken links the traditional psychoanalytic couple, mother and son, rather than female friends who enact the relationship of mother and daughter. Mr. Ramsay's sudden appearance at the window and his abrupt declaration, "But it won't be fine" reiterates Peter Walsh's sudden appearance at the window and his abrupt question, "Star-gazing?" (10). The literal father has replaced his surrogate in the Oedipal drama Woolf has transferred to the son and seemingly rendered canonical. The male violence that revises the Oedipal story in *Mrs. Dalloway* confirms it in *To the Lighthouse*. James's response to his father's interruption, "Had there been an axe handy, or a poker, any weapon that would have gashed a hole in his father's breast and killed him, there and then, James would have seized it," is more overtly violent than Clarissa's "It was like running one's face against a granite wall in the darkness! It was shocking; it was horrible!"; yet the conventional Oedipal rhetoric easily contains James's fantasy of violence within familiar contours (10). We are situated safely in this discourse; we know how to read its metaphors. Even the imagery of the violent phallic duel, when James stands "very stiff" between his mother's knees watching his father's "beak of brass, the arid scimitar of the male" plunge into the fountain of his mother's sympathy, ritualizes the conflict between father and son (59). If Justin Parry is obscurely, but explicitly, responsible for his eldest daughter's death, James and Mr. Ramsay will never come to blows. The Oedipal narrative appears to have achieved new orthodoxy.

Yet Woolf's docility is deceptive, for although she alters neither the action nor the motives of her Oedipal cast, she inflects the narrative differently from James and questions the values he derives from it. Counterposed to the construction of a tale in which father-son conflict is resolved through a masculine identification that tallies with maturity—the prevailing critical reading of this narrative—is a darker account of the psychic, cognitive, and ethical wages of repression.[8] Moreover, by accenting the outlines of the Oedipal narrative *and* directing our gaze behind them, Woolf suggests the narrative repressions that inhere in the narrative of repression. In choosing repression as her focus, Woolf is revaluing the Freudian paradigm, assessing its costs for its masculine subject and for his female accomplices—both the female characters within the narrative and the female author who experiments with it.

James reads his developmental story as a positive accession to his father's philosophical realism.[9] By grafting the Oedipal narrative onto the epistemological quarrel that traverses *To the Lighthouse,* Woolf seems to endorse his interpretation. In the parental debate about the weather, Mr. Ramsay intervenes between mother and son, bans the pleasure principle they implicitly assume (that nature mirrors human desire; thus Mrs. Ramsay's reassurance, "But it may be fine—I expect it will be fine" [11]), and claims his son for "reality" ("But it won't be fine" [10]). The novel validates Mr. Ramsay's philosophical position in the ten dark years that interrupt the action and divide the lighthouse at which James finally arrives from the object of his boyhood fantasy. Woolf ties the Oedipal framework—the paternal no that forbids the son's desire and the mother's complicity in it, the decade of suspended desire, and its resurgence toward an altered goal—to the triumph of Mr. Ramsay's conviction that a gulf splits the world from our desires. According to this logic, the voyage to the lighthouse must await Mrs. Ramsay's death, for the visionary lighthouse that son and mother see partakes of the fantasy world they share, the "marvel" of the lighthouse beam dovetailing perfectly with the conclusion of the fairy tale Mrs. Ramsay reads to James. The "stark tower on a bare rock" at which James arrives seals his separation from his mother (277). A point in actual space and time, this lighthouse is no longer the mirroring eye ("I") that his mother embraces in ecstatic subjectivity but an icon of separation and factuality. "Barred with black and white," it incarnates a visual reminder of the father's prohibition, as well as representing "that loneliness which was for both of them the truth about things" (277, 301). Stark and solitary paternal reality replaces fantasmatic union with the mother. The story joins the triumph of the father's authority, his successful engineering of the resented trip, to the transmission of authority to the son. In the rite of passage that begins with the revival of James's anger at his father for disturbing "the perfect simplicity and good sense of his relations with his mother" (58), James assumes the position of authority at the tiller of the boat; the rite is completed with the only words Mr. Ramsay addresses to his son, the long-awaited "Well done!" (306). In the course of part 3, James increasingly identifies with his father: "[H]e had come to feel, quite often lately, . . . there were two pairs of footprints only; his own and his father's" (274–75). "[A]s a matter of fact," James thinks with pleasure as he watches the stark black and white lighthouse rising in front of him, "it's like that. . . . They shared that knowledge" (302).

But what is "that knowledge" which the lighthouse seems so unproblematically to represent, and how exactly is it gained? Complicating the alliance she constructs between Freud and Mr. Ramsay's philosophy, Woolf writes an Oedipal narrative that severs its protagonist from "reality." Against the overt function of James's Oedipal story—to narrate the achievement of objectivity—she plays a covert function—to narrate the accession to subjectivity. Her insistence on repression undermines the comedy of James's reconciliation with Mr. Ramsay. Anticipating Lacan, Woolf shifts her accent from the empirical reality the black-and-white lighthouse seems transparently to signify to the status of the lighthouse as a signifier that depends on a disjunction from reality.

The Oedipal drama in part 3 is condensed into a single section that recreates the scene of interruption at the window in part 1. Section 8 of part 3 is staged as a narrative hiatus: in the "middle of the bay," the wind falls, motion stops, and James's imagination reverts to the novel's opening scene. The narrative interlude parallels the scene of Clarissa Dalloway's withdrawal from the party: a retrospective moment rewrites the interruption in the past. Woolf's Oedipal plot requires this division: to be resolved, the Oedipal scene must be recalled and revised; the narrative splits between two moments, the second of which rewrites the first. That recognition should occur through recollection is faithful to the structure of the Oedipus story and to that of psychoanalysis itself, but Woolf insists recollection is revision. By dividing the Oedipal moment from its effects on consciousness, she conflates the repression of desire, deferred from the original scene to the scene of its recollection, with a deliberate process of revision. Recognition thus becomes misrecognition, dually entailed by the birth of the unconscious through repression and by a conscious process of revision.

James's scene of recollection begins as his attempt to understand his ambivalence toward his father: "They alone knew each other. What then was this terror, this hatred?" (275). Framed thus, as the son's effort to reconcile filial hatred and identification, the remembered scene both requires and proscribes the mother's presence; needed to account for one stance, she must be banished to allow the other. Set in the dead center of the bay, the scene on the boat is haunted by the mother whose memory must be repressed if James is to seal his identification with his father, break the stasis in the middle of the bay, and move toward the lighthouse and the future rather than remaining attached to the past. The maritime setting underscores the lure and the danger of this maternal past which, siren-like, could suck him back into its hold; the Odyssean ambiance is heightened by the line Mrs. Ramsay cites in part 1 from William Browne's "Siren Song."[10] James's conflict finds expression in the repetitive structure of this drama of consciousness, which plays the fleeting memory of a veiled, alluring maternal presence against the vivid image of a harsh paternal censor.

James first explains his conflict with his father hypothetically and impersonally: "Suppose then that as a child sitting helpless . . . he had seen a waggon crush ignorantly and innocently, some one's foot . . . anybody's foot. One sat and watched it" (275). Disavowing both his father's responsibility and his own pain, James offers only the disguised reminder of an Oedipal story in the swollen foot (the literal meaning of "Oedipus") that is not his own. Working to situate this scene, James remembers first an Edenic garden (the loss of the mother is a Fall), then a house from whose interior, enclosed by a "leaf-like veil," he can see "a figure stooping, hear, coming close, going away, some dress rustling, some chain tinkling" (276). It is night: a faintly sketched scene of childhood desire, the barely hinted moment of the mother's nighttime kiss, James's last encounter with his mother in the text. As the adolescent James imaginatively approaches this unnamed, scarcely visible, maternal center of memory, this evanescent figure whose coming and going enacts his own ambivalent (because forbidden) desire, the recollection of his father as a fixed "something" that "stayed and darkened over him . . . arid and sharp" returns him to the present and the image of the lighthouse as a "tower, stark and straight" (276). In the present as in the past, the father dispels this intimacy, prohibiting the mother who beckons now to the awakening of unconscious desire. Drawn downward and pulled up, shuttling psychically back and forth in the immobilized boat for which his father, he believes, holds him responsible, James is torn between remembering "the rustle of some one coming, the tinkle of some one going" and fearing his father's expected interruption: "For in one moment if there was no breeze, his father would slap the covers of his book together, and say: 'What's happening now? . . .' as, once before he had brought his blade down among them on the terrace" (277).

The crisis is averted not, as appears, by the sudden liberating gust of wind that sends the boat on its course toward the lighthouse but by James's internalization of paternal censorship. The final descent into memory begins as an evasion of Mr. Ramsay's imagined surveillance: "At any moment Mr. Ramsay (he scarcely dared look at him) might rouse himself, shut his book and say something sharp; but for the moment he was reading, so that James stealthily, as if he were stealing downstairs on bare feet, afraid of waking a watchdog by a creaking board, went on thinking what was she like, where did she go that day?" (278). Pursuing his mother mentally "from room to room," James finally sees her standing "in a blue light, . . . saying simply whatever came into her head" (278). The vision allows James to identify "the source of her everlasting attraction for him": "She alone spoke the truth; to her alone could he speak it" (278). The veil is torn; Mrs. Ramsay stands revealed as truth. But her truth cannot be heard; the moment of disclosure is the moment of repression; the internalized censor bars knowledge and desire. "But all the time he thought of her, he was conscious of his father following his thought, surveying it, making it shiver and falter. At last he ceased to think" (278). Having made the "happy world" of childhood "shrivel and fall," (276) the father makes its memory "shiver and falter" (278). The image behind the veil—mother, memory, truth, desire—is apprehended and concealed.

Such an unabashed account of repression directs our attention to the ellipsis at the center of the section's final paragraph: "A rope seemed to bind him there, and his father had knotted it and he could only escape by taking a knife and plunging it. . . . But at that moment the sail swung slowly round" (279). In this unarticulated moment, James is released by the unexpected, unexplained gust of wind. Seemingly external, and divided by two sentences from the preceding cessation of thought, this resolution conceals the logic that connects it to the triumph of paternal censorship. Having "ceased to think" about his mother, James can proceed to his destination and complete his identification with his father, despite some enduring hostility toward him. The ellipsis reenacts the moment of repression, which reenacts the original scene of interruption. The narrative hiatus concealed by three dots condenses and reiterates the interlude of "Time Passes." James's future is precariously purchased by repression. In the middle of the journey, at the center of the bay, and of the novel, lies the submerged image of the mother, over which the son sails on his course to masculinity.

James's celebrated recognition that the lighthouse is both his father's black-and-white tower and his mother's silvery tower with a yellow eye must be read within this narrative context. Introducing the final descent into memory that ends with the erasure of his mother's image (and thus of her image of the lighthouse), the assertion marks a stage within a psychological balancing act, not the conclusion of that process. Woolf uses the Oedipal narrative to subvert the affirmations that surround James's development, to puncture the illusion that he can both be his father's heir and retain his mother's heritage. By dramatizing the mental act that inaugurates the unconscious and by repeating as a single moment of repression the ten-year gap that bisects *To the Lighthouse,* Woolf inserts discontinuity into the heart of James's story, confounding the impression of a linear journey and compromising the resolution achieved by the arrival at the lighthouse. As in *Mrs. Dalloway,* Woolf underlines the shift that enables the seemingly affirmative resolution. After the ellipsis, the narrative perspective veers away from James, returning only in section 7 to record his reconciliation with his father. James is absent from the moment of release; the image of renewed potency is displaced to the ship. The interruption has been interrupted; the journey resumes, but only through a process of revision. The paragraph concludes with an image of Mr. Ramsay mysteriously transformed from a tyrant and intruder into a conductor of a secret symphony, a man attuned to the music of the spheres. Echoing the shift from the intrusive Peter Walsh to the heroic Richard Dalloway in the parallel scene of reconstruction in *Mrs. Dalloway,* Mr. Ramsay is finally redeemed. The "But" that introduces the change of weather ("But at that moment the sail swung slowly round") liberates the boat and recalls Mr.

Ramsay's opening position about the weather ("But it won't be fine"), reversing the original scene of interruption, transforming rupture into release.

Woolf works her revision of the Oedipal scene for James rather than through him, remaining more distant from her male protagonist than she had been from Clarissa Dalloway. Reversing the sexual politics of *Mrs. Dalloway*, where Septimus's sacrifice provides the terms that enable Clarissa to revise and relinquish the past, Woolf has Mrs. Ramsay, Lily, and Cam clarify the cost of James's passage rather than obfuscating, and thus facilitating, it. The mother whose image James consigns to oblivion provides an absence through which James's loss can be articulated. As her image behind the veil haunts his scene on the boat, her voice haunts his text. James does not record the pure, unmediated "truth" Mrs. Ramsay speaks in memory: any particular verbal formulation would compromise its integrity. We hear Mrs. Ramsay's voice indirectly, however, from beyond the margins of the text. The scene on the boat refers us to another scene—that of Mrs. Ramsay's reading in the final section of "The Window." If the nautical setting of the revisionary Oedipal scene enables us to hear between the lines of James's reverie the "Siren Song" that articulates the dangers posed by memory, the imagery that introduces James's search for memory redirects us to the other text that Mrs. Ramsay reads.

James seeks an aesthetic shape to organize his terror, hatred, and understanding of his father. "Turning back among the many leaves which the past had folded in him, . . . he sought an image to cool and detach and round off his feeling in a concrete shape" (275). The imagistic sequence mirrors his mother's. As Mrs. Ramsay "opened the book[,] . . . she felt that she was climbing backwards, upwards, shoving her way up under petals that curved over her" (178–79). Her reading progresses from Browne's "Siren Song," whose opening line she quotes, to Shakespeare's Sonnet 98, which answers the need that motivates her search: "How satisfying! How restful! . . . she held it in her hands, beautiful and reasonable, clear and complete, the essence sucked out of life and held rounded here—the sonnet" (181). The echoes between the passages present Shakespeare's sonnet as the "concrete shape" James seeks for his feelings. The maternal voice as unsullied truth that cannot be represented speaks in James's text through two other texts that articulate the crossroads at which he is poised: between the dangers of engulfment and the pain of separation, between a past defined by (maternal) presence and a future defined by the (maternal) absence that enables and inaugurates textuality.

Through its metaphors of language ("tell," "praise," "figures"), Sonnet 98 translates a lament over absence into a reflection on representation. Mrs. Ramsay quotes from the final quatrain and the couplet, but the entire sonnet clarifies the issues that confront her son.

From you have I been absent in the spring,
When proud-pied April, dressed in all his trim,
Hath put a spirit of youth in everything,
That heavy Saturn laughed and leapt with him;
Yet nor the lays of birds, nor the sweet smell
Of different flowers in odor and in hue,
Could make me any summer's story tell,
Or from their proud lap pluck them where they grew:
Nor did I wonder at the lily's white,
Nor praise the deep vermillion in the rose;
They were but sweet, but figures of delight,
Drawn after you, the pattern of all those.
    Yet seemed it winter still, and you away,
    As with your shadow I with these did play.

As the season of rebirth, the renewal of presence, spring should signify itself; its natural signs should embody their conventional significance; the "lays of birds" and "sweet smell" of flowers should tell, and thus inspire, a "summer's story." But the speaker's subjective situation, an "I" separated from a "you," disrupts this unity, transforming signs of presence into a play of substitutes, "figures," signs of absence that compensate poorly for a vanished "pattern." By recalling this sonnet in a scene whose primary metaphor is a veil and whose pivotal rhetorical device is an ellipsis, Woolf signals James's entry into a realm of figuration that (inadequately) substitutes for maternal presence.[11]

The scene on the boat is framed by two descriptions that link repression with representation through the image of a steamer erased from the horizon, an image associated with Mrs. Ramsay, whom Lily had pictured at the dinner party as a ship that fades beneath the horizon and then returns to life. At the end of section 7, directly prefacing the scene on the Ramsay boat, Lily observes that

> A steamer far out at sea had drawn in the air a great scroll of smoke which stayed there curving and circling decoratively, as if the air were a fine gauze which held things and kept them softly in its mesh, only gently swaying them this way and that. And as happens sometimes when the weather is very fine, the cliffs looked as if they were conscious of the ships, and the ships looked as if they were conscious of the cliffs, as if they signalled to each other some message of their own. For sometimes quite close to the shore, the Lighthouse looked this morning in the haze an enormous distance away. (271)

This is a scene of absolute presence; consciousness takes no toll of physicality; the landscape sustains and integrates the signifiers it produces. This coherence requires the lighthouse to be distant; its proximity, the conjunction "For" suggests, would disrupt this system of communication. The scene allegorizes two mutually exclusive signifying systems: one, which excludes the lighthouse, is based on presence; the other, which incorporates the lighthouse, is based on absence. After James's section, Lily describes the scene again, with a difference: "The steamer itself had vanished, but the great scroll of smoke still hung in the air and drooped like a flag mournfully in valediction" (279–80). With the passage of the steamer, and the concurrent erasure of Mrs. Ramsay's image from James's memory, the scroll of smoke announces the advent of a system that mournfully salutes the presence it has lost. The lighthouse that marks James's destination is the central figure in this system; the more emphatically it signifies empirical reality, the more it displays its function as a signifier. The descriptions of the steamer register James's passage into a realm of figuration that undercuts his equation of his destination with his father's version of "reality."

James's voyage to the lighthouse, however, does replay his father's philosophical venture: the literal and figurative journeys together reveal the gesture that underlies the culture James inherits. Mr. Ramsay's solitary speculative venture, section 6 of "The Window," provides an important parallel to the scene on the boat. Our most extended access to Mr. Ramsay's consciousness, the scene is depicted through metaphors that are actualized in James's voyage. The intellectual fortitude required to reach R, represented through tropes of masculine heroism, prefigure the stance required of James. "Qualities that would have saved a ship's company exposed on a broiling sea with six biscuits and a flask of water" (54) become those needed on the boat that "slapped and dawdled there in the hot sun" (274); the "desolate expedition across the icy solitudes of the polar region" (54) becomes the "waste of snow and rock very lonely and austere" where James comes to feel "there were two pairs of footprints only" (274–75). Both scenes proceed through erasures of the mother, the material antithesis to symbolic systems, and both select language (or its rudiments) as the metaphor for knowledge gained by the repression of her.

Mr. Ramsay's solitary search for R is framed by two encounters with Mrs. Ramsay: the argument about the weather and the request for sympathy. Mrs. Ramsay's role as mother is explicit in the second scene, which pictures her as a "nurse carrying a light across a dark room" to assure "a fractious child," and portrays Mr. Ramsay being "filled with her words, like a child who drops off satisfied" (60). During his own meditation, Mr. Ramsay repeatedly returns to the image of mother and son sitting in the window. If James's drama of consciousness is structured as a conflict between memory and censorship, Mr. Ramsay's unfolds as a conflict between the image of the mother and speculative thought, which he imagines as a heroic quest beyond the material world. The opposition maternity/philosophy is recurrent in the novel. Mr. Bankes allegorizes Mr.

Ramsay's deviation from the straight path of philosophy by the story of the mother hen spreading her wings around her chicks, "upon which Ramsay, stopping, pointed his stick and said 'Pretty—pretty'. . . . After that, Ramsay had married" and divested himself "of all those glories of isolation and austerity which crowned him in youth to cumber himself definitely with fluttering wings and clucking domesticities" (34–35, 37). The insistence of Charles Tansley, Mr. Ramsay's philosophical protégé, that "[w]omen made civilisation impossible with all their 'charm,' all their silliness" is a direct response to Mrs. Ramsay's maternal sympathy (129).[12] In Mr. Ramsay's scene, we shift from Mrs. Ramsay's consciousness to the philosopher's with a description of escape: "He was safe, he was restored to his privacy" (52); male subjectivity is here defined in opposition to the mother. The scene concludes by echoing Mr. Ramsay's "Pretty—pretty." Returning from "the intensity of his isolation," the philosopher again "does homage to the beauty of the world" incarnate in the mother who tries unsuccessfully throughout the novel to call his attention to physical beauty, especially to the flowers that serve in this passage as an emblem of the material world he struggles to transcend (57).

Between the moments of withdrawal and return, the scene of philosophy proceeds through oppositions: between heroism and domesticity, transcendence and immanence, death and life, language and image. Reaching R, a philosophical goal and a psychosocial identity (Ramsay), is a question of transcending the bonds of matter and *mater*. Despite his promise "to talk 'some nonsense' to the young men of Cardiff about Locke, Hume, and Berkeley, and the causes of the French Revolution" (70), despite his insistence on basing meteorological predictions on scientific fact, Mr. Ramsay's need to establish his identity in opposition to the mother muddies his respect for material reality. In his fantasies, Mr. Ramsay is a solitary hero, leading his men through an increasingly rarefied landscape (the sea, the "icy solitudes of the Polar region," the arctic mountain from which he sees "the waste of ages and the perishing of the stars") away from the grasp of the material world (54, 57). The fantasy culminates in solitary death (celebrated elsewhere in his favorite refrain, "We perished each alone"), the affirmation of heroic male identity as the severance of ties to maternal/material origins. Separation becomes rarefaction; a metaphorics of transcendence compromises faith in "facts uncompromising"; and the discourse of realism yields to the discourse of Platonism.[13] Juxtaposing images of distance and proximity, the scene stages philosophical thought as the search for what is "scarcely visible to mortal eyes" (53).

Shifts in focus organize the scene, which oscillates between the image of mother and son in the window and Mr. Ramsay's search for R— for philosophy, symbolic structure, and masculine identity. By metaphorizing philosophy as language ("For if thought . . . like the alphabet is ranged in twenty-six letters all in order" [53]), Woolf not only underscores the linear character of Mr. Ramsay's quest but also insists on the exclusionary basis of speculative thought: the replacement of thing by word, of the image of the mother by the language of the father, by the Name of the Father, Ramsay, R. Image and sign cannot coexist: the perception of the mother must be displaced for R to be manifest. The section opens as Mr. Ramsay situates his wife in the domain of the visual, exterior to language, although supportive of it: she is to language as "illustration" is to "printed page" (53). As the metaphor of language is introduced in the following paragraph, the image of Mrs. Ramsay and James is distanced in both space and time: "[H]e saw, but now far, far away, . . . his wife and son, together, in the window. . . . But after Q?" (53). Mother and son do not come back into focus until the heroic search through the polar wastes for R has been renounced and "the hero puts his armour off, and halts by the window and gazes at his wife and son, who, very distant at first, gradually come closer and closer, till lips and book and head are clearly before him" (57).

Although Mr. Ramsay returns to the material world, he outlines for James the masculine journey into the symbolic terrain represented by language, the sign of material/maternal absence. Mr. Ramsay's scene, moreover, is the site of an unannounced but pivotal transition in his son's identity. When the novel opens, James sits tranquilly at his mother's knees cutting out pictures from an "illustrated catalogue," learning under her supervision to "guide his scissors neatly round the refrigerator," learning, that is, about boundaries (9, 10). After Mr. Ramsay's discouraging pronouncement about the weather, Mrs. Ramsay tries to console her son by looking through the catalog for "something like a rake, or a mowing-machine, which, with its prongs and its handles, would need the greatest skill and care in cutting out" (26–27). Out of this activity, and this relationship, James will become an artist, his mother fantasizes: "[A]nd why should he not? He had a splendid forehead" (49). As if the fantasy provokes a paternal counterpart, Mr. Ramsay instantly appears at the window and claims James as his heir while tickling his bare leg: "'James will have to write *his* dissertation one of these days,' he added ironically, flicking his sprig" (50). Speculative discourse will displace the apprenticeship in negotiating boundaries James pursues under the aegis of his mother, and the visual imagination will devolve exclusively on Lily, the artist-daughter. Prefacing Mr. Ramsay's solitary scene, this miniature drama is resolved through it. Mother and son return into Mr. Ramsay's focus engaged with texts rather than with images and outlines, a transformation seemingly wrought by the power of the philosopher's gaze, which has pressed his wife into service. The "lips and book and head" that return to Mr. Ramsay's view are the only sign of an enduring change: Mrs. Ramsay reads to James for the duration of their time together in "The Window." At the end of the preceding section, Mrs. Ramsay had kissed

James on the forehead (the very organ that presages his artistic vocation) and suggested they find "another picture to cut out" (48). The term that mediates between mother and son has changed through the father's intervention from a picture to a book, which now divides the mother's lips from the forehead of her son, replacing a kiss by the reading of a text.

It is not only the mother whose relationship to James is mediated by texts, however. Cam also comes to discern a textual filter in her exchanges with her brother, although as sister she is the auditor rather than the reader. Cam records the conclusion of the process Mrs. Ramsay initiates. As James assumes his father's position in "The Lighthouse," Cam feels increasingly burdened by the pact she and James have made, for father and son divide between themselves the double bind governing the destiny of daughters: to learn to desire the father and to abstain from desiring him. Mr. Ramsay plays the father-seducer who subjects Cam to an "extraordinary temptation. . . . For no one attracted her more; his hands were beautiful, and his feet, and his voice, and his words" (253); James plays the father-prohibiter, tapping his own filial defiance for the moral authority to proscribe the daughter's love. Cam perceives the transformation of son into father as an accession to language and law: "James the lawgiver, with the tablets of eternal wisdom laid open on his knee (his hand on the tiller had become symbolical to her), said, Resist him. Fight him. He said so rightly; justly" (251). If Mrs. Ramsay's pictures metamorphose into a book, the tiller/phallus passed from father to son evolves into *the* "symbolical" patriarchal text, the "tablets of eternal wisdom" that conflate Mosaic with Oedipal law. As a Mosaic figure issuing commandments etched in stone, the son enunciates the father's law that forbids the sister's desire, reducing her to silence, rendering her unable to "move some obstacle that lay upon her tongue" and to give her father, "unsuspected by James, a private token of the love she felt for him" (252).

II

The voyage to the lighthouse caps James's drama exclusively. Cam, who has never longed for this journey, drifts suspended between the text's dual resolutions: the arrival at the lighthouse and the completion of Lily's painting. The characterization of Cam appears to indicate some irresolution on Woolf's part: minimally outlined in part 1, Cam nevertheless joins the finale in part 3, although as such a shadowy, attenuated presence it is not clear why she is included. Yet, far from evincing artistic incoherence, her plight brilliantly exposes the sources of the daughter's silencing.

Cam is an enigma throughout the novel. Less central than James, she is also less programmatic: no ritualistic images or phrases allegorize her consciousness. Her developmental course, subtler than James's, entails sacrificing agency. As a child, Cam is fiercely independent: "She would not 'give a flower to the gentleman' as the nursemaid told her. No! no! no! she would not!" (36). Hence her appellation by Mr. Bankes: "Cam the Wicked" (83). Indecipherable even to her mother (and perhaps the only character who is), Cam seems wholly present to herself as she dashes through part 1 like a projectile guided by some urgent private desire: "She was off like a bird, bullet, or arrow, impelled by what desire, shot by whom, at what directed, who could say? What, what? Mrs. Ramsay pondered, watching her" (84). This defiant energy has dissipated by part 3; Cam sits passively in the boat while her brother navigates, her father reads and chats with Macalister, and Macalister's boy catches fish. Like the boat that bobs up and down in place, Cam's thoughts circle back on themselves as she aimlessly dabbles her hand in the water and watches the fish that objectify her feeling of mutilation.[14] Whereas the narrative holds James psychically responsible for the interrupted progress of the boat by linking his drama of memory and repression to the fall and rise of the wind, thereby according him the task of reshaping the past to enable the future, Cam's internal drama, which follows and depends on her brother's, is severed from this narrative teleology. James faces the lighthouse and navigates toward it; Cam sits in the bow and gazes back toward the island. Although brother and sister share the task of reconstructing memory, Cam's efforts in no way impinge on the action. Her project is purely historical.

At the beginning of "The Lighthouse," the cowed and angry siblings share a single will, although Cam's syntactic subordination—"He would be impatient in a moment, James thought, and Cam thought" (242), "So James could tell, so Cam could tell" (245)—indicates the brother's dominance. Woolf chooses the occasion of an interpolated masculine "text" to introduce Cam as an independent consciousness. Macalister's tale of maritime rescue and disaster, prompted by Mr. Ramsay's questions about the great storm at Christmas, weaves an alliance between the two old men, overcoming class and ethnic differences to constitute a homogeneous narrative voice as Mr. Ramsay adjusts his gaze and speech to Macalister's and mimics his Scottish accent. Shared pleasure in the sexual division of labor and its representation in narrative outweighs other differences: Mr. Ramsay "liked that men should labour and sweat on the windy beach at night; . . . he liked men to work like that, and women to keep house, and sit beside sleeping children indoors, while men were drowned, out there in a storm" (245). Woolf dramatizes the impact of this story not on James, who can aspire to a future role in it, but on its more problematic female auditor, whose access to this explicitly masculine discourse requires mediation. The imaginative arena the story opens frees the carefully guarded love Cam feels for her father, but this release is qualified by the mental act it presupposes. Cam can enter this discourse only by displacing herself as its potential subject, transfering her childhood love of adventure to an idealized image of her (elderly) father, with some consequent mystification of her own emotion. "Cam thought, feeling proud of him *without knowing quite why,* had he been there he would have launched the lifeboat, he would have reached the wreck. . . . He was so brave, he was so adventurous" (246; emphasis added).

Cam's idealization of Mr. Ramsay, moreover, provokes a return of what it has repressed: the knowledge of his tyranny. This knowledge is Cam's as well as James's and the "compact" that declares it and that suddenly checks her surge of affection for her father has presumably been forged by both of them. Yet Cam perceives the agreement as a text she can neither revise, revoke, not fully endorse, a coercive force that evolves into the tablets of eternal wisdom lying on her brother's knee, silencing her. Cam is complicit in this silencing. Although the compact *does* represent James's perspective more fully that her own and *does* reflect his greater authority, Cam's desire to evade her own anger obscures her part in the creation of an unwritten text that records a strand of her relation to her father. As she projects her former adventurousness onto her father, she projects onto her brother her former defiance, the voice that had said "No! no! no!" to the gentleman, and divides her salient childhood characteristics between two men and two texts in which her participation can lead only to her alienation. Denying herself the roles of both protagonist and author, she colludes with the assumptions of patriarchal textuality.[15] The scene on the boat reflects some prior learning.

Paralyzed by the standoff between her father and her brother, Cam recovers her own memories only after this drama is resolved in section 8 and the boat is speeding toward the lighthouse once again. In section 10 the motion sparks Cam's imagination, which converts the growing distance into time and reverts to a single privileged scene, her counterpart to James's epiphanic vision of his mother. Cam, however, remembers her father, not her mother, and a study rather than a garden. Eden to her is the garden's aftermath, although the narrative suggests that this revision is delusion. "Sometimes she strayed in from the garden purposely to catch them at it. There they were (it might be Mr. Carmichael or Mr. Bankes who was sitting with her father) sitting opposite each other in their low armchairs. . . . Just to please herself she would take a book from the shelf and stand there, watching her father write" (281). In Cam's imagination, fathers know best, and they speak the knowledge of the printed text. "They were crackling in front of them the pages of *The Times,* when she came in from the garden, all in a muddle, about something some one had said about Christ, or hearing that a mammoth had been dug up in a London street, or wondering what Napoleon was like" (281). "Straying" from garden to study, from nature to culture, from the private muddle to the public text, Cam reenacts Clarissa Dalloway's symbolic moment of transition, but Cam's is a voluntary shift from one developmental era to another.

In Cam's memory, closure is gentle, a gradual transition from one sphere to another, a gradual translation of experience to thought that unfolds organically like a leaf that has regained its natural environment. As a child in the study Cam had felt that "one could let whatever one thought expand here like a leaf in water" (282). Yet the tension between her metaphor and her literal description undercuts her evolutionary model, reasserting a distinction she would blur. Throughout the text Woolf associates the leaf with Mrs. Ramsay. In "The Window" Cam carries a leaf when she responds to her mother's call; in "The Lighthouse" the leaf is her recurrent image for the island that incarnates the receding past: "It lay like that on the sea, did it, with a dent in the middle and two sharp crags, and the sea swept in there, and spread away for miles and miles on either side of the island. It was very small; shaped something like a leaf stood on end" (280). Cam's simile revises but does not conceal a prior, less overt metaphorization of the island as a female body from which she is slowly drawn away as James steers the boat toward the tower on the rock. With a sea-swept dent in the middle of two crags, the island hovering behind the leaf is a figure of the mother. As a child, Cam hoped to extend, articulate, and assess the past identified with the garden and the mother by translating the leaf into the language of the father—and, in so doing, to imitate her father's own translations of hedges into periods, of geranium leaves into "scraps of paper on which one scribbles notes in the rush of reading," of nature's leaves into the pages of a book (66). When she repeats this gesture in the present, a fissure opens. It is the image of the leaf-shaped island that triggers her adolescent memory: "Small as it was, and shaped something like a leaf stood on its end with the gold-sprinkled waters flowing in and about it, it had, she supposed, a place in the universe—even that little island? The old gentlemen in the study she thought could have told her. Sometimes she strayed in from the garden" (281). The rift between the gold-sprinkled island and the old men in the study reveals what has been lost in the translation and what now is lost more emphatically in Cam's attempt to situate one domain of experience within the discourse of another.

Only these repercussions of the past in the present lend credibility to the hints of a Fall. If the young Cam "strays" from the garden in search of information, this knowledge is not forbidden, nor is she expelled. The garden, moreover, is no unfallen natural paradise, for voices within it have produced the muddle that sends her in search of clarification. If there is a Fall, it does not pertain to the search for knowledge, or even to its source (the study is a logical, perhaps inevitable, resource to enlist), but to its consequences. The historical questions that arise in the garden—about

Christ, Napoleon, and a prehistoric mammoth—are appropriately carried to the study, but they differ from the issue the older Cam mentally refers to the same place: a question of personal history, of the private past, of the mother's place "in the universe." However passionately motivated her search for knowledge and however legitimate her indebtedness to her father, Cam's apprenticeship in the study ensnares her as well as liberating her, sanctioning certain modes of thought, discouraging others, creating an intellectual framework that becomes her single frame of reference. The old gentlemen in the study reinforce Cam's interest in history, priming her for the position she assumes in the boat.[16] Studying the past, she also learns to privilege it. By the time of "The Lighthouse" Cam is expert at gazing backward, at translating images of a shifting present into the framework of the past, at extending in adolescence patterns learned as a child.

The scene in the study both mirrors and prepares the scene in the boat. Moreover, Cam's psychological position in the present, as well as her literal one, finds a precedent in her father's study. In both situations Cam's curiosity and responsiveness draw her imaginatively into a conversation between men, with a consequent erosion of her own subjectivity. As the two scenes blur in her mind, similarities emerge between her relation to the story spun by Mr. Ramsay and Macalister, and her relation to the dialogue between Mr. Ramsay and an old gentleman "who might be Mr. Carmichael or Mr. Bankes," whose identity matters less than his structural position opposite her father—Macalister's position. (This location is indicated obliquely through stage directions: when James fears his father's admonition about a slackening sail, he imagines that Mr. Ramsay "would say sharply, 'Look out! Look out!' and old Macalister would turn slowly on his seat"—presumably to look at the drooping sail; when Mr. Ramsay listens to Macalister's story, he leans forward—presumably to catch every word [244].)

In the study ambiguity obscures who talks with whom. Cam wants to believe that her questions received answers, but the text suggests that the gentlemen conversed primarily with one another. Whom did they address when they turned their papers, crossed their knees, "and said something now and then very brief" (281). An almost identical phrase in the next sentence records a conversation between the two old men: Mr. Ramsay said something "briefly to the other old gentleman opposite" (281). Only in Cam's final recapitulation of the scene does someone explicitly answer her question: "The old gentleman, lowering the paper suddenly, said something very brief over the top of it about the character of Napoleon" (283). Is this a wishful secondary revision, part of her project of rescuing her father from James's hostile fantasy? The substance of the interaction reinforces its structural ambiguity. Cam's only question to be answered, and the only specified content of any verbal exchange, concerns the character of Napoleon—ominous, since Woolf elsewhere depicts him as the paradigmatic figure who excludes women from history.[17] That his character should be the climax of a scene in which Cam struggles to learn history reveals the pathos of her eagerness for access to a discourse whose terms diminish her and for a place in an exchange that undermines her status as interlocutor.

The apprenticeship in the study is not the only source of Cam's attenuation in language. It may be her fate as youngest daughter to serve as a vehicle of messages rather than their sender or recipient, and her willing metamorphosis into a blank page encourages her use as a transparent medium. The significant variable is the gender of the speakers. In "The Window" Woolf briefly sketches an alternative semiotic context for Cam. When sent by Mrs. Ramsay to ask the cook if Andrew, Paul, and Minta have returned from the beach, Cam mimics for her mother the cook's exact response. But between the question and the answer, she inserts her own story, and "it was only by waiting patiently, and hearing that there was an old woman in the kitchen with very red cheeks, drinking soup out of a basin, that Mrs. Ramsay at last prompted that parrot-like instinct which had picked up Mildred's words quite accurately and could now produce them, if one waited, in a colourless singsong" (85). A diminutive female Hermes shuttling between two female speakers, Cam nevertheless succeeds in imposing her own embryonic narrative. Its subject, "an old woman in the kitchen," resonates against Woolf's first description of the vision to which Cam is heir: the father in a boat. The text associates the red-cheeked old woman with the bibulous elderly cleaning woman, Mrs. McNab, who in "Time Passes" remembers being "always welcome in the kitchen," where the cook, at Mrs. Ramsay's request, kept a plate of milk soup for her (206).[18] Though stripped of Mrs. Ramsay's arabesquing consciousness, Mrs. McNab serves in "Time Passes" as a bare corporeal remainder and reminder of her mistress, an incarnation of memory who tears the "veil of silence" that has fallen on the Ramsay home (196). As the lowest common denominator of female artistry, the work of preservation whose psychological correlate Mrs. Ramsay calls "the effort of merging and flowing and creating" (126), Mrs. McNab is the figure who by sheer determination (and the help of Mrs. Bast and her son) rescues the Ramsays' home from "the sands of oblivion" and connects the first part of the novel to the third (209).[19] As Cam's kitchen muse, she fleetingly inspires a story that refuses to be squelched. In the same way that her position in the novel inscribes the traces of female labor in a bleakly inhuman textual center, her position in Cam's circuit as messenger raises the prospect of a third rendition of the novel's three-part form.

Cam's vision of the island as a sea-swept dent between two crags hints at this rendition. The configuration of mass and space shows a family resemblance to James's "night's darkness" between two days and to Lily's "question . . . how to connect this mass on the right hand with that on the left," but Cam represents the center as a place of origin. Her glimpse of the island shares with her miniature narrative a buried notion of female engendering. These echoing accounts could evolve into Cam's counterpart to the narrative formulas offered by James and Lily; they could become Cam's story, her metanarrative, her version of history. But this nascent narrative design never emerges, and cannot. Cam's muted presence in the text is no accident, for it is precisely when she first perceives the island as a body ("She had never seen it from out at sea before" [280]) that she turns to the memory of the study.

Cam's poignancy derives from a narrative perspective that blends sympathy with irony. It is less that we see options to which Cam is blind (to whom should she refer her questions about history?) than that we can gauge the cost of choices she has made, interpret metaphors opaque to her, and register her pleasure as an index of her innocence. Although Cam's course may look easier than James's—the death of their mother appears less devastating to her, and her father is less peremptory with her—we can nevertheless observe that if her suffering is less sharply focused and articulate, it is also less empowering. Cam enters the realm of discourse less successfully than James. Her own metaphors betray that her father's study, in which she takes such pleasure, offers her the material of language more readily than its significance.[20] Within this sanctuary Cam relishes the tangible signs of language, with no expectation that their meaning is available. She represents the old gentlemen's clarification of her muddle as a tactile, rather than a verbal, intervention: "Then they took all this [muddle] with their clean hands (they wore grey-coloured clothes; they smelt of heather) and they brushed the scraps together" (281). Instead of reading the book she takes from the shelf "just to please herself," she watches her father write and admires the evenness of his lines without attempting to decipher their meaning.

The scene on the boat mirrors this relation to paternal texts. Cam is both thoroughly familiar with, and ignorant of, the book in which her father is engrossed, "the little book whose yellowish pages she knew, without knowing what was written on them. It was small; it was closely printed. . . . But what might be written in the book which had rounded its edges off in his pocket, she did not know. What he thought they none of them knew" (283). The father as text, like the father's texts, remains hermetic to her, and her attempt to generalize this condition cracks against James's conviction that he and his father "alone knew each other" (275). Cam's image of the tiller's transformation into tablets marks her only conscious recognition of their father's differing legacies. These differences crystallize in the children's final interactions with Mr. Ramsay. Cam's relationship with her father culminates in a silent gesture of paternal courtship, as Mr. Ramsay hands her "a gingerbread nut, as if he were a great Spanish gentleman, she thought, handing a flower to a lady at a window (so courteous his manner was)" (305). The father-son relationship concludes with the breaking of silence in the long-withheld "Well done!" that answers James's unspoken desire for paternal recognition and praise (306). Despite (or because of) Cam's delight in her father's courtly gesture, this resolution of their relationship implies that her apprenticeship did not fulfill its promise of knowledge and authority.

The "most touching" of the "life-giving affinities" between Leslie Stephen and his youngest daughter, according to Leon Edel, was Sir Leslie's gift on Virginia's twenty-first birthday of a ring and a declaration: she was, he averred, "a very good daughter." Oblivious to the dissonance of his metaphors, Edel explains: "It was as if there were a marriage and also a laying on of hands, a literary succession. The father . . . performed a marriage between Virginia and the world of letters."[21] Woolf herself, however, was well aware that being wed to a tradition was not being its heir, and she dramatized this difference in the Ramsay children's destinies. The personal inclinations of daughter and of father have little relevance to the course of events; Cam's education in the study prepares her to inherit her mother's position rather than her father's. Whether overtly enacted as dialogue or mediating more subtly between a masculine authorship and readership, the textual tradition transmitted by the study returns its female initiate to a position between two gentlemen: between Ramsay and Macalister, between Ramsay and the generic old gentleman, between Ramsay and his son—the nuclear masculine pair.[22] The daughter's position thus slides imperceptibly into the mother's. Although the father-mother-son triad that prevailed in "The Window" gives way in "The Lighthouse" to a father-daughter-son triad, the median feminine position is unchanged. As the scene on the boat gradually recreates its predecessor at the window, where Mrs. Ramsay is wedged between father and son, the characters psychically alter their positions. Having explicitly established that Mr. Ramsay sits "in the middle of the boat between them (James steered; Cam sat alone in the bow)" (242), Woolf inconsistently rearranges the protagonists to conform with the emotional topography. Cam's "brother was most god-like, her father most suppliant. And to which did she yield, she thought, sitting between them, gazing at the shore" (251). As Cam inherits her mother's median position, for which her training in the study paradoxically has groomed her, Woolf dissects the configuration that prevents Cam from articulating her desires.

Ostensibly, Mr. Ramsay tries during the boat trip to engage his daughter in conversation, but Woolf portrays the scene as an unvoiced dialogue between Mr. Ramsay and his son. After Mr. Ramsay's opening question, we shift directly to James's response: "Who was looking after the puppy today? [Mr. Ramsay] asked. Yes, thought James pitilessly, seeing his sister's head against the sail, now she'll give way. I shall be left to fight the tyrant alone" (250). Mr. Ramsay's second question similarly returns us to James's consciousness. Sliding pronouns (*she, her, they, somebody*) replace Cam with Mrs. Ramsay as the pressure of the struggle recalls its prototype: "She'll give way, James thought, as he watched a look come upon her face, a look he remembered. They look down, he thought, at their knitting or something. Then suddenly they look up. There was a flash of blue, he remembered, and then somebody sitting with him laughed, surrendered, and he was very angry. It must have been his mother, he thought, sitting on a low chair, with his father standing over her" (251). Having blurred his sister with his mother, James succeeds in adolescence where he failed as a child and prevents his father's victory. Torn between the irreconcilable demands of her father and his son, Cam succumbs to silence, unable to find a language for her own split desire.

Mr. Ramsay appears humble, not apparently engaged in any struggle, eager only to converse with his daughter. His motivation, however, mirrors his son's: like James, he uses Cam to replay and repair the past, although he tries to make reparation to Mrs. Ramsay through Cam rather than exacting reparation from Cam. When Cam's uncertainty about the points of the compass recalls Mrs. Ramsay's imprecision about the weather, Mr. Ramsay merges daughter and mother: "He thought, women are always like that; the vagueness of their minds is hopeless. . . . It had been so with her—his wife" (249). Grieving for his wife, and feeling remorse over his anger at her, Mr. Ramsay craves the solace of his daughter's approval. The boat thus stages a seduction scene that locates Cam between two men struggling to redo their relation to her mother: "I will make her smile at me, Mr. Ramsay thought" (250). His manner is courteous, but his project is coercive. Although he struggles to suppress his longing for confirmation, Cam reads it clearly: "And what was she going to call [the puppy]? her father persisted. He had had a dog when he was a little boy, called Frisk. . . . [S]he wished, passionately, . . . to say, Oh, yes, Frisk. I'll call him Frisk" (251–52). In this competition for her tongue, Cam can be silenced by Mosaic tablets or echo a paternal language that suggests an Adamic ritual of naming: "So she said nothing, but looked doggedly and sadly at the shore" (253).[23] Paralyzed between father and son, she can escape only out of the body, the desire motivating the suicidal fantasy latent in her envious gaze at the island, where people, it seems, "had fallen asleep, . . . were free like smoke, were free to come and go like ghosts. They have no suffering there, she thought" (253).

Only the resolution of the father-son conflict that places Cam psychically between the two men frees her from these fantasies. Cam's section 10, which follows the resolution of James's drama, opens with a sense of liberation, a "sudden and unthinking fountain of joy" whose "gold-sprinkled waters" illumine both the dark shapes of the future and the leaf-shaped island that embodies the past (281). Gazing at the island transformed by her anticipation of the future, Cam identifies her distinctive narrative task: to hinge the maternal shape of the past with the fleetingly illumined shapes of the future by articulating the central place she occupies, turning her historical aptitude to an unwritten history. It is here that she remembers her father. The section ends with the disappearance of the island: "the leaf was losing its sharpness. . . . The sea was more important now than the shore" (284). The final words return to Macalister's story and to Mr. Ramsay's refrain, as Cam "murmured, dreamily half asleep, how we perished, each alone" (284). Swerving away from a story that would link the "shapes of a world not realised" with the shapes of a feminine past beyond the study, Cam discloses her enclosure in paternal narratives.[24]

A certain circularity marks Cam's narrative activity, for the story she tells is the story of how she came to tell that story. It is a paradigmatic story of the daughter who thinks back through her father, a story of narrative imprisonment.[25] Only a differently affiliated daughter could begin to negotiate an escape. Through Lily, who was added to the novel as its focus began to shift to Mrs. Ramsay, Woolf breaks the narrative decree that governs Cam's (and Clarissa's and Elizabeth's) fate.

4

SPATIAL RELATIONS:
LILY BRISCOE'S PAINTING

So it became clear that if painting is concerned with the feelings conveyed by space then it must also be to do with problems of being a separate body in a world of other bodies which occupy different bits of space: in fact it must be deeply concerned with ideas of distance and separation and having and losing.

Joanna Field [Marion Milner], *On Not Being Able to Paint*

For how could one express in words these emotions of the body? express that emptiness there? (She was looking at the drawing-room steps; they looked extraordinarily empty.) It was one's body feeling, not one's mind. The physical sensations that went with the bare look of the steps had become suddenly extremely unpleasant. To want and not to have, sent all up her body a hardness, a hollowness, a strain.

Virginia Woolf, *To the Lighthouse*

Woolf's description of her plan to "thicken" *To the Lighthouse* with "branches" and "roots" coincides with her account of Adrian Stephen's visit after the completion of Klein's London lectures. Ten days later, on 30 July 1925, she notes that she has begun to "vacillate between a single and intense character of father; and a far wider slower book."[1] By the following week, her narrative plan reveals that her interest has gravitated from the father to the mother: "The theme of the 1st part shall *really* contribute to Mrs. R's character. . . . The dominating impression [of part 3] is to be of Mrs. R's character." To sustain Mrs. Ramsay as the novel's "dominating impression," Woolf created Lily Briscoe.[2]

Lily's narrative consistently foregrounds Mrs. Ramsay. In contrast to James, who compounds his mother's death with his own psychological necessity, and to Cam, who assumes her mother's function rather than remembering her, Lily negotiates a relationship with her surrogate mother from the novel's beginning to its end. Ambivalence toward Mrs. Ramsay pervades Lily's experience; she is buffeted by opposing impulses toward merger and autonomy in a pattern unbroken (and perhaps even intensified) by Mrs. Ramsay's death. Although Lily is older than James and Cam, her story reaches further back to the earliest rhythms of subjectivity. Lily functions simultaneously as the middle-aged artist whose completed painting "of" Mrs. Ramsay concludes the novel that assuages Woolf's adult obsession with her mother and as an infant longing both to fuse and to separate. If the adult voice prevails, the accents of unsatisfied infantile desire are audible in Lily's reiterated, uninflected verbs, intransitive because their object incorporates everything: "To want and not to have. . . . And then to want and not to have—to want and want. . . . Oh, Mrs. Ramsay!"[3] Here, the object of desire is the mother who has died, but its origin is ancient—for the longing, like its language, is repetitive. "'Mrs. Ramsay! Mrs. Ramsay!' she cried, feeling the old horror come back—to want and want and not to have. Could she inflict that *still?*" (300; emphasis added). Never adequately available, Mrs. Ramsay confirms in death an absence that begins at birth.[4]

Lily finds in the "language" of painting (both the spatial relations on the canvas and the discourse they generate) a means of representing the boundary negotiations that characterize the mother-infant bond. As in the significantly titled "Sketch of the Past," where the relations of foreground and background articulate the earliest delineation of ego boundaries, *To the Lighthouse* thematizes the difference between visual and verbal representation in a way that privileges painting.[5] Yet Lily's painting is represented in a text that betrays no anxiety about this contradiction. Painting functions in this novel as an alternative not to language but to Woolf's account of language acquisition, which she depicts through James and Cam as both compelling and dismaying. By making Lily the central figure of the artist, and Lily's completed painting the central figure of the text, Woolf implicitly affiliates her writing with a mode of representation that her representation of language contradicts.[6]

By conflating Lily's aesthetic and psychological tasks, Woolf engages issues Klein was exploring simultaneously. Klein's shift of focus from the Oedipal triad to the phantasies produced within a mother-infant dyad marked by fluctuating boundaries made visual art a privileged field for the enactment and disclosure of developmental processes.[7] Klein's 1929 essay "Infantile Anxiety-Situations Reflected in a Work of Art and in the Creative Impulse"—which contains a reading of "The Empty Space," Karin Michaelis's study of Ruth Kjär's abrupt discovery that she could paint—offers striking parallels to Lily's experience as a painter. The essay traces painting (especially women's) to the desire to repair a maternal image damaged by aggressive phantasies. Kjär's chronic feeling "that something was lacking in her body," her melancholy sense of an inner vacancy produced by the lack of an internalized good mother, is intensified by the removal of a painting from her wall: "The empty space grinned hideously down at her."[8] By suddenly and feverishly beginning to paint—first a life-size image of a naked black woman, then other maternal images—Kjär succeeds in filling the empty external and internal spaces. Lily must similarly confront an empty space after a maternal loss produced by death rather than aggression: the "hideously difficult white space" on the canvas "glared at her" as she struggles to represent the "emptiness" on the drawing-room steps and within her own body, "a hardness, a hollowness, a strain" (238, 255, 265–66). Like Ruth Kjär (although through more abstract forms of representation), Lily replenishes herself by reconstituting a figure of the mother. But the painting also serves the different process of Lily's separation from Mrs. Ramsay; the line that solves the problem of the empty space at the center of the canvas at once restores Mrs. Ramsay and asserts Lily's autonomy.

Despite its parallels with Klein, the story of Lily's painting more closely prefigures the school of object relations that, in the half century following Klein's early work, diverged from Freud more radically than Klein, its founder, could. Most articulately represented by D. W. Winnicott, this school discarded the biological features of Klein's theory (especially her emphasis on a death instinct manifested as aggression) and heightened her insistence on interpersonal ("object") relations and on the mother-infant origins of creativity.[9] Theorizing a distinctive pre-Oedipal relationship in which hunger and aggression have been muted, Winnicott reconstructs the depressive position as a zone of creativity enabled by the "good enough" mother's gradually waning support of infantile illusions of omnipotence. In this hypothetical "transitional space," populated by "transitional objects" (such as teddy bears and blankets) that mediate between the infant and its mother, and thus between subjective and objective worlds, the infant learns to negotiate between fantasy and fact, between "inner psychic reality" and "the external world."[10] In this intermediate zone in which subject and object are only partially distinct, we play, we make our symbols, we conduct our cultural lives, for "playing leads on naturally to cultural experience and indeed forms its foundation."[11] To figure the transitional space, Winnicott chooses lines by the poet Tagore—"On the seashore of endless worlds, children play"—that echo the liminal landscape of Woolf's text, set at the thresholds of a house on an island at twilight during summer's end, a landscape whose subjective correlative Lily articulates as she paints.[12]

To define the "place" of cultural experience, Winnicott elaborated a metaphorics of space that he supplemented frequently with diagrams. The special status of spatial relations in the discourse of object relations becomes explicit in the work of his contemporary, Marion Milner, whose *On Not Being Able to Paint* (published under her pseudonym, Joanna Field), a blend of autobiography and psychoanalytic theory, reads like a case history of Lily Briscoe's work on her painting. Milner meticulously parallels the compositional tasks of painting with the psychological tasks of drawing boundaries. As the art "concerned with the feelings conveyed by space"— "the primary reality to be manipulated for the satisfaction of all one's basic needs, beginning with the babyhood problem of reaching for one's mother's arms, leading through all the separation from what one loves that the business of living brings"—painting deals directly with the "problems of being a separate body in a world of other bodies which occupy different bits of space[,] . . . with ideas of distance and separation and having and losing."[13] Composition requires manipulating distance and relationship, which in turn requires facing "certain facts about oneself as a separate being, facts which could often perhaps be successfully by-passed in ordinary living"; outline and color both arouse anxieties about shifting boundaries, about "one personality merging with another."[14] The successful painter must be able to move easily between defining and dissolving boundaries, between feeling separate and feeling merged, since painting enforces recognition of the limits of one's body and of their flexibility. By delimiting a space that works with separation to restore the illusion of unity, painting replays, without resolving, the dialectic of autonomy and continuity.

Winnicott and Milner extend the privileged status of visual representation in Klein's matricentric discourse; Lacan theorizes, and fortifies, the status of language in Freud's patricentric discourse. By playing Lily's narrative against those of James and Cam, Woolf both juxtaposes these discourses and further genders them. In *To the Lighthouse* the cultural space of mother and infant is preeminently a daughter's habitat: whereas James quits his place as "artist" at his mother's side to embrace his father's linguistic domain, Lily remains embedded in the drama of shifting boundaries. Cam's self-effacement calls out for a different daughter narrative. James's and Lily's stories anticipate a distinction not drawn clearly in psychoanalytic theory until the work of Nancy Chodorow. According to Chodorow, the daughter's experience of oneness with her mother, intensified and prolonged by the mother's own gender identification with her daughter, ensures that "separation and individuation remain particularly female developmental issues."[15] In contrast to the son, whose initial separation from his mother is assimilated to and consolidated by the Oedipal rite of passage, the daughter (Chodorow claims) never surmounts her primary identification with her mother, although she may supplement it with an erotic attachment to her father. Because she does not give up her pre-Oedipal bond with her mother, the girl maintains her earliest relational mode of primary identification and continues to experience permeable ego boundaries; the primary sense of self she carries through life is one of self-in-relationship. The undulating rhythms of the mother-daughter narrative rock from birth to death.

Lily's version of this narrative is complex, for superimposed on the mother-daughter story is the different story of how Lily identifies and represents it. Through the history of Lily's paintings, a *Künstlerroman* intersects and reconstructs the developmental narrative.[16] To read Lily's story we must read her visual creations—both their spatial composition of narrative and the narrative of their composition. "The Window" and "The Lighthouse" describe two paintings and two compositional processes. In "The Window," which culminates for her in a fantasied aesthetic solution she fails to implement, Lily cannot align her story and her medium. The aesthetic subjects and theories that contend for her allegiance are focused in a single extended scene of painting (section 9). "Time Passes" wipes her uncompleted canvas clean. In "The Lighthouse" she begins again, confronting a point of origin that was blocked from our vision in part 1. By returning to the beginning, and thereby reversing the courses of James and Cam, who both acquiesce in "The Lighthouse" to some occulting of the past, Lily succeeds in representing her ambivalence in paint.

I

The scene of painting in "The Window" culminates in a discussion with Mr. Bankes of the project Lily has completed for that day. Lily's explanation of her painting retroactively restructures the section it concludes as a palimpsest that contracts different pictorial and psychoanalytic scenes and different aesthetic discourses. The layered structure of the painting connects Lily's aesthetic impasse to the layers of consciousness whose cultural status was the subject of contemporary psychoanalytic controversy.

The first scene, in the reverse order this organization imposes, is the concluding discussion between Lily and Mr. Bankes of the nearly completed canvas. Lily's explanation of her methodology and goals has been widely read as evidence of her adherence to the reigning aesthetic doxa of Bloomsbury, specifically the doctrines of Roger Fry, which diverge dramatically from object relations theory by restricting painting to a timeless formal "plasticity" divorced from both psychology and narrative.[17] Lily's emphasis on structural relationships allies her with Fry's hero, Cézanne, who (in Fry's words) "saw always, however, dimly, behind this veil [of color] an architecture and a logic."[18] Lily "saw the colour burning on a framework of steel; the light of a butterfly's wing lying upon the arches of a cathedral" (75). Her position, more importantly, dissociates her art from the aesthetic of verisimilitude: painting, she insists at this stage of her work, is to be an autotelic whole, freed from the claims of representation and assessable by purely formal criteria. Making "no attempt at likeness" and insisting on the formal relations of masses, lights, and shadows, Lily echoes Fry's belief that "our reaction to a work of art is a reaction to a relation and not to sensations or objects or persons or events," that the aesthetic effect arises from "self-contained, self-sufficing" structures which are "not to be valued by their reference to what lies outside."[19]

Woolf represents Fry's aesthetic, however, as a factor in Lily's *struggle* with her painting, not as the adequate exposition of the painting. By conflating Lily's formalism with her choice of an Oedipal iconography, Woolf uses Freud to (dis)qualify Fry.[20] Lily responds to Mr. Bankes's surprise at her choice of a purple triangle to represent Mrs. Ramsay reading to James by offering a formal explanation: "[I]f there, in that corner, it was bright, here, in this, she felt the need of darkness" (81). But she does not account for her choice of this particular dark form, which displaces her earlier image of Mrs. Ramsay in the window wearing "the shape of a dome" (80). Triangles and domes are not culturally uncoded. Rejecting verisimilitude does not free art from the iconography that Bankes's apparently innocent query discloses. Seemingly neutral dispositions of form betray the cultural construction of sexuality: one of Lily's solutions to the painting's formal tensions, breaking "the vacancy in the foreground by an object (James perhaps)," for example, echoes the phallic fantasies evoked in James by his position, "very stiff," between his mother's knees (83, 59). Distilling "her picture" from the accidents of nature by "subduing all her impressions as a woman to something much more general," Lily discovers less a neutral language of form than abstractions that universalize masculinity (82).

At the next level of the palimpsest, Woolf further subverts the ideal of a disinterested aesthetic vision by associating it with a distancing, objectifying, but deeply interested masculine gaze. "Behind" Lily's nearly completed canvas is the carefully composed, motionless scene of Mrs. Ramsay and James, presented as Lily imagines it appears to the rapt gaze of Mr. Bankes, for whom the sight of mother and son in the window had "precisely the same effect as the solution of a scientific problem, so that he rested in contemplation of it" (74). The reverential male gaze, idealizing its subject, elevates this scene beyond the flux of life, grants it the steady contemplation only works of art receive, and aestheticizes it as a proto-painting whose status as art is underscored by the analogy to science, a staple of Fry's aesthetic. By literalizing the metaphor of point of view, Woolf both reinforces the impression of a painting behind the painting and sutures gender to perspective. For only after "looking along the level of Mr. Bankes's glance" does Lily add "her different ray" to "his beam," dissolving the perfect scene he aestheticizes and substituting her daughterly perspective for the formal criteria linked to the erotics of a masculine gaze that reverently reifies woman as (son's) mother (75, 76, 75).[21]

Seeking the "essential thing" that differentiates Mrs. Ramsay from "the perfect shape which one saw there," Lily considers Mrs. Ramsay from her own angle of vision, "thinking of her relations with women," especially with that "younger . . . insignificant person" who is Lily Briscoe. To "start the tune of Mrs. Ramsay in her head," Lily rejects static shapes for the drama of mobile boundaries in which Mrs. Ramsay's "tune" originates: "She opened bedroom windows. She shut doors" (76). After shaking free from Mr. Bankes's gaze, Lily regains the experience of penetrating the "sanctuary" of her own relationship with Mrs. Ramsay, where she can see Mrs. Ramsay from her own perspective, at once more intimate (the sanctuary is ambiguously situated both within them and between them) and more confused ("all one's perceptions, half way to truth, were tangled in a golden mesh") (78). Her memories come to rest in a paradigmatic mother-daughter scene of intimacy and conflict, assimilation and exclusion: Mrs. Ramsay's nocturnal visit to Lily's bedroom, the scene of their dispute over the "universal law" of marriage, a dispute that for Lily generates the contrary impulse toward identification that the perception of difference generates (77). Erasing the scene that she paints, Lily now sees herself at Mrs. Ramsay's knees, occupying James's position. Motion stops, conflict subsides, and the remembered scene that replaces son with daughter is arrested as a tableau, framed by the descriptions that open and conclude it: "Sitting on the floor with her arms round Mrs. Ramsay's knees"; "leaning her head on Mrs. Ramsay's knee" (78, 79). Within this frame, nothing stirs but the flood of metaphors produced by Lily's passionate desire to merge with Mrs. Ramsay. Beneath the formalist aesthetic and the Oedipal scene that alike occlude a prior level of experience is the daughter's story, the bottom layer of the palimpsest, psychically and aesthetically submerged. Peeling off the layers of the palimpsest—from abstract formal composition, to the idealized scene of mother and son perceived in the present through the rapt male gaze, to the recollected scene of mother and daughter—Woolf constructs a painterly analogue to Freud's archaeological metaphor of the Minoan-Mycenean civilization behind that of classical Greece.

Within the buried, unactualized sketch, Woolf renders Lily's adult consciousness as a sequence of present-tense questions which voice a desire that, sparked by separation, defies restriction to a single era. The rapid flux of metaphors of fluidity unwrites the language of structured relationships in a scene which reveals that during Mrs. Ramsay's life Lily feels the same impossible longing for oneness that she expresses after Mrs. Ramsay's death. Pressing "close as she could get" to Mrs. Ramsay, Lily articulates an insistent, powerful desire to (re)enter a sealed maternal space, to liquify the boundaries of mind and flesh: "What art was there, known to love or cunning, by which one pressed through into those secret chambers? What device for becoming, like waters poured into one jar, inextricably the same, one with the object one adored? Could the body achieve, or the mind, subtly mingling in the intricate passages of the brain? or the heart? Could loving, as people called it, make her and Mrs. Ramsay one?" (78, 79). Lily's metaphors of boundaries thinned to nothingness come from the same psychological lexicon as those of Mrs. Ramsay herself, who in a later scene describes "that community of feeling with other people which emotion gives as if the walls of partition had become so thin that practically (the feeling was one of relief and happiness) it was all one stream" (170). At different moments the two women speak a similar language of desire, yet Lily's wish is more urgent and acute. She seeks a specific reincorporation: her exclusive focus—"the object one adored," the mother seen only as impersonal container—reveals the simplified geography of infantile desire.

The scene Lily remembers draws a crossroads, in the text, for contending systems of metaphor. Seeking to articulate her own relation to Mrs. Ramsay, Lily starts by discarding the metaphors associated with James and Mr. Ramsay. Initially, she imagines knowledge of Mrs. Ramsay as a decoding of hermetic texts: "[I]n the chambers of the mind and heart of the woman who was, physically, touching her, there stood, like the treasures in the tombs of kings, tablets bearing sacred inscriptions, which if one would spell them out, would teach one everything, but they would never be offered openly, never made public" (79). Maternal wisdom is inscribed in a language that presupposes maternal death: Mrs. Ramsay's secrets are legible only as tablets in a tomb, in a body turned repository, "chambers" housing gravestones/texts.[22] Lily's fantasy at first bears the traces of the Oedipal scene she paints: the "tablets bearing sacred inscriptions" adumbrate the "tablets of eternal wisdom" that James inherits and that cause and reward his renunciation of his mother; and they recall Mr. Ramsay's solitary scene, which substitutes philosophy, symbolized as language, for Mrs. Ramsay's presence. Yet as the scene unfolds, Lily rejects the metaphors of textuality, linked with maternal absence (or death), for metaphors of spatial relationships, of porous, fluctuating boundaries between two coexistent, commingling presences. Mapping Lily's wish for the deliquescence of inscriptions into fluids, difference into unity, symbolic structure into intimacy, the scene "behind" the scene of mother and son concludes as a manifesto of pre-Oedipal desire, figuration, and epistemology: "[I]t was not knowledge but unity that she desired, not inscriptions on tablets, nothing that could be written in any language known to men, but intimacy itself, which is knowledge, she had thought, leaning her head on Mrs. Ramsay's knee" (79).

The unpainted scene thus constitutes an extraordinary juncture in the text: as Lily moves backward in memory, displacing James from his mother's side, her metaphors anticipate the conclusion of his story and articulate his unrepresented transition from the drama of aesthetic and human boundaries, metonymically enacted in his play with the scissors, to the symbolic domain of texts, in which he participates as Lily paints. As James evolves into his father's heir and assumes a place in the register of language and law, Lily appropriates his position at his mother's knees, the spot in this text where for both daughters and sons the work of art originates. Art's sources are traced to the task of drawing boundaries; its sphere is a relation of the mother that is the *female* child's *enduring* legacy. As an art whose aesthetic construction of space articulates the tensions between proximity and distance that delineate human space, painting now opposes the formalist aesthetic and the Oedipal economy with which it was allied. Lily's painting spatializes the psychoanalytic debate beginning to emerge in Woolf's environment: if the surface of the canvas conforms to psychoanalytic orthodoxy, its visual pre-text relocates the origins of cultural experience in preverbal boundary negotiations with the mother. With the unacknowledged sketch for Lily's painting we leave the Freudian domain, which casts prelinguistic experience as shadowy, unrecoverable, and culturally inconsequential prehistory, and enter the domain first mapped by Klein.

Woolf guides us in this section against the current of Lily's thought; the painting itself, however, assumes the aspect of a cover-up and consequently remains unfinished in "The Window" despite her gleeful discovery of a formal solution. To implement this solution and complete her canvas, Lily must reverse the sequence of the palimpsest and confront the underlying issues of boundaries repressed by the Freudian domain. Starting again from the beginning in "The Lighthouse," Lily will be doubly returned to origins: through the struggle with Mrs. Ramsay's death and the confrontation with the empty space displayed by a virgin canvas.

II

The moment of truth in painting, Lily's language repeatedly suggests, is the first mark on the canvas. Between conception and enactment falls the shadow: "She could see it all so clearly, so commandingly, when she looked: it was when she took her brush in hand that the whole thing changed. It was in that moment's flight between the picture and her canvas that the demons set on her who often brought her to the verge of tears and made this passage from conception to work as dreadful as any down a dark passage for a child" (32). The first brushstroke is a commitment to the material world, to an embodiment of mental images, to an incarnation, a birth resembling a child's progress "down a dark passage" linking conception to the world. In "The Lighthouse" the birth metaphor receives a Neoplatonic gloss: right before painting, Lily always has "a few moments of nakedness when she seemed like an unborn soul, a soul reft of a body" (237). Painting demands a radical disjunction, a risky fall into immediacy, a leap from a haven where conflict is buffered by detachment from the world into the painful turmoil of inhabiting a body. "One line placed on the canvas committed her to innumerable risks, to frequent and irrevocable decisions. All that in idea seemed simple became in practice immediately complex; as the waves shape themselves symmetrically from the cliff top, but to the swimmer among them are divided by steep gulfs, and foaming crests" (235). The plunge from cliffs to waves measures the distance from idea to practice, from the safe appreciation of visual forms to their perilous creation, the process whose origins "The Window" does not represent. Figured as birth, this process conjures terrors not only for oneself but also for the sanctuary one has quit. At the other end of the passage may be the mother's death—as in the novel's only direct account of maternal death: "(Mr. Ramsay, stumbling along a passage one dark morning, stretched his arms out, but Mrs. Ramsay having died rather suddenly the night before, his arms, though stretched out, remained empty)" (194).

When Lily characterizes painting as a process, rather than as an autotelic product, she describes a medium whose paradoxes constitute the ideal discourse for the mother-infant bond. On the one hand, the materiality of paint appears to bypass the separation that Freud and Lacan define as the origin of language. In "The Lighthouse" Lily contrasts the gestures of painting with those of language, which "fluttered sideways and struck the object inches too low," and associates her art with "a dancing rhythmical movement, as if the pauses were one part of the rhythm and the strokes another, and all were related" (265, 236). The canvas records this rhythm in the relationships of spaces and lines that constitute its visual vocabulary. On the other hand, the act of painting entails the separation that the language of paint is intended to heal. It is this paradoxical simultaneity of maternal absence and presence, not a magical vanquishing of absence, that in this novel differentiates visual art from words.

Lily's metaphors suggest that the material strokes of paint not only encode separation but also impose a confrontation with their visual antithesis: empty space, that "formidable ancient enemy of hers" (236). No sooner do Lily's first lines settle "than they enclosed (she felt it looming out at her) a space," as indissolubly united with the lines as the "steep gulfs" are with the "foaming crests" of the waves that represent the painter's practice. The first brushstroke defines the canvas dialectically as a space signifying a fundamental loss, a blankness behind paint, behind any mark of presence. For Lily, this blankness is tangible, "this truth, this reality, which suddenly laid hands on her, emerged stark at the back of appearances and commanded her attention" (236). A sign simultaneously of origin and exile, the glaringly empty space demands confrontation with the knowledge she resists in the bedroom scene—that she and Mrs. Ramsay are not one. The circumscribed vacancy in the foreground of the original canvas has expanded to "a centre of complete emptiness" (266), a space of absence so intense it provokes a fantasy of return: "[T]he space would fill; those empty flourishes would form into a shape; if they shouted loud enough Mrs. Ramsay would return. 'Mrs. Ramsay!' she said aloud, 'Mrs. Ramsay!' The tears ran down her face" (268). Paint no more than words can conjure this return, except momentarily in fantasy; yet the signs of paint do not seal maternal absence, as the language allegorized within the novel does, but enforce a repeated confrontation with it as a condition of the medium. Every line generates new spaces in the continuously shift-ing configurings of absence and presence that compose an art whose modality is space.

Lily defines her return to painting at the opening of "The Light-house" as a project of translation between media and genders. The course back to painting begins with an overheard refrain, Mr. Ramsay's decla-mation of Cowper: "We perished each alone" (219). The quotation (at-tributed, in Woolf's diary, to her father) summarizes the masculine separation narrative outlined in the novel by Mr. Ramsay's quest for R, a fantasied adventure which retreats from Mrs. Ramsay to culminate in lonely, heroic death. Lily mentally inscribes the two words she hears, "Alone," "Perished," on the grey-green walls and identifies her task as the construction of a grammar: "If only she could put them together, she felt, write them out in some sentence, then she would have got at the truth of things" (219). She knows the existing syntax; what she seeks is an altered set of rules that expand the logic of the sentence to include back-ground as well as foreground, the walls on which the text is written as well as discrete words. Her syntax breaks down logical relations of subordina-tion to emphasize embeddedness, contextualizing meaning within vacancy. "Perished. Alone. The grey-green light on the wall opposite. The empty places. Such were some of the parts, but how bring them to-gether?" (220). Referring simultaneously to the spaces between words and the places carved by death at the Ramsay table, "empty places" be-come integral parts of Lily's visual "sentence," which revises the gram-matical and narrative sequence of the masculine sentence that designates death (only) as its terminus. As the final step in her translation, Lily recalls her painting. "Suddenly she remembered. . . . There had been a problem about a foreground of a picture. . . . She would paint that picture now" (220). The contending claims of foreground and background, sign and space, have emerged within a medium that adjudicates them differently: the medium of paint translates the linear sentence whose prototype is Mr. Ramsay's alphabet, where the course from A to Z charts a course from birth to death, into "one of those globed compacted things" whose empty places constitute the ground on which its figures play (286).

Ground becomes foreground in Lily's second painting, crafted as a struggle with origins, with the empty space, in the knowledge of Mrs. Ramsay's death. Having regained her project, Lily more assertively claims it as her own. The formal critical discourse she had shared with Mr. Bankes yields to an idiom that infiltrates aesthetics with autobiography in her narrative account of an encounter with a canvas that "glares" at her like an adversary/twin with an "uncompromising white stare" (234), imposing on her vision an empty space that "loomed before her; . . . pressing on her eyeballs" (237). As the distance dividing painting from painter is radically foreshortened, and the blankness of the canvas mirrors emptiness, the material of art is imaged as experience, pigment its tangible accompaniment: "[H]er mind kept throwing up from its depths, scenes, and names, and sayings, and memories and ideas, like a fountain spurting over that glaring, hideously difficult white space, while she modelled it with greens and blues" (238). As Lily continues "tunnelling her way into her picture, into the past" (258), she locates on the canvas the memories of her nighttime visit with Mrs. Ramsay, the scene locked behind her original painting. Dissolving the dissonance between painting and sketch, between mother/son triangles and mother/daughter memories, Lily realigns her memory, her medium, and her altered iconography of empty space, painfully reconstructing her painting from the ground up.

Lily's narrative in "The Lighthouse" deliberately, if fluidly, revises each layer of the palimpsest. Having redefined her medium in metaphors drawn from a moment unrepresented in "The Window," Lily reconstructs the crucial scene that had been framed as a tableau beneath her canvas. Her first memory is of Mrs. Ramsay, Charles Tansley, and herself on the beach. That this scene should come to mind seems arbitrary even to herself: "Why, after all these years had that survived, ringed round, lit up, visible to the last detail, with all before it blank and all after it blank, for miles and miles?" (254). Yet the very framing of the scene as scene, its rescue from the blankness of history, links it to the bedroom tableau—and, like it, the beach scene "stayed in the mind affecting one almost like a work of art" (240). Lily uses the scene as a double point of departure for her memories, recounting it in section 3 and returning to and revising it in section 5, where specific verbal echoes evoke the bedroom tableau despite the obvious differences in setting. The scene at the beach alters the primary memory informing Lily's painting. Having consciously worked through a moment of origin, with the knowledge of separation (and death) it confers, Lily recognizes that there is no "art" for becoming one with the object one adores. In "The Lighthouse" she retrieves a more enabling memory of a more enabling mother. Constructing Mrs. Ramsay in her own image, Lily fashions the mother she now needs, one who, neither engulfing nor diminishing, actively joins in the creation of a shared imaginative space.

Lily's memory of playing ducks and drakes with Charles Tansley in a moment of uncharacteristic harmony casts Mrs. Ramsay, creator of this harmony, in a new role. She no longer looms larger than life, privy to secret wisdom, but is a fallible human presence, strangely dwarfed (she sits while Lily stands) and nearsighted (she cannot distinguish the object in the waves), less the object of Lily's myopia than a myopic subject herself. Although demystified as mother, however, Mrs. Ramsay is idealized in a different capacity. Writing letters as she sits on the beach, she is magnified through Lily's gaze into the author of the script that Lily and Tansley act: "When she thought of herself and Charles throwing ducks and drakes and of the whole scene on the beach, it seemed to depend somehow upon Mrs. Ramsay sitting under the rock, with a pad on her knee, writing letters. . . . That woman sitting there writing under the rock resolved everything into simplicity" (239). No longer the Great Mother whom Lily worships as a suppliant entreating entry, Mrs. Ramsay has evolved in Lily's eyes into a mirror image: "Mrs. Ramsay saying, 'Life stand still here'; Mrs. Ramsay making of the moment something permanent. . . . She [Lily] owed it all to her" (240–41).

Instead of merger, the scene highlights seeing, a mode of interaction that requires separation. Previously, seeing has not been reciprocal: although Lily has scrutinized the subject of her painting, Mrs. Ramsay has kept her head bowed over the book she reads to James. At other times when Mrs. Ramsay has looked at Lily, she has seen only fixed cues ("With her little Chinese eyes and her puckered-up face, she would never marry; one could not take her painting very seriously" [291]), or she has caught her eye at dinner only to enlist her assistance managing men. Now, Lily constructs a reciprocal gaze: "Every now and then Mrs. Ramsay looked up over her spectacles and laughed at them[,] . . . watching them. She [Lily] was highly conscious of that. Mrs. Ramsay, she thought, stepping back and screwing up her eyes" (239). The two women gaze at one another across a hypothetical transitional space that mediates between two persons and two eras, and in this suddenly constituted moment, Lily paints, grounding her art in the dialectic of maternal difference and continuity.[23] This imaginary moment of mother-daughter seeing counterpoints the unvoiced conversation between James and Mr. Ramsay on the boat: the mother-daughter gaze across a mutually constituted intermediate space fosters painting; the father-son dialogue across a silent female body transmits the knowledge of language and law.

In her replay of the scene on the beach, Lily elaborates this transitional space and, in so doing, revises the bedroom scene. Returning to her memory of the beach as she returns to her canvas in section 5, Lily situates herself differently: "And she began to lay on a red, a grey, and she began to model her way into the hollow there. At the same time, she seemed to be sitting beside Mrs. Ramsay on the beach" (255). Tansley has disappeared, and Lily has assumed in memory a position that echoes the bedroom scene. In the present coincident with memory, she jubilantly names the central problem of the painting, which the work of memory will mirror and resolve: "Heaven be praised for it, the problem of space remained. . . . The whole mass of the picture was posed upon that weight." The scene on the beach pivots on a clearly designated moment of seeing—Mrs. Ramsay finds her spectacles, and with this sharpened vision unlocks the door to the space she and Lily share: Mrs. Ramsay "began hunting round for her spectacles. And she sat, having found them, silent, looking out to sea. And Lily, painting steadily, felt as if a door had opened, and one went in and stood gazing silently about in a high cathedral-like place, very dark, very solemn" (255). In a Proustian moment that collapses past and present, Lily sits next to Mrs. Ramsay and stands across from her in their private refuge, screened from time and world. Imaged as a cathedral, this hallowed mutual space looks forward to the geography of childhood Woolf would later chart in "A Sketch of the Past" ("Certainly, there she was, in the very centre of that great Cathedral space which was childhood; there she was from the very first")[24] and backward to the scene with Mrs. Ramsay in the bedroom ("But into what sanctuary had one penetrated?" [78]). But the nature of the space has changed between the bedroom and the beach. The "cathedral-like place" that links Lily's painting with the scene on the beach does not modulate into a sealed maternal space. The locus of desire has shifted from biology to art and from the asymmetry of infantile longing to a mutually constituted space of seeing in which Lily, having perceived Mrs. Ramsay as perceiver, now is "painting steadily."

As she enters this transitional space, Lily completes her revision of the bedroom scene that had offered the stillborn sketch for her uncompleted canvas. Seated next to Mrs. Ramsay on the beach in a world constituted by the two of them, Lily now is as self-contained and silent as the older woman. Her flood of impassioned questions has been stilled; her desire for "intimacy, which is knowledge," the resounding conclusion of the former scene, has evolved into a question that acknowledges the irreducibility of difference: "Mrs. Ramsay sat silent. She was glad, Lily thought, to rest in silence, incommunicative; to rest in the extreme obscurity of human relationships. Who knows what we are, what we feel? Who knows even at the moment of intimacy, This is knowledge" (256). In this bittersweet but fertile moment of parity and silence that has become the new icon of their relationship ("it seemed to have happened so often, this silence by her side"), the two women form an impenetrable pair, gazing not at one another but together out to sea.

As she continues through "The Lighthouse" to model the empty space on which her picture hangs, Lily moves through stages of acute and softened grief, culminating in her vision of Mrs. Ramsay's return to her former position at the window: "Mrs. Ramsay—it was part of her perfect goodness—sat there quite simply, in the chair, flicked her needles to and fro, knitted her reddish-brown stocking, cast her shadow on the step. There she sat" (300). Traditionally read as a stage in the process of mourning, the vision also alters the subject of Lily's painting by reconstructing the scene she paints, the next layer of the palimpsest.[25] Lily's vision of Mrs. Ramsay is a significant revision. For although Mrs. Ramsay occupies the same position in the window, James has disappeared. Knitting by herself in the window, Mrs. Ramsay returns as Lily's final mirror: alone, no longer bowed over the text she reads to James but facing toward the daughter out to sea.

Only as Lily revisualizes this scene, and in the process directs our attention to the nearly completed canvas, does the iconography of the original painting return, recontextualized. As the (still unidentified) presence settles at the window, it throws "an odd-shaped triangular shadow over the step. It altered the composition of the picture a little. It was interesting. It might be useful" (299). Its utility asserted in the conditional, the triangle (here mentioned for the first time in "The Lighthouse") has become an uncertain feature of the composition. The shadow, moreover, is cast by Mrs. Ramsay alone. It now echoes her private (in)version of the Oedipal triangle, the "wedge-shaped core of darkness, something invisible to others" that introduces her single scene of solitary contemplation and communion with the lighthouse beam (95). Brilliantly situated between James's departure for bed and Mr. Ramsay's appearance at the window, this solitary scene translates Mrs. Ramsay's structural position between husband and son into a space of eroticized interiority that the Oedipal narrative elides.[26] In Lily's vision of Mrs. Ramsay's shadow, the triangle changes from the representative form that situates the canvas at a certain intersection of Freudian theory and formalist aesthetics to a contingent and private piece of iconography that explodes that intersection by encoding a maternal scene exterior to it—a scene apprehended only by the female artist, whose brushstrokes reproduce the sensual "strokes" of the lighthouse beam.[27]

Until the final paragraph of her narrative, Lily describes her painting in terms of space and color. Only in the concluding gesture that follows Mrs. Ramsay's return does she revive the solution she had imagined ten years earlier: the line "there, in the centre" (310). The central line is usually read as a superimposition of the vertical line of the lighthouse on the feminine space of the window, and thus as the completion of an androgynous work of art.[28] However, the line has already been contextualized more thoroughly in the narrative of Lily's relationship with Mrs. Ramsay, and that more fully elaborated context subsumes the discourse of androgyny. Within this context, Lily's imaginative participation in the journey to the lighthouse, which "had stretched her body and mind to the utmost," is one means of distancing herself from Mrs. Ramsay (308). The line "in" the center is far more ambiguous than a perfect androgynous symmetry, which would resituate the painting in a realm of formal perfection severed from the incompletion of experience. Where, first, does the line in the center go? Moving the tree to the center, Lily's primary gloss on it, suggests a vertical line, yet her actual description of moving the tree suggests a horizontal line: "It was a question, she remembered, how to connect this mass on the right hand with that on the left. She might do it by bringing the line of the branch across so" (82–83).

This ambiguity points to a more fundamentally indeterminate aspect of the representation. The painting ostensibly is "of" Mrs. Ramsay, and the parallel accounts of her return ("There she sat") and of the concluding line ("there, in the centre") associate the painting's final stroke with Mrs. Ramsay. A connecting horizontal line would further consolidate this association with the mother who takes upon herself "the whole of the effort of merging and flowing and creating" (126). As a version of the tree moved to the center, however, a vertical line has been just as definitively associated with Lily's separation from Mrs. Ramsay: "[S]he would move the tree to the middle, and need never marry anybody. . . . She had felt, now she could stand up to Mrs. Ramsay" (262). Yet Mrs. Ramsay has also been identified with trees (she "rise[s] in a rosy-flowered fruit tree" [60], and she "grew still like a tree which has been tossing and quivering" [177]), and with verticality ("Holding her black parasol very erect, and moving with an indescribable air of expectation" [19]; "Often and often Lily had seen her go silently . . . [,] very upright" [291]). The carefully preserved indeterminacy in the painting's subject and appearance refuses a decision, for the painting is not "of" either woman separately but of the dual unity, mother and daughter, that has been the subject of Lily's narrative. Lily paints (in Winnicott's words) a "separation that is not a separation but a form of union," a relationship, not an individual.[29] Articulating the poignant, paradoxical "place where it can be said that *continuity* is giving way to *contiguity*,"[30] the line "there, in the centre" of the painting both connects and divides the canvas and its subject, a counterpart to the interdependent absence and presence that for Lily has come to constitute the medium of paint.

5

THE POETICS OF HUNGER, THE POLITICS OF DESIRE: WOOLF'S DISCURSIVE TEXTS

> All this should be discussed and discovered; all this is part of the question of women and fiction. And yet, I continued, approaching the bookcase again, where shall I find that elaborate study of the psychology of women by a woman?
>
> Virginia Woolf, *A Room of One's Own*

> For as Professor Grensted gave his evidence, we, the daughters of educated men, seemed to be watching a surgeon at work—an impartial and scientific operator, who, as he dissected the human mind by human means laid bare for all to see what cause, what root lies at the bottom of our fear. It is an egg. Its scientific name is 'infantile fixation'.
>
> Virginia Woolf, *Three Guineas*

Instead of "that elaborate study of the psychology of women by a woman," the narrator of *A Room of One's Own* finds "at the very end" of her bookshelf *Life's Adventure,* the first novel by Mary Carmichael, Woolf's representative contemporary woman novelist and Lily Briscoe's successor in *Room.*[1] Like Lily's painting, *Life's Adventure* redefines the subject of narrative: "'Chloe liked Olivia,' I read. And then it struck me how immense a change was there. Chloe liked Olivia perhaps for the first time in literature. Cleopatra did not like Octavia. And how completely *Antony and Cleopatra* would have been altered had she done so!" (86). Mary Carmichael also breaks the narrative sequences established by her foremother Jane Austen, yet her novel stands at both the end and the beginning of a female line: "[O]ne must read it as if it were the last volume in a fairly long series, continuing all those other [women's] books. . . . For books continue each other, in spite of our habit of judging them separately" (84). The new work of fiction generates a discourse of merger and rupture that stands in the place of a feminine psychoanalysis.

By invoking and unmasking that discourse, *Room* "continues" *To the Lighthouse* and breaks with it. The later text both theorizes and challenges the mother-daughter story Lily narrates as she paints. In *To the Lighthouse,* as in object relations theory, the ambivalence that emerges with the mother's narrative centrality is located benignly in the negotiation of boundaries and finds resolution in a work of art. Through the

1920s, however, Woolf's texts reverse the sequence of psychoanalytic history by proceeding toward increasingly primitive, passionate, Kleinian renditions of ambivalence toward the mother. By articulating a plaint about material nurture, *Room* discloses retrospectively what Lily's discourse of boundaries has failed to address: that only men are represented eating at the dinner in *To the Lighthouse*, for example; that although Mrs. Ramsay is depicted alternately nurturing her husband until he is "filled with her words, like a child who drops off satisfied," and starving him until he is "the very figure of a famished wolfhound," Lily represents her longing for the mother only in the language of merger, never hunger.[2] The polemical framework that simplifies *Room*'s representation of maternal origins paradoxically permits the analysis of conflicts that Woolf's poetics of detachment banished from her fiction.

Room is Woolf's most complete and complex interpretation of matrilineage; it is also her last. In its sequel, *Three Guineas*, the mother as both origin and feeder disappears; women in this text no longer have nor are mothers. The boundary discourse jeopardized in *Room* by hunger is transformed in *Three Guineas* by sexuality and recentered in a father who assimilates the mother. From representing patriarchy's other, the mother shrivels to the "egg" that figures patriarchy's source. The mother's contamination diminishes Woolf's argument with Freud: the search for a female-authored psychology of women yields to the discourse of "infantile fixation."

Read together, *Room* and *Three Guineas* disclose some of the pressures on the figure of the mother that mediated Woolf's encounter, across two decades, with the fictions of psychoanalysis. The two texts also recast the traditional division of Woolf's career between the "tug to vision" in the 1920s and the claims of "fact" in the 1930s.[3] By outlining the forces guiding Woolf's trajectory from matrilinear to patrilinear definitions of the daughter, the discursive texts resituate her career, and its diverse intersections with psychoanalysis, within the social history of gender. To highlight and to explicate the break in this career, this chapter proceeds from the feminization of origins through which Woolf counters Freud's authority in *Room* to the reversals *Three Guineas* performs; it then returns to *Room* to disturb this opposition by uncovering an ambivalent discourse of nurture that qualifies the celebration of maternal origins; the chapter concludes by exploring how *Three Guineas*'s redefinition of the female subject as the "daughter of an educated man" allies Woolf, in the late 1930s, problematically with Freud.

I

For a text on women and fiction, *Room* presents surprisingly few scenes of writing. Except for the description of Jane Austen hiding her manuscripts under the blotter, the only representation of a text in production is Professor von X's treatise, *The Mental, Moral, and Physical Inferiority of the Female Sex,* which stands synecdochically for the masculine discourses the narrator discovers in the British Museum. The narrator's sketch of the German professor links the act of writing with fury: "His expression suggested that he was labouring under some emotion that made him jab his pen on the paper as if he were killing some noxious insect as he wrote, but even when he had killed it that did not satisfy him; he must go on killing it; and even so, some cause for anger and irritation remained" (31). Writing proceeds from a surplus of anger that motivates and exceeds the flow of signifiers. This parody of a psychoanalytic theory of the text is the site of the text's one (parodic) allusion to Freud: "Had he [Professor von X] been laughed at, to adopt the Freudian theory, in his cradle by a pretty girl?" Invoking Freud against a Freudian text on sexual difference, *Room* links the scene of writing with a retaliatory masculinity.

Woolf's account of contemporary fiction, typified by Mr. A, Professor von X's counterpart from the opposite end of the alphabet, contextualizes the professor's private history. In her description of Mr. A's new novel, the scene of writing dissolves into the subject it re-presents. The pen has become the authorial ego—"a straight dark bar, a shadow shaped something like the letter 'I'"—incarnate in the protagonist, *A*lan, who obliterates the heroine, Phoebe, in the "flood of his views" and his passions (103–4).[4] The erotic scenes, like the scene of writing, are tinged with sadism, for in contrast to "Shakespeare's indecency," which expresses and evokes "pleasure," Alan's phallic mastery of Phoebe betrays his author's aggressive purpose: "He is protesting against the equality of the other sex by asserting his own superiority" (105). Exposing its origins in a decade when "the Suffrage campaign . . . must have roused in men an extraordinary desire for self-assertion," Mr. A's novel discloses the political unconscious of the professor's gender theory (103).[5]

Room attempts to counter, while it tries to describe, a defensively misogynist construction and conflation of gender and textuality. Woolf challenges the written text's authority by insisting on *Room*'s status as a lecture to women and (in a way reminiscent of Lily Briscoe's painting) by privileging the visual arts as metaphors for writing. It is no accident that a drawing discloses the truth of Professor von X's text or that literary forms are represented architecturally as structures "built now in squares, now pagoda shaped, . . . now solidly compact and domed like the Cathedral of Saint Sofia at Constantinople" (74). Woolf quite explicitly regenders textuality by figuring fiction as "a spider's web, attached ever so lightly perhaps, but still attached to life at all four corners" (43). The weaving that Freud contemporaneously translates from a conventional trope of women's generative primacy, of (in Bachofen's words) the "labour of great material primordial mothers," into a compensatory cultural achievement motivated by the desire to conceal an "original sexual inferiority," is reclaimed by Woolf as a feminized figure of the text.[6]

Texts are mothered, not authored, in *Room,* although Woolf opposes textual maternity to biological maternity. "Masterpieces are not single and solitary births; they are the outcome of many years of thinking in common, of thinking by the body of the people" (68–69). A potential masterpiece typically miscarries, since "[e]verything is against the likelihood that it will come from the writer's mind whole and entire. . . . [P]robably no book is born entire and uncrippled as it was conceived," yet birth figures an ideal textual autonomy (53–54). Unlike the pen that serves authorial self-expression, the mind-as-womb separates texts from their creators; eluding its author's ego, the externalized text assumes an embodied and autonomous position in the world. The maternal metaphor reconciles Woolf's disdain for confessional works with her privileging of subjectivity.[7] Successfully giving birth to a text is synonymous, finally, with the androgyny *Room* openly propounds.[8] For the formal expression of androgyny, epitomized by the plays of Shakespeare—"the type of the androgynous" and the antitype of Mr. A—is the purging of the authorial self from the "whole and free" text generated by the "naturally creative" mind (102).

The weighting of androgyny toward the maternal is in fact implicit throughout Woolf's discussion. The very sexuality on which her language insists—the "intercourse" and "marriage" of masculine and feminine that qualifies the meaning of their "collaboration"—returns to the metaphor of birth. The site of textual production is figuratively the womb: the taxicab into which the man and woman enter in Woolf's allegory of the androgynous mind; the imaginative chamber whose "curtains must be close drawn" so that the mind can "celebrate its nuptials in darkness" and the "marriage of opposites . . . be consummated" (108). Androgyny is proposed as a corrective to a masculinization of discourse represented, at one end of the decade, by the pen's attack on the female body and, at the other, by the "horrid little abortion. . . . [t]wo heads on one body" that reflects the fascist poem's double paternity (107). In practice, if not in theory, androgyny entails the assimilation of maternal generativity—and not some more general notion of the feminine—consistently contrasted with "the dominance of the letter 'I' and the aridity that, like the giant beach tree, it casts within its shade" (104).

Woolf's privileging of the maternal metaphor rests, however, on her discomfort with biological maternity, a discomfort already implicit in *To the Lighthouse,* where it is Lily (not Cam) who thinks back through Mrs. Ramsay, who is not her biological mother, whom she reimagines in terms that gravitate from biology to art. In *Room* Woolf historicizes the rhetoric of gender: as she locates exaggerated claims for masculinity in the context of the suffrage victory, she contextualizes the maternal metaphor within postsuffrage feminism. Biological motherhood in *Room* disqualifies literary maternity: childlessness, the narrator observes, is the only link among the four great nineteenth-century women novelists; Judith Shakespeare's suicide reiterates the fate of Mary Hamilton (the unnamed Mary of the Child ballad from which Woolf draws her narrative persona), who went to the scaffold for murdering her illegitimate child.[9] Through her choice of authors for *Life's Adventure,* Woolf situates *Room* in relation to the birth control movement that emerged in England in the 1920s, for Mary Carmichael (whose name is mandated by the Child ballad—"Call me Mary Beton, Mary Seton, Mary Carmichael or by any name you please" [5]) is also the pseudonym under which Marie Stopes, the most famous birth control advocate in England, had published her novel, *Love's Creation,* the year before *Room* came out.[10] *Life's Adventure* is politically more adventurous than *Love's Creation,* but the echoes in title and setting, as well as in the authors' names, affiliate women's literary production with a social discourse in which issues of reproduction have shifted from the margins to the center. In marked contrast to the single-minded focus on political equality that galvanized the suffrage movement, postsuffrage feminists endorsed the birth control movement, economic support for mothers, protection in the workplace, and family allowances in order to redress the social penalties that women incur biologically. Fueling the maternal metaphor that opposes masculine authorship is the position of the mother in the "new feminism" of the 1920s.[11]

Through Mary Carmichael's fiction of Chloe and Olivia, which shares Alan and Phoebe's emblematic status, Woolf suggests a further context for the oppositional figure of the mother: a female intimacy intensified in the postwar world by a disenchantment with masculinity.[12] The figuration of Chloe's affection for Olivia intimates an originary space constructed and inhabited by two women: "For if Chloe likes Olivia and Mary Carmichael knows how to express it she will light a torch in that vast chamber where nobody has yet been. It is all half lights and profound shadows like those serpentine caves where one goes with a candle" (88). Jane Marcus has uncovered the lesbian implications of Woolf's having prefaced the statement that "'Chloe liked Olivia'" with a reference to Sir Chartres Biron, who presided over the obscenity trial Radclyffe Hall's *Well of Loneliness* had provoked the preceding year, and of Woolf's alluding to the *Well* in Fernham's female pastoral.[13] The romantic "cave" of Chloe and Olivia, and the garden world of Fernham, where daffodils and bluebells wave in the wind and purples and golds "burn in windowpanes like the beat of an excitable heart," are pockets of exclusive and impassioned femininity that substitute for the heterosexual couple a fantasy of double motherhood (16).

Woolf elaborates this fantasy by asymmetrically feminizing the con-

THE POETICS OF HUNGER, THE POLITICS OF DESIRE

cept of androgyny. For despite her declaration that "some marriage of opposites has to be consummated," she calls into question the hetero-sexual prototypes of women's literary maternity (and hence of androgyny) by never representing a marriage with the masculine, by including no women in her list of androgynous writers, and by implying through her epithets that "powerful and masterly" but infertile feminist texts require some intercourse with the *feminine* (108). When she rewrites from a contemporary feminine perspective the vision of sexual difference that underlies androgyny—an "illustrious man" renewed by "her" as the "centre of some different order and system of life" in the "drawing-room or nursery"—both the room and its viewer are feminine (90). It is the sight of sameness, not difference, that now refreshes and invigorates, the sight of a femininity that craves articulation in the public world but no insem-ination by the masculine. A vision of illicit linguistic birth registers the circumvention of paternity: "[W]hole flights of words would need to wing their way illegitimately into existence before a woman could say what happens when she goes into a room" (91).

Suggestions of parthenogenesis also write men out of the figures of birth pervading *Room*. The narrator's purse, for example, supplied with money by her aunt, procreates autonomously: "[I]t is a fact that still takes my breath away—the power of my purse to breed ten-shilling notes auto-matically. I open it and there they are" (37).[14] Parthenogenetic or lesbian, the mothers that figure origins in *Room* are not mothers who reproduce biologically. When biological maternity was glorified by fascism in the 1930s, an oppositional maternal metaphor became untenable. In conse-quence, Woolf's antipatriarchal figure shifted from the (nonbiological) mother to the chaste daughter, the heroine of *Three Guineas*.

II

The itinerary of Woolf's argument to and within *Three Guineas* can be condensed to a route first followed in *Room:* the construction of a cultural text's human origin. The "text" in *Three Guineas* is pictorial: a 1936 photograph from the beleaguered Spanish government illustrating the horrors of war. The adult body, whose mutilation obliterates any trace of gender, the dead children, and the bombed-out house form a meeting place for the narrator and her male correspondent, a text they interpret identically. At her letter's end, however, the narrator draws an image of this picture's origin, foregrounding difference rather than commonality. The horrors of war recede into the background.

> For . . . another picture has imposed itself upon the foreground. It is
> the figure of a man; some say, others deny, that he is Man himself, the

quintessence of virility, the perfect type of which all the others are imperfect adumbrations. He is a man certainly. . . . His eyes are glazed; his eyes glare. His body, which is braced in an unnatural position, is tightly cased in a uniform. Upon the breast of that uniform are sewn several medals and other mystic symbols. His hand is upon a sword. He is called in German and Italian Führer or Duce; in our own language Tyrant or Dictator. And behind him lie ruined houses and dead bodies—men, women, and children.[15]

Both iconographically and formally, this "figure of a man" that generates and consequently explicates a violent text recalls a predecessor: "the face and the figure of Professor von X . . . jab[bing] his pen on the paper as if he were killing some noxious insect." The pen that figuratively killed its female subject has been converted to a sword.

The decade that has intervened, however, has altered the gender ideology. By the mid-1930s the feminist movement was too depleted to excite retaliation against women's bodies. Woolf's footnote in the passage quoted above to "he is Man himself" explains: "The nature of manhood and the nature of womanhood are frequently defined by both Italian and German dictators. Both repeatedly insist that it is the nature of man and indeed the essence of manhood to fight. Hitler, for example, draws a distinction between 'a nation of pacifists and a nation of men.' Both repeatedly insist that it is the nature of womanhood to heal the wounds of the fighter" (186n. 48). Unlike the defensive and punitive rhetoric of Professor von X, these paraphrased male voices are calm and assured; the "mental, moral, and physical inferiority of women" has yielded to a discourse of "natural and eternal law" that acclaims a biologically grounded female power of nurturance which serves, rather than interrogates, masculine heroics.[16] The sword is lifted against men instead of women, whose solace and assistance it presupposes.

In this footnote Woolf quotes from two items in the three volumes of newspaper clippings she compiled between 1931, when she first envisaged a sequel to *Room,* and 1938, when she published *Three Guineas.*[17] A recurrent motif in this compendium of pronouncements on gender and social institutions is the fascist ideology of sexual difference as an innate and immutable polarity enjoined by nature and ratified by providence. "The Natural and Eternal Law in Germany" is her title for a *Times* clipping that reports a speech by Dr. Woerman, counsellor of the German embassy, justifying Hitler's expulsion of women from the professions in 1933: "It was the aim of National-Socialism to let man's work be done by men and not by women. To believe that a woman's principle work was family life and bringing up the young generation was simply to return to natural and eternal law."[18]

Intended to legitimate the complementary figures of warrior hero and prolific mother that Hitler's imperial mission required, the Nazi rhetoric of sexual difference, as biologistic as its racial rhetoric, celebrated women's procreative power. As a Nazi propaganda pamphlet designed by and for women succinctly declares: "In woman's womb rests the future of the people."[19] The Third Reich officially acknowledged maternal valor in 1938 by designing the Medal of Honor for prolific German mothers (bronze for more than four children, silver for more than six, gold for more than eight), entitling its possessor to mandatory respect and the privileges accorded special military groups, since the mother "risks her body and her life for the people and the Fatherland as much as the combat soldier does in the roar and thunder of battle."[20] Giving birth is thus represented as tantamount to, not (as in Freud) compensatory for, the hero's sword. Designed to counteract the falling birthrate that the dissemination of birth control and the spreading aspiration for a higher standard of living (hence smaller families) had produced in the 1920s, the Nazi glorification of maternity served the expansionist goal implied in the other clipping from which Woolf draws—Hitler's speech, at the celebration of the fifteenth anniversary of the Rosenheim branch of the Nazi party, extolling Germany's new military resolve by representing the Fatherland as no longer "a nation of pacifists but . . . a nation of men."[21]

Woolf's political agenda in *Three Guineas* is less to articulate a pacifist response to the fascist threat, her stated goal, than to bring the impending war home, to resituate the battlefield in the British family and workplace. Her most iconoclastic gesture is to subvert the distinction between political antagonists by discovering the mystique of gender difference, represented as fascism's core, in democratic England. Characterizing the British revival of domestic ideology as a response to the postwar depression and record unemployment that England shared with Germany and Italy, *Three Guineas* quotes three newspaper articles whose authors complain that the First World War afforded women "too much liberty" and who proclaim that "[h]omes are the real places of the women who are compelling men to be idle" (51). Pair these declarations with another one, Woolf directs, drawing again from her notebooks to quote Hitler's 1936 speech to the Nazi women's association: "There are two worlds in the life of the nation, the world of men and the world of women. Nature has done well to entrust the man with the care of his family and the nation. The woman's world is her family, her husband, her children, and her home." Woolf then insists, "One is written in English, the other in German. But where is the difference? Are they not both saying the same thing?" (53).[22]

The fascist promotion of two gender worlds contaminates the maternal metaphor that Woolf could differentiate from biological maternity in *Room*. The discourse of natural and eternal law disqualifies her strategy of reversal: the more profoundly other the mother, the more she now serves the interests of the same. Instead of marking a position anterior or exterior to patriarchy, the mother has become, in Oswald Mosley's words, "one of the main pillars of the state."[23] Woolf translates Hitler's two gender worlds, and their counterparts in England, into variants of a single world: a private house and a public house that are equally paternal, that afford no uncontaminated place of residence. A new geography articulates these changes: for the room that had delineated a private feminine space Woolf substitutes a bridge that affords an anthropologist's perspective on social institutions perceived at a distance but not from any native ground. The bridge demarcates a liminal zone "between the old world and the new," between "the private house and the world of public life" (16, 18). But the private house is no longer maternal; the "final slam of the door" behind the Ibsenesque daughter seals a point of origin that is always already paternal, that epitomizes patriarchy rather than opposing it (138). *Three Guinea*'s topography of doubled fathers, prefigured in the twofold paternity of the fascist text, inverts *Room*'s fantasy of double mothers, a fantasy sustainable only in a context that permitted new ways of envisaging maternity.[24]

Woolf's metaphors linking fascism to England signal her anxiety about maternal complicity. In the newspaper clippings assigning women to the home, she insists, "is the egg of the very same worm that we know under other names in other countries. . . . Dictator as we call him when he is Italian or German. . . . And he is here among us, raising his ugly head, spitting his poison, small still, curled up like a caterpillar on a leaf, but in the heart of England" (53). By consistently figuring the origins of fascism in England as an egg, Woolf implicates the mother in her own appropriation.[25] The insect that in *Room* represented the unambiguous victim of misogyny has metamorphosed into the egg-laying caterpillar-fascist (elsewhere called "insect" and "worm") who figures the collapse of the sexual polarities that his discursive "eggs" propound. *Room*'s sequel hints at a monstrously literalized androgyny that furthers, rather than tempers, the achievements of masculinity. The literalization is consistent with the diminished faith in imagination suggested by Woolf's embrace of an aesthetic of fact in the 1930s; but the reconstruction of androgyny as a patriarchal appropriation of maternity also demonstrates the problem of merger under the aegis of the father. "Husband and wife are not only one flesh; they are also one purse" in the domestic arrangements the text criticizes by insisting on women's economic autonomy (54). But although Woolf devises strategies for separating incomes, the text is haunted by the vision of the single flesh, which returns in a pervasively eroticized rhetoric that assimilates the single purse (no longer breeding parthenogenetically) to an image of sexually appropriated, and acquiescent, femininity.

Three Guineas emphasizes economic tactics for dismantling England's protofascist social structures. Designating 1919 a "sacred year" not because of the suffrage victory but because it was the year of the Act of

Parliament that unbarred women's entry into the professions (the anti-thesis to Hitler's expulsion of women from the professions), the text privileges an entry to the public sphere that subverts, rather than inverts, the cultural construction of sexual difference. To guide the daughter beyond the private house, Woolf maps the discourse of female sexual conduct onto the novel economic terrain, but the erotic rhetoric eclipses the economic framework it should serve. Woolf presents as uncomplicatedly figurative the chastity she recommends: "By chastity is meant that when you have made enough to live on by your profession you must refuse to sell your brain for the sake of money" (80). The body that should serve as a trans-parent vehicle repeatedly asserts its own distracting literality, however: "[T]o sell a brain is worse than to sell a body, for when the body seller has sold her momentary pleasure she takes good care that the matter shall end there. But when a brain seller has sold her brain, its anaemic, vicious and diseased progeny are let loose upon the world to infect and corrupt and sow the seeds of disease in others" (93).[26] The dangers of economic seduction pale beside those represented as reproduction, which in the imagery of this text inevitably breeds disease. *Three Guineas* argues that the daughter must penetrate the public world to break her economic dependence on her father and unsettle a repressive and deceptive separa-tion of spheres; a fixed opposition between the virgin and the whore conversely proscribes the reproduction of the private sphere, for an invar-iant language of sexual revulsion assimilates the mother (present in this text only as a sexual being) to the whore.[27] Losing control over the object of her irony, Woolf implicitly sanctions the discrimination she condemns against married women in the government: "As for 'Mrs.,' it is a contami-nated word; an obscene word. The less said about that word the better. Such is the smell of it, so rank does it stink in the nostrils of Whitehall, that Whitehall excludes it entirely. In Whitehall, as in heaven, there is neither marrying nor giving in marriage" (52).

The smell that both signals and confirms a masculine fantasy is a symptom of a pervasive social illness Woolf diagnoses variously as mis-ogyny and incest (variations on one theme, as we shall see) but figures consistently as female reproductive sexuality. Traced ultimately to the eggs laid by caterpillars curled in the "heart of England," the rank smell calls attention to the text's other site: the garden that represents the "heart" of the city, whose buildings and processions, seen from a distance, constitute the foregrounded urban spectacle.[28] The nostalgic discourse of the garden "heart of England" seems to contradict the text's emphatic cosmopoli-tanism, but the garden that (like Fernham) might situate some unfallen sexual or national identity rehearses, instead of opposing, the politics of the urban sphere. If the garden heart is a passive feminized body invaded by the phallic caterpillar-dictators, it also displays an unruly female sexu-ality; the leaves on which the caterpillars lay their eggs have been destroyed through sins of prostitution as well as through predation. The "glory . . . of war lies curled up in the rotten cabbage leaves of our prostituted fact-purveyors"—that is, of the daughters Woolf charges with "adultery of the brain" while she images a bodily unchastity that recasts the invading caterpillars as the prostitutes' progeny (97, 93). *Three Guineas*'s ruined garden echoes *Hamlet*'s "unweeded garden / That grows to seed," possessed by "[t]hings rank and gross in nature" (1.2.135–36); both texts invoke the garden trope to write the mother's guilt into a charge ostensibly against the fathers. *Room* revises *Antony and Cleopatra* through Chloe's affection for Olivia; *Three Guineas* borrows, without changing, *Hamlet*'s vision of corruption—a vision, as Janet Adelman argues persuasively, of a maternal sexuality indistinguishable from adultery.[29]

Like *Hamlet*, moreover, *Three Guineas* displays, in a nightmare parody of androgyny, great anxiety about the power of sexuality to obliterate difference. The loss of Hamlet's idealized father, Adelman suggests, removes Hamlet's defense against archaic fears of the engulfing mother, whose sexuality (newly confirmed for Hamlet by her adultery) threatens to erase all boundaries; hence Claudius appears to Hamlet, "My mother—father and mother is man and wife, man and wife is one flesh, and so, my mother" (4.3.50–51). In *Three Guineas* the confrontation with maternal heterosexuality—the loss, that is, of the idealized, autonomous mother—evokes a parallel fear of merger, but for the daughter, the father is dominant: "Husband and wife are" both "one flesh" and "one purse." The protective responses are also akin. Woolf's charge of chastity to the daughter echoes Hamlet's to Ophelia, at times quite literally. "I say we will have no more marriage," Hamlet declares (3.1.150). Woolf's rhetoric is similar, though somewhat unpersuasively disowned: "In Whitehall, as in heaven, there is neither marrying nor giving in marriage."

In the fantasy Woolf elaborates in *Room* two women regender origins; in *Three Guineas* origins are equated with disease; the later text exhorts an end to paternal power more urgently than it does a new beginning. As the sexual and political ideologies of the 1930s underscored for Woolf both the intractability of patriarchy and the mother's position in perpetuating it, her feminism shifted from valorizing mothers to confronting "the infantile fixation of the fathers," now "massed together in societies, in professions," and "even more subject to the fatal disease than the fathers in private" (137–38).[30] Before following Woolf's turn to the fathers, however, we must return to *Room* to uncover its own criticism of the mother. Simply to polarize the feminist texts would undervalue their complexity, for the matrilineage acclaimed by *Room* conceals—though imperfectly—the ambivalence triggered by the problem of maternal nurture.

III

The mind in *Room* is both a womb and a stomach; writing is digestion as well as birth. Contesting the representation of texts gestating within an enclosed interior is an insistence on the mind's need to feed on something exterior, "to absorb the new into the old without disturbing the infinitely intricate and elaborate balance of the whole" (89). If the mind's self-enclosure privileges the figure of the mother, however, digestion privileges an access to the world that has been the male writer's prerogative.

To give birth to texts in *Room*, one must eat. *Room* locates discourse consistently in a particular relation to the body: "[A] good dinner is of great importance to good talk" (18). Not altogether playfully criticizing fictional conventions for emphasizing language ("something very witty that was said") or action ("something very wise that was done") over "what was eaten," the scenes of eating that precede the scenes of reading launch an argument about representation and an account of literary production that are repeatedly declared in terms of money and dramatized in terms of food (10). Hunger and the anger it generates, however, are gendered impediments to writing in *Room*. For men such as the "well-nourished, well-educated" Mr. A, and even for his less coddled predecessors, Woolf depicts the obstacles to "free and unimpeded" creation as a wounded and intrusive ego which must be purged by an incandescent flame that leaves "no foreign matter unconsumed" (103, 58). But the metaphorics of eating, problematized for women, activate the secondary meaning of the word "consume" and suggest a different ecology of writing. By enabling "the more profound, subtle and subterranean glow, which is the rich yellow flame of rational intercourse" to vanquish "that hard little electric light which we call brilliance, as it pops in and out upon our lips," the scene of lavish eating at Oxbridge contextualizes incandescence as an effect of consumption rather than its cause (11).

Leaving "no foreign matter" textually unconsumed always requires adequate consumption, but appetite's object is shaped historically. The nineteenth-century woman writer hungered catastrophically for experience: when Charlotte Brontë "remembered that she had been starved of her proper due of experience," *Jane Eyre* miscarried; Brontë "will never get her genius expressed whole and entire. Her books will be deformed and twisted" (76, 72). In the postsuffrage present of the narrative, however, the object of women's hunger, and anger, has changed. The new woman represented by Mary Carmichael's Olivia "sees coming her way" precisely what Brontë hungered for: "A piece of strange food—knowledge, adventure, art" (89). Woolf preserves the suffrage movement's privileging of hunger as a figure of feminine desire; but whereas the suffragettes made hunger, theatricalized through hunger strikes, a metaphor of women's intellectual starvation and a sign of their resistance to patriarchal food, of refusal to accept nurture for the body when the spirit went unfed, Woolf situates the hunger of the postsuffrage woman in a different register.[31] In contrast to Judith Shakespeare, who escaped to the city from the advantageous marriage arranged by her father because "her genius was for fiction and lusted to feed abundantly upon the lives of men and women and the study of their ways," or to Jane Eyre, who, in the passage Woolf cites, escaped to the roof "when Mrs. Fairfax was making jellies and looked over the fields at the distant view"—in contrast, that is, to an intellectual hunger that exceeds and repudiates material sustenance—the women at Fernham, to whom the fathers have granted food for thought, hunger instead for material food they (illogically) blame their mothers for withholding (50, 71). In a reversal produced by women's new cultural location, Woolf literalizes hunger and returns it to its original relation to "our mothers," now charged with the task of feeding daughters recently admitted to cultural institutions that both stimulate and frustrate the longing for maternal nurture.

In *Room*'s complex representation of the present, a chasm between two female generations simultaneously promotes a celebration of matrilineage and aggravates a complaint about nurture. To protect the mother as origin from anger at the feeding/withholding mother (the least rational and most deeply prohibited anger in the text), Woolf separates the discourses of descent and hunger, locating each in one of the Marys that constitute her narrative persona. Through Mary Carmichael she identifies the changes that made it newly attractive for a writing daughter to celebrate a relationship to mothers whose lives she had recently been safeguarded from reproducing. The subject Woolf proposes for Mary Carmichael's next novel, "a very ancient lady crossing the street on the arm of a middle-aged woman, her daughter, perhaps. . . . No biography or history has a word to say about it," underlines the emergence of a distinctive mother-daughter plot, for the first time in literary history, in women's fiction of the 1920s (92–93).[32] Woolf outlines this narrative in the context of literary history through Mary Carmichael's continuation of, and rupture with, Jane Austen. To protect the narrative's benign dynamics, Woolf systematically depicts the writing daughter only as negotiating issues of difference and continuity with her female precursors, not as hungering for sustenance from them. Reading is eating only if the substance is provided by men: "Lately my diet has become a trifle monotonous; history is too much about wars; biography too much about great men," the narrator complains, to exhort her female audience "to write all kinds of books." But her discourse swerves from eating to genealogy to characterize the female tradition: every exemplary woman writer of the past "is an inheritor as well as an originator, and has come into existence because women have come to have the habit of writing naturally" (112–13).[33] Unlike Lily Briscoe, *Room*'s narrator does investigate what the discourse of descent excludes, but she concentrates her investigation in the reproaches she addresses on her own behalf and that of Mary Seton, a science don at Fernham, to Mary's mother, Mrs. Seton, a Victorian mother of thirteen.

Represented iconically through a photograph on Mary Seton's mantlepiece, Mrs. Seton, the only biological mother in *Room*'s cast of fictional characters, assumes a generic character. In a text that employs portraiture almost exclusively for feminist satire (the sketch of Professor von X is a typical example), the unusual visual image of a woman, enforcing a pause in the narrative, calls attention to the portrait of "a homely body; an old lady in a plaid shawl" sitting, with her dog, in a basket-chair (21). Vivid but silent, Mrs. Seton cannot answer the questions she attracts about the "reprehensible poverty" of "our mothers" (23). Instead, she is a vehicle for Woolf's translation of maternal poverty into insufficient feeding: "If only Mrs. Seton and her mother and her mother before her had learnt the great art of making money and had left their money, like their fathers and their grandfathers before them, to found fellowships and lectureships and prizes and scholarships appropriated to the use of their own sex, we might have dined very tolerably up here alone off a bird and a bottle of wine" (21–22). The preoccupation with "our mothers" that hunger exacts is regressive, not progressive, an obstacle, not an alternative, to the newly available and valued masculine discourses: if Mrs. Seton "had left two or three hundred thousand pounds to Fernham, we could have been sitting at our ease tonight and the subject of our talk might have been archaelogy, botany, anthropology, physics, the nature of the atom, mathematics, astronomy, relativity, geography"—instead of mothers (21).

The narrator recognizes that "our mothers" are not to blame for their culturally inflicted inability to feed. In the language of economics she reasons that "in the first place, to earn money was impossible for them, and in the second, had it been possible, the law denied them the right to possess what money they earned" (23). But the images provoked by hunger reinscribe maternal poverty in the register of feeding. The figuration of the scanty meal at Fernham simultaneously exonerates the mothers by examining how culture has constructed the relation between food and money and articulates the anger that has been disavowed. The imagery evoked by the tasteless meal about which the narrator insists "there was no reason to complain" is that of emotional as well as economic meanness, of a voluntary rather than imposed withholding (18). Resentment speaks loudest during the dessert that should gratify desire rather than need. "[S]tringy as a miser's heart and exuding a fluid such as might run in misers' veins who have denied themselves wine and warmth for eighty years and yet not given to the poor," the prunes that constitute dessert figure a withered and implicitly masculinized heart. The sources of this desiccated mothering are intimated by the meal's main course: beef, greens, and potatoes, "a homely trinity, suggesting the rumps of cattle in a muddy market, and sprouts curled and yellowed at the edge, and bargaining and cheapening, and women with string bags on Monday morning" (17). The dinner refers us to a prior scene: the marketplace, a scene of scarcity and exchange that positions women as consumers rather than producers. As the string bags evolve into the stringy hearts, women are written out of the picture entirely. Collapsed with the images evoked by the prunes, the scene recurs as "*lean* cows and a muddy market and withered greens and the stringy hearts of old men" (19; emphasis added). The loss of the status of nurturer imposed by the shift from production to consumption implies a final degendering, depicted as a violation of and by the mothers.[34]

The scene of exchange has a counterpart at Oxbridge. During the discussion of maternal poverty in Mary Seton's room, the narrator confesses: "While these things were being said, however, I became shame-facedly aware of a current setting in of its own accord. . . . [T]wo pictures, disjointed and disconnected and nonsensical as they were, were for ever coming together and combating each other and had me entirely at their mercy" (19). The two pictures the narrator sees at Fernham—one of lean cows and a muddy market, the other of kings and nobles pouring treasure under the Oxbridge earth—echo and revise the Tennyson and Rossetti poems she "hears" at Oxbridge when listening "not entirely to what was being said, but to the murmur or current behind it" (12). The two pictures translate sexual difference into an economic frame by pairing images of founders instead of lovers, shifting the frame of reference from the phallus, linked with the poems through the narrator's speculation on the Manx cat's missing tail, to the "chest" in which food passes through the circuit of money. If the Fernham scene implies that at some hypothetical moment in history the marketplace has intervened in the transmission of food from mother to child, the Oxbridge scene, elaborated through the luncheon, reveals that this intervention has constituted fathers as, lamentably, the better nurturers, the more effective mothers.

The complete account of the founding moment of Oxbridge, quite literally the construction of its foundation, describes a flow of gold and silver that transforms nature to culture: "Once, presumably, this quadrangle with its smooth lawns, its massive buildings, and the chapel itself was marsh too, where the grasses waved and the swine rootled. . . . An unending stream of gold and silver, I thought, must have flowed into this court perpetually to keep the stones coming and the masons working" (9). The represented moment of cultural origins depends, however, on some prior ones: the privatization of property, the accumulation of wealth, and the creation of gold and silver as a means of exchange. Subsequent economic developments simply displace the flow from one paternal chest to another: "[T]he gold and silver flowed now, not from the coffers of the king, but from the chests of merchants and manufacturers, from the purses of men who had made, say, a fortune from industry" (9). Juxtaposed scenes transpose the ceaseless flow of money into the ceaseless flow of food in the lavish Oxbridge luncheon, distinguished not only by its bounty and excellence but by the magical nature of its provenance, the sense of a return to some originary plenitude now produced under the aegis of the fathers. Gratification is known before desire is felt. With no command uttered, and agency scarcely revealed, course follows course in a prelinguistic economy of desire. "Meanwhile the wineglasses had flushed yellow and flushed crimson; had been emptied; had been filled" (11). In an unruptured trajectory from chest to glass, the two-colored flow of wine highlights the aridity of biscuits, cheese, and water with which Fernham dinner unceremoniously terminates. The meals perform a symmetrical regendering: mothers dispossessed by the marketplace shrivel into the stringy hearts of aged men; paternal chests metamorphose into breasts that reconvert gold and silver to wine and food.

That the luncheon fleetingly reconstitutes a prelapsarian moment is further suggested by the barred return that frustrates the narrator's first attempt to enter the Oxbridge sanctum. As she opens the door of the library "instantly there issued, like a guardian angel barring the way with a flutter of black gown instead of white wings," a gentleman denying women access (7). After the luncheon that suspends the banishment from Eden, the narrator is gently but decisively expelled from a campus whose description telescopes the dining hall and library: "Gate after gate seemed to close with gentle finality behind me. Innumerable beadles were fitting innumerable keys into well-oiled locks; the treasure-house was being made secure for another night" (13). The drama of women's exclusion from the sanctuaries of culture also images a lost maternal Eden, for the scene of prohibited reading shares the feminization of the scene of gratified eating. In contrast to the accessible British Museum, under whose "vast dome" the narrator feels like "a thought in the huge bald forehead which is so splendidly encircled by a band of a famous [male] names," the Oxbridge library, "with all its treasure safe locked in its breast" is figured not as a masculine brain but as a maternal "treasure-house" possessed and guarded by the fathers (26, 8). The image of hoarded maternal treasure recalls Lily Briscoe's fantasy that "in the chambers of the mind and heart" of the unresponsive Mrs. Ramsay "were stood, like the treasures in the tombs of kings, tablets bearing sacred inscriptions, which if one could spell them out, would teach one everything, but they would never be offered openly, never made public."[35] Mrs. Ramsay's enigma in this scene, however, is not produced by her submission to the fathers but by a discourse of knowledge that Lily rapidly rejects for the language of mother-daughter merger. The surfacing of hunger in *Room* generates a new perception of maternal withholding.

Room's insistence on hunger for and anger at a mother kept from feeding constitutes the historicized terrain on which Woolf intersects with

Klein. Through the figure of Mrs. Seton, Woolf examines the constriction
of maternal nurture in a context *Room* images as the marketplace but
analyzes more precisely as a postindustrial economy that divides material
production from human reproduction.[36] The long list of wishful clauses
that follow the conditional "If only Mrs. Seton" and her foremothers
"had learnt the great art of making money" concludes abruptly with
"there would have been . . . no Mary" (22). Mrs. Seton can either bear
children or earn the wages that enable her to feed them: to give birth to
children is to starve them; to feed them is to forgo bearing them. Instead of
inhabiting and consecrating the reproductive mother, as in contemporaneous sentimental anthropological theories, the nurturant mother has
become her antithesis.[37] Lacking liquid treasure to pour into the earth,
the founding mothers of Fernham exhaust their resources giving birth to
buildings: "To raise bare walls out of the bare earth was the utmost they
could do" (23).

The imaginative solution *Room* proposes to this split returns us to
the fantasy of the double mother, but from the vantage point of lack
instead of plenitude. This fiction of the double mother both echoes and
revises Klein. Reversing the projections of the Kleinian infant—who splits
the inevitably frustrating maternal body into an idealized "good" breast
and a withholding "bad" breast that, by drawing anger to itself, protects
the fantasy of the "good" mother—Woolf compensates for a socially inflicted maternal failure by constructing the woman who *can* feed: the
woman who is *not* biologically a mother. *Room*'s narrator inherits a legacy
of five hundred pounds a year from the third Mary, her aunt, Mary Beton,
"for no other reason than that I share her name" (37). *Room* suggests,
however, that the namesake is as much an effect as a cause of the legacy, a
way of registering a maternal descent produced by nurture rather than by
birth. That the narrator bears the name of neither her mother (represented
in the text by the generic Mrs. Seton), nor her father (whom the text does
not represent), but of her father's sister—a single woman, presumably,
since she shares her brother's last name and leaves her money to her
niece—constitutes her as the daughter of two mothers: the one who bears
her, and therefore cannot nurture, and the one who feeds her, but does not
give birth.[38] The aunt is the mother's necessary cultural complement: her
legacy enables the narrator not only to write, the function Woolf describes,
but also to eat, the function that Woolf dramatizes. The legacy is introduced during the text's third scene of eating, which mediates between the
paternal lavishness of Oxbridge and the maternal penury of Fernham.
Situated in a restaurant near the British Museum, and costing precisely
"five shillings and ninepence," this modest luncheon of chicken and coffee
redeems the conversion of food into money by providing nourishment "in
return for a certain number of pieces of paper which were left me by an
aunt" (37). Enabling the negotiation of hunger in society, the aunt pays

the deficit incurred by reproduction; the purse in which the legacy money "breeds" translates generation into nurture. Although the declared value of the legacy is freedom from corrosive work and thus from anger and bitterness toward men, the dramatized value is freedom from hunger and thus from anger and bitterness toward women.[39] The last scene of eating, at the end of chapter 2, clears the way for the construction of the literary matrilineage that dominates the next three chapters, a task performed more safely after the management of appetite, gratified and regulated by a small fixed income, has been staged.

Protecting the literary mothers as points of origin, however, displaces the dynamics of hunger and anger through the text, colonizing distant arenas. The question "what food do we feed women as artists upon?," a question whose explicit reference to "that dinner of prunes and custard" seems to require by analogy some account of a maternal literary tradition, is rigidly segregated from that tradition (54–55). The answer is drawn instead from the textual food produced by the literary fathers, and specifically by the patriarchs studied earlier that day at the British Museum: Lord Birkenhead, Dean Inge, and Mr. Oscar Browning. Comparing the textual nurture of women and men to "the effect of ordinary milk and Grade A milk upon the body of the rat. . . . [O]ne was furtive, timid and small, and the other was glossy, bold and big," the narrator undoes the opposition between the breast of the Oxbridge library and the forehead of the British Museum by representing misogyny in the language of maternal food (54). Literary fathers, not mothers, feed their daughters inferior milk, a displacement less astonishing, perhaps, in view of one function of the chapter on the British Museum: to deflect onto the fathers the anger at the mothers with which the preceding chapter concludes. Literal fathers who repeat the words of Mr. Oscar Browning to legitimate their own attempts to keep their daughters from leaving home participate in the politics of feeding that will be replaced by sexuality in *Three Guineas*, where the father-daughter dyad acquires its own dynamics. In *Room*, through a certain poetic justice, the fathers are subsumed to the economy of eating they appropriate.

Room incorporates contrary currents, of course. The legend of Judith Shakespeare, which fits the classic pattern of the traffic in women, depicts the daughter exchanged by men and undone by masculine desires. But this fiction is circumscribed historically. Judith's vulnerability resides in her body, not (in contrast to *Three Guineas*) in her sexuality. This body, *Room* suggests, has been recently protected by the development of contraception, and Judith's story has been less recently revised by that of Aphra Behn, whose life is represented as an exemplary text that (like Judith's) "outweighs anything that she actually wrote" (67). Aphra Behn succeeds, where Judith Shakespeare fails, in "com[ing] to town and . . . mak[ing] her living by her wits" and proving the factitiousness of chastity.

Demonstrating women's erotic and economic autonomy, Behn should be *Room*'s heroine, her life a pattern for her literary daughters. But *Room* grants Behn no literary heirs, even when Woolf's imagination has free reign; Mary Carmichael's novel is affiliated instead with Behn's opposite, Jane Austen, who "never travelled; . . . never drove through London in an omnibus" and had the gift "not to want what she had not" (71). Behn's victories are compartmentalized as *Room*'s own undigested foreign matter because they are not the issues with which this text, despite its declarations, is concerned: sexuality is not yet the problematic female desire (and chastity is therefore represented as a constraint rather than a choice); autonomy is not yet the economic goal. For despite Woolf's claim that women should earn five hundred a year by their wits (69), a proposal that Behn's life explicitly authorizes, she chooses to dramatize the legacy rather than a salary, to figure money not as the earned and consequently "chaste" sixpence that in *Three Guineas* represents economic and erotic freedom from the fathers but as the magically inherited self-reproducing ten-shilling notes that situate money within the problematics of mothering. Hence the economic event that in *Room* overshadows the suffrage victory is not (as in *Three Guineas*) the 1919 Act unbarring the professions but the receipt of the aunt's legacy "about the same time that the act was passed that gave votes to women" and "infinitely the more important" (37).

"A solicitor's letter fell into the post-box and when I opened it I found that she had left me five hundred pounds a year for ever," the narrator explains, the "for ever" signaling the fairy-tale character of this text's economic strategy. The distancing of the aunt's death "by a fall from her horse when she was riding out to take the air in Bombay" removes any sense of loss from the fulfillment of the wish for sustenance (37). But even the fantasy enacts, rather than resolving, the dynamic of hunger and anger, for it is Woolf herself who must murder the aunt to gratify her narrator's desire. Although hedged with irony, the narrator's acknowledgment that "this writing of books by women . . . leads to the murder of one's aunts" articulates one of the text's most profound unconscious fears: that the daughter's hunger will annihilate the mother (112).[40]

The reproduction of the problem of hunger within its solution does not engender new inquiries, however. *Three Guineas* is profoundly split from *Room*. Woolf never mentions hunger in the later text, never hints that her final disillusion with the reproductive mother is anticipated by that mother's inability to feed. Instead, the failure of maternal nurture fuels Woolf's shift of attention from the mother to the father. Weakened by the unresolved problem of hunger and undermined politically by fascism, the figure of the mother disappears as an antidote to the father, whose resurgence in Woolf's discourse in the late 1930s both promotes and reflects her new engagement with Freud.

IV

"Began reading Freud last night," Woolf noted in her diary late in 1939; "I'm gulping up Freud" she confessed the following week; "Freud is upsetting: reducing one to whirlpool; & I daresay truly. If we're all instinct, the unconscious, whats all this about civilisation, the whole man, freedom &c?" she grudgingly conceded the following day in deference to the evidence of irrationality afforded by world politics in the late 1930s.[41] But the politics of sexuality, rather than of nations, defined the terms of Woolf's encounter with Freudian theory a few years earlier. The unconscious represented in *Three Guineas* is not a generalized whirlpool of instinct but a product of explicitly Oedipal relationships. A medical discourse prevails at the end of *Three Guineas*: cases, symptoms, and diagnoses supersede the discussion of unemployment; "infantile fixation," "castration complex," "Oedipus complex" become the critical terms. It is to investigate father-daughter sexuality that Woolf for the first time turns openly to Freud.

"A good deal of p[sycho]. a[nalysis]. talked; & I liked it. A mercy not always to talk politics," Woolf noted about a dinner party given by Adrian and Karin Stephen in 1936; the "talk" similarly shifts to psychoanalysis in the political text she began composing two weeks later.[42] Near its end *Three Guineas* returns to its beginning to reopen a question it has not resolved: the question of discourse between the sexes, the question posed by the book's epistolary form. The return initiates the explicitly psychoanalytic moment of the text. The form of *Three Guineas* itself, however, is imbricated in a dialogue with psychoanalysis. Woolf opens her text with a question posed by a letter she claims to have received three years before: "How in your opinion are we to prevent war?" (3). The question echoes one posed to Freud five years earlier: "Is there a way of delivering mankind from the menace of war?" Albert Einstein had written to Freud in accordance with an epistolary project sponsored by the League of Nations to foster international exchange among intellectuals. Freud begins his response, published with Einstein's letter in a League of Nations pamphlet entitled *Why War?* (1933), by protesting his surprise and uncertainty: "[T]he question which you put me—what is to be done to rid mankind of the war menace?—took me by surprise. And, next, I was dumbfounded by the thought of my (of *our,* I almost wrote) incompetence."[43] Woolf begins similarly by expressing hesitation: "A whole page could be filled with excuses and apologies; declarations of unfitness, incompetence, lack of knowledge, and experience"; but she decides to reply nevertheless, "since when before has an educated man asked a woman how in her opinion war can be prevented?" (3). By both writing and departing from Freud's position, while recasting a discussion across disciplinary boundaries into an exchange across gender lines, Woolf inscribes the question of war in a dialogue conducted with psychoanalysis across and about the sexual division.[44]

This dialogue becomes explicit when, after characterizing women's proposed double membership in society and the Society of Outsiders as "a movement . . . among educated men's daughters against the Nazi and the Fascist," the text quietly returns to its beginning in the midst of what should be its conclusion (119). The return occurs at a moment when the economic discourse falters, when the narrator admits the inadequacy of her earlier definition (and dismissal) of feminism as the completed struggle for "the only right, the right to earn a living" (101). Feminism returns in a psychoanalytic guise that, in contrast to *Room,* replaces, rather than parallels, the economic frame; Woolf marks the return by quoting her original account of the abyss that divides her from her male correspondent. A veil still intervenes in discussions between men and women even when they "talk, as we have boasted, about 'politics and people, war and peace, barbarism and civilization,'" the issues raised by her correspondent's letter (120, 4). She reproduces the ellipsis that had undermined the already achieved economic parity by "mark[ing] a precipice, a gulf so deeply cut between us that for three years and more I have been sitting on my side of it wondering whether it is any use to try to speak across it" (4). The gap widens in the repetition: ". . . Again there are three dots; again they represent a gulf—of silence this time, of silence inspired by fear" (120). Each time the narrator elects to approach the gulf obliquely, by choosing someone else through whom to speak. Her first interpreter is Mary Kingsley, whose comments on the differential education of daughters and sons introduces the economic perspective according to which "the noble courts and quadrangles of Oxford and Cambridge often appear to educated men's daughters like petticoats with holes in them" (5). The second interpreter is the 1935 Report of the Archbishops' Commission on the Ministry of Women, whose appendix by Dr. Grensted, an eminent professor of theology at Oxford, introduces a (sub)version of Freud that translates possession and lack into the psychoanalytic language that informs the supplement to Woolf's own text.

Charged with presenting the psychological reasons for the church's refusal to admit women to the ministry, Dr. Grensted iconoclastically invokes psychoanalysis to diagnose, rather than to apologize for, patriarchy. Insisting that the resistance to admitting women to the ministry is evidence of a "powerful and widespread subconscious motive" connected to the "infantile fixation," Dr. Grensted improvises a psychoanalytic explanation of misogyny: "'[W]hatever be the exact value and interpretation of the material upon which theories of the "Oedipus complex" and the "castration complex" have been founded, it is clear that the general acceptance of male dominance, and still more of feminine inferiority, resting upon subconscious ideas of woman as "man manqué," has its background in infantile conceptions of this type. These commonly, and even usually, survive in the adult, despite their irrationality'" (126). In Grensted's reconstruction, the perception of woman as a man manqué—for Freud the precondition for a credible castration threat and hence for normative male sexuality—becomes the source of a pathology whose pervasive symptom is women's exclusion from positions of authority.

Dr. Grensted's reading of Freud not only offers a clinical rendition of Woolf's own claim in *Room* that "women have served all these centuries as looking-glasses possessing the magic and delicious power of reflecting the figure of man at twice its natural size" (35) but also provides the psychoanalytic materials for constructing a theory of the masculine desire that produces the dominant gender ideology. Grensted's intervention allows Woolf to reinterpret three Victorian "cases" that illustrate "these very ancient and obscure emotions . . . which the Professors have only lately brought to the surface and named 'infantile fixation,' 'Oedipus complex,' and the rest" (130). The well-known cases of Elizabeth Barrett Browning and Charlotte Brontë are relatively straightforward, although their relation to psychoanalytic theory is oblique: the father opposes his daughter's marriage, struggling to manage her erotic life and implicitly to be its exclusive object. The case of Sophia Jex-Blake is less familiar and more subtle, for the father overtly opposes his daughter's economic rather than erotic autonomy. Yet "we will call it a case of infantile fixation," because Mr. Jex-Blake's final aim is to maintain erotic power: "The case of Mr. Jex-Blake shows that the daughter must not on any account be allowed to make money because if she makes money she will be independent of her father and free to marry any man she chooses" (131, 133). The desire of the father is fundamental to the Jex-Blake case and to the section of *Three Guineas* it epitomizes; the daughter's desire to marry is represented as incidental to the narrative. If history interpreted psychoanalysis through the figure of Professor von X, psychoanalysis interprets history through the figure of Dr. Grensted, who—in contrast to his predecessor—distinguishes male dominance from male superiority. Woolf's case histories, read through Grensted's lens, suggest that the object of adult male desire is not the procreative wife, totally absent from these accounts, but the daughter kept at home for covert erotic motives that are screened, in particular historical situations, by domestic ideology. Freudian theory—reconstructed—has acquired new truth-value. Extending Dr. Grensted's equation of the infantile fixation and the castration complex (redefined as belief in women's castration), Woolf intimates a theory of male desire that reorders the Oedipus and castration complexes. Rather than terminating incestuous desire (as in Freud), the perception of female "castration" seems in Woolf's account to fixate desire on an image of inferiorized femininity most fully realized in the daughter.[45] Misogyny and father-daughter incest are twin faces of the same, and conspire in constructing the home as woman's sphere. The infantile fixation has come to signify fixation on, not of, the infant—or, rather, the chain that links the son's eroticized perception of maternal lack to the father's eroticized investment in his daughter.

Woolf's reading of the Victorian family romance returns psychoanalysis to its preanalytic origins in the seduction theory, which locates desire in the father rather than in the daughter.[46] Woolf's embrace of Freudian theory restores its proto-feminist prehistory. The anger and fear that Woolf insists inhibit conversation between women and men attest to the explosiveness of this restoration, for simple claims to sexual equality would be too familiar by the 1930s to produce such violent emotions. Fear definitely intervenes in Woolf's dialogue with Freud. To complete the "bisexual private conversation" (128) enacted by the epistolary form that links *Three Guineas* to Freud, the narrator proposes: "[L]et us lower the veil of St. Paul between us—in other words take shelter behind an interpreter" (120). Dr. Grensted is the interpreter who allows Woolf to work her revision of Freud obliquely; but the psychoanalytic veil entangles as well as shelters her, delimiting as well as enabling her revision.

Dr. Grensted is juxtaposed overtly against Saint Paul, the archbishops' authority for barring women from the church, and played covertly against Freud; but the veil metaphor itself is Paul's, and also Freud's. Woolf is of course in mock compliance with Paul's command that women veil their heads in public to mark their deference to male authority, but she cannot quite sustain ironic mastery of the figure. Her selective quoting from and gloss on the Letter to the Corinthians highlights the echoes between Paul and Freud, especially in the context of the discourse on castration. Veiling, for Paul as for Freud, is the sign that both conceals and reveals woman's secondariness. Veils reproduce in culture the natural function of women's hair, which "'is given her for a covering'" (167n. 38); the "shame" of unveiling is the exposure (and defiance) of female secondariness—or, as Freud would explain in less veiled terms, the shame of the "genital deficiency" which has provoked women to excel at weaving. Freud's reversal of Bachofen actually repeats the reversal Paul adapts from *Genesis:* "'For the man is not of the woman; but the woman of the man . . . : for this cause ought the woman to have a sign of authority on her head'" (166–67n. 38). However, whereas *Room*'s privileging of the text as web reverses Freud's reversal, *Three Guineas*'s adaptation of the psychoanalytic veil unexpectedly complies with the presumption of female lack.

Woolf invokes Grensted's veil to unveil paternal sexuality by deriving it from the son's sight of the mother's genitals. But she never questions that the son perceives a lack. The mother's body in *Three Guineas* is the site of both a horrifying excess and a lack; whether disgustingly prolific or castrated—extremes that collapse into each other—it consistently fails to possess positive attributes of its own. Woolf can criticize the father's sexuality, but she cannot redeem the mother's.

The loss of the mother as a specific term of difference both situates Woolf on Freud's terrain and constricts her remapping of that terrain. A certain specularity haunts *Three Guineas:* father and daughter, Freud and Woolf, male and female correspondents face each other across an abyss that can be negotiated only in the discourse of the father. Grensted's veil enables Woolf to redesign the ethics but not the structure of the father-daughter exchange. Resituating desire in the father is an insufficiently radical act. Although Woolf reverses the reversal that founded psycho-analysis, she safeguards the libidinal economy that locates desire in either the daughter or the father; her theory of paternal desire at once excludes the mother and precludes (a theory of) the daughter's desire.[47]

Such asymmetries are unstable. In her final novel, Woolf implicates the daughter in the structure of desire without, however, exonerating the father: *Between the Acts* transforms aversion toward the father into ambivalence. As the father, who now overshadows the mother as a point of origin, comes to join her as an object of ambivalence, Woolf's transition from Kleinian to Freudian fictions is complete.

6

THE LADY VANISHES: MATERNAL ABSENCE AND FREUDIAN NARRATIVES IN *BETWEEN THE ACTS*

> But this turning from the mother to the father points in addition to a victory of intellectuality over sensuality—that is, an advance in civilization.
>
> Sigmund Freud, *Moses and Monotheism*

> Society it seems was a father, and afflicted with the infantile fixation too.
>
> Virginia Woolf, *Three Guineas*

Woolf was reading widely in Freud during the years she worked on *Between the Acts*, and his language echoes throughout her depiction of civilization's instinctual underlay, "something hidden, the unconscious as they call it."[1] (Hetero)sexuality is repeatedly insinuated as our covert truth:

> I know where the tit nests, . . .
> In the hedgerow. I know, I know—
> What don't I know?
> All your secrets, ladies,
> And yours too, gentlemen . . .

the village idiot sings from the pageant stage, leering at the audience and plucking at Queen Elizabeth's skirts (86). Yet Freud's discourse figures diversely in Woolf's text, for the repudiation of the mother's body that aligns Woolf with Freud generates both a new insistence on female heterosexuality and a new portrait of the disembodiedness produced by the "victory of intellectuality over sensuality."

In *Between the Acts*, as in *Three Guineas*, society is "a father," and sexual relations between men and women reproduce the father-daughter bond. Rather than positioning desire only in the father, as in *Three Guineas*, however, Woolf now rewrites the Oedipus complex by situating both love and hatred in the daughter. The warring passions echo the

Freudian instincts, eros and thanatos; but the introduction of hate into this context reconstructs the Oedipal situation. Freud imagines an uncontaminated daughterly desire for the father and reserves ambivalence for, on the one hand, the son's relation to the castrating father and, on the other, the daughter's relation to the "castrated" mother.[2] Woolf, however, represents the daughter's ambivalent relation to the father as Freud's plot. In an autobiographical text contemporary with her work on *Between the Acts*, she claims to have discovered Freud and ambivalence simultaneously. "It was only the other day when I read Freud for the first time, that I discovered that this violently disturbing conflict of love and hate is a common feeling; and is called ambivalence," she notes. The object of her ambivalence is unambiguous: "[T]he tyrant father—the exacting, the violent, the histrionic, the demonstrative, the self centered, the self pitying, the deaf, the appealing, the alternatively loved and hated father that dominated me then."[3] The strangeness of her claim to have just read Freud "for the first time" (since she had been reading him for at least a year), and the ambiguous antecedents of her next clause—"But before I analyze our relation as father and daughter"—suggest, however, that Woolf's ambivalence extends to Freud. In *Between the Acts,* Woolf both redefines Freud's plot and, more importantly, embraces it as the final story of her final text.

This narrative surfaces at the novel's end, when the curtain rises on the central couple, Isa and Giles, who perform the first act of Miss La Trobe's new play. But despite this resolution, which distills and proclaims the erotic undercurrents that have rippled through the text, the psychological world of *Between the Acts* is characterized primarily by passionlessness, emptiness, and disembodiedness.[4] Overtly, the dissociation within and between characters is caused by the horror of the impending world war, but the text intimates another cause, one that extends Woolf's critique of the fascist appropriation of the mother's body. Fascism lurks in this text, as in *Three Guineas,* in a domestic (as well as in a foreign) guise, personified most fully in the aggressively virile Giles Oliver, who is, as Alex Zwerdling notes, "very close to the Fascist threat he fears[,] . . . a good indigenous example of the ethos Woolf had seen in the first days of Italian Fascism."[5] During a centrally symbolic interlude in Miss La Trobe's pageant, Giles asserts his mastery over a world of embodiment gone wrong:

> There, crouched in the grass, curled in an olive green ring, was a snake. Dead? No, choked with a toad in its mouth. The snake was unable to swallow; the toad was unable to die. A spasm made the ribs contract; blood oozed. It was birth the wrong way round— a monstrous inversion. So, raising his foot, he stamped on them. The mass crushed and slithered. The white canvas on his tennis shoes was bloodstained and sticky. But it was action. Action relieved him. (99)

Annihilating the grotesque body generates, however, a longing for ideal embodiment; both Giles and his father, Bart, are attracted to a purified image of maternal generativity. The novel's mothers struggle to dissociate themselves from this ideal, but neither they nor the novel offers an alternative construction of maternity. Lucy Swithin, Bart's elderly sister, is heir to Mrs. Ramsay's faith in human connectedness: "For she belonged to the unifiers, he to the separatists," Bart declares in an echo of the Ramsay couple's distribution of sexual difference (118). But Lucy embraces an ethereal notion of disembodied unity, split—in contrast to her precursor's—from any practice of motherhood and lodged instead under the aegis of a patriarchal God. In refusing to participate in the co-optation of the maternal body, the mothers ultimately reinscribe the father's superiority and join in the dissociation from the body.

By adopting both a critical and an elegiac stance toward the mother's body, Woolf places her novel in a complex relation to Freudian narrative. In Freud's contemporaneous text, *Moses and Monotheism* (1934–38), his psychoanalytic history of Judaism, the disembodiedness produced by the turn from mother to father is an "advance in civilization" endangered by the course of recent history. Rather than appearing as the culmination of patriarchy (as it is depicted in *Three Guineas* and *Between the Acts*), fascism emerges in Freud's text as the endpoint of an era marked by the erosion of paternal authority: what had peaked with the acceptance of the Jewish father God finds its nadir in an anti-Semitic world that has reinstated the worship of the body. Written in the last dark years of the 1930s, *Between the Acts* and *Moses and Monotheism* are both crisis texts that share a sense of a world that is ending, but they interpret this demise antithetically: as Woolf is conceding patriarchy's triumph, Freud is deploring its decline.

Moses and Monotheism was on Woolf's mind as she drafted *Between the Acts*. On 15 July 1939, she wrote to John Lehmann, who since 1938 had replaced her as Leonard's partner at the Hogarth Press, "My nose is not among the flowers, but on the grindstone. Moses had a very good show—I'm reading it."[6] That same year the Hogarth Press published the English translation of *Moses and Monotheism:* the "Moses" Woolf mentions must have been Freud's. Indeed, Woolf borrows directly from Freud's text: the pageant's opening playlet about a "babe in the basket," a "rightful heir" rejected by a hostile father and rescued from the water by an aged crone, exactly reproduces Freud's summary of the essential features of hero myths, which he glosses as fantasies of birth (88). Both texts are preoccupied with the question of origins, but they historicize this question differently. Prefacing a reading of Woolf's final full-length text with a reading of history's course in Freud's enables us to outline the shape of both careers and to map their final intersection.

I

Moses and Monotheism is a chaotic text that retells stories, reiterates conclusions, and returns to problems restlessly. Its first two essays are primarily concerned with arguing, on dubious historical and linguistic grounds, that Moses was an Egyptian who joined with the pharaoh Akhenaten in consolidating the worship of the sun god Aten into a monotheistic religion. Following the biblical historian Ernst Sellin, Freud argues that Moses was murdered by the Semitic tribes to whom he brought the new religion; generations later these tribes revived the worship of Moses's God.[7] Dissatisfied with this account, Freud shifts in the third essay from an historical to a psychoanalytic framework and replaces the discourse of biblical scholarship with that of *Totem and Taboo*. The story of the Mosaic God now represents the reestablishment of the primal father, and the murder of Moses becomes a repetition of the original patricide. In contrast to *Totem and Taboo*, however, the focus of this narrative is not the murder of the father and the internalization of paternal law but the contrast between the Mosaic God and the forms of worship he replaced. In this context gender assumes a new centrality, and matriarchy (which Freud uses interchangeably with goddess worship) replaces polytheism as the term that opposes Moses's God.

In *Totem and Taboo*, Freud is unconcerned about his inability to specify the place of "the great mother-goddesses, who may perhaps in general have preceded the father-gods."[8] The problem dismissed so cavalierly in *Totem and Taboo* is squarely addressed in *Moses and Monotheism*: the worship of mother goddesses is positioned between the murder of the primal father and the worship of the Mosaic God, and the relative status of mothers and fathers moves to center stage. The question of gender, repressed by the assumption of a single paternal origin in *Totem and Taboo*, is implicit in the subject of *Moses and Monotheism*, the triumph of a father God; but it transcends these historical parameters to become a governing thematic of the text.[9] In a section entitled "The Advance in Intellectuality," whose special status is indicated by its prior separate publication, Freud represents the distinctiveness of Judaism as the difference between patriarchal and matriarchal social orders.[10]

The section is designed to provide a fuller answer to the issue that dominates the entire third essay: "how the special character of the Jewish people arose."[11] Having discussed the high self-esteem produced in the Jews by their role as the "chosen people," Freud now examines the impact of the Mosaic prohibition on making images of God, "the compulsion to worship a God whom one cannot see" (112–13). This stricture, which distinguishes Mosaic from Egyptian monotheism, has a critical effect: "For it meant that a sensory perception was given second place to what may be called an abstract idea—a triumph of intellectuality over sensuality or, strictly speaking, an instinctual renunciation" (113). Freud offers three analogies to amplify the import of the mind's triumph over the body; the second (and central) one encapsulates his gendering of history. "[I]t came about that the matriarchal social order was succeeded by the patriarchal one—which, of course, involved a revolution in the juridical conditions that had so far prevailed. . . . But this turning from the mother to the father points in addition to a victory of intellectuality over sensuality—that is, an advance in civilization, since maternity is proved by the evidence of the senses while paternity is a hypothesis, based on an inference and a premise. Taking sides in this way with a thought-process in preference to a sense perception has proved to be a momentous step" (113–14). Freud's source for these claims is Johann Jakob Bachofen, the most famous theorist of matriarchy, whom Freud practically quotes, although without acknowledgment.[12] Matriarchy and its theorists, written out of *Totem and Taboo*, are now allowed a limited scope in the interests of recontaining them. But as Freud attempts to delineate the place of the maternal in cultural history (as he had demarcated that place in individual history), his text reveals a seepage that cannot be contained.

The Mosaic constitution of God as a father, and the concomitant elevation of intellect over the senses, stands in *Moses and Monotheism* as a cultural high point toward which history proceeds and from which it declines. As in *Totem and Taboo*, Freud turns from the religion of the father God to that of the son, and in both narratives, the replacement of the father by the son reflects the ambivalence the father evokes: "Judaism had been a religion of the father; Christianity became a religion of the son. The old God the Father fell back behind Christ; Christ, the Son, took his place, just as every son had hoped to do in primaeval times" (87–88). In *Totem and Taboo*, however, the Oedipal fiction has a cast of two, and the story concludes with the father's displacement by the son; in *Moses and Monotheism*, the shift from father to son screens and promotes the mother's return. Christianity, in this account, feminizes religion, both in the modes of worship it fosters and in the conception of God it offers. The new religion marks a "lightly veiled" reintroduction of polytheism and a recrudescence of magic and superstition, a decline from "the high level in things of the mind to which Judaism had soared" into "the very puzzling emotional phenomenon of faith"; it also transforms the image of God from a stern paternal figure who demands instinctual renunciation to a loving, consoling, self-effacing presence, a son with the psychic features of the mother (88, 118).[13] Christianity, moreover, relegitimates the icons that Moses prohibited and that for Freud epitomize the dominance of mothers. These diverse signs of the mother's return crystallize in Mary's position within the Christian pantheon. Never mentioned in *Totem and Taboo*, Mary now represents the reestablishment of "the great mother-goddess" eradicated by Judaism (88).[14] By analogy to Christ's own sacrifice, which replaces the father it would appease, Mary's selfless mothering advances maternal authority.

This advance endures and burgeons darkly in the present. Begun in Vienna in 1934 in the shadow of an impending Nazi invasion, *Moses and Monotheism* inevitably comments only obliquely on contemporary politics. Freud's fear of jeopardizing the already endangered future of psychoanalysis is apparent in the text's prefatory notes and in his decision to withhold publication of the third essay until he was safely ensconced in London. Nevertheless, his language reaches out to incorporate the present within the historical patterns he constructs. In striking contrast to what was becoming a psychoanalytic commonplace, Freud aligns fascism not with authoritarian patriarchal figures, who might reproduce in the secular world a single paternal deity, but with the primitive (dis)organizing principles Judaism superseded.[15] In a section whose title, "The Great Man," resonates eerily against the political backdrop of this text, Freud describes the Jews' response to Moses and his God in language that sounds like an apology for Hitler: "We know that in the mass of mankind there is a powerful need for an authority who can be admired, before whom one bows down, by whom one is ruled and perhaps even ill-treated. . . . It is a longing for the father felt by everyone from his childhood onwards" (109). The present crisis in Germany derives, in Freud's account, from the dispersion, not the consolidation, of patriarchal authority.

Freud refers explicitly to Nazi Germany only three times in this text, but the references constitute a matrix of associations that characterize the present day as a "relapse into almost prehistoric barbarism" (54). In his first prefatory note to the third essay, Freud differentiates Hitler's Germany from other repressive regimes by its absence of "any progressive ideas"; in contrast to the USSR and Italy, it is an instance of undiluted regression (54). Freud also distinguishes Germany by its form of barbarism. Although he emphasizes the authoritarianism of Soviet Russia and of Mussolini's Italy, he makes no such claim about the state that would appear to deserve it most. Instead, the Nazis regress to a "barbarous polytheism" (91). Anti-Semitism is, in this account, a hatred of monotheism. "[A]ll those peoples who excel to-day in their hatred of Jews," he explains, are descendants of those who were forcibly converted to Christianity: "Their hatred of Jews is at bottom a hatred of Christians, and we need not be surprised that in the German National-Socialist revolution this intimate relation between the two monotheist religions finds such a clear expression in the hostile treatment of both of them" (91–92). The worship of a single, deified father that constitutes monotheism is set in antithesis to fascism, which emerges as a principle of disorder rather than control.

This disorder is analogous to the body's, to sense and instinct ungoverned by authority, to the disposition of matriarchy. In the final

113

paragraph of "The Advance in Intellectuality," Freud contrasts the Jewish emphasis on "intellectual labours," which has held the "scattered people together," with "the brutality and the tendency to violence which are apt to appear where the development of muscular strength is the popular ideal" (115). In a clear allusion to the Aryan ideal in a context that has celebrated the "victory of intellectuality over sensuality" achieved by Moses and patriarchy, the Nazi cultivation of body over mind is aligned with the principles of matriarchy. The "prehistoric barbarism" Freud saw reborn in his environs marked regression to more than brutality. The world that for Woolf had newly consecrated patriarchy was for Freud reviving the sensuous chaos of archaic matriarchy.[16]

II

Like *Moses and Monotheism,* Woolf's *Between the Acts* emphasizes the disintegration of the contemporary social fabric, but it refuses integration under the aegis of fathers, and it laments the loss of a concept of mothering that could serve as an alternative source of unity.[17] During the same interval in which Giles kills the snake and toad, his wife, Isa, elaborates the pageant's musical refrain: "Dispersed are we. . . . All is over. The wave has broken. Left us stranded, high and dry. Single, separate on the shingle" (96). Throughout the novel, as throughout the autobiographical texts contemporary with it, water functions as a figure of a longed-for mother whose return might undo separation.[18]

The world of *Between the Acts* is parched. "This dry summer the path was hard as brick across the fields. This dry summer the path was strewn with stones" (98). Like the landscape, the incantatory repetition echoes T. S. Eliot—surprisingly, for an author whose version of modernism has always emphasized fluidity. Even the novel's opening lines call attention, more satirically, to the lack of water, by reporting a dialogue about a cesspool that the county council has failed to provide. Set inland "in the very heart of England," thirty-five miles from the sea—although "[i]t seems more," Isa observes, "It seems from the terrace as if the land went on for ever and ever"—*Between the Acts* inverts the topography of *To the Lighthouse,* exchanging the flow of consciousness and nature for a gendered (and gentler) version of *The Wasteland*'s aridity (16, 29). Scarce, water becomes an object of female memory and desire. Lucy Swithin nostalgically recalls her childhood "living in a house by the sea," where they ate lobsters "fresh from the lobster pots" and fish so fresh (in contrast to those Isa now orders for lunch) that lice still lived in their scales (29). Lucy likes the fable that, even inland, one can hear a wave break after a storm. "Hearing the waves in the middle of the night he saddled a horse and rode to the sea. Who was it," she asks her brother, "who rode to the sea?" (29). Not susceptible to his sister's fantasies, Bart does not respond.

He, by contrast, dreams of a different past which repeats and exaggerates the dryness of the present. Dwelling on his youth as a soldier in India, rather than as a child living by the sea, he sees "himself, a young man helmeted; and a cascade falling. But no water; and the hills, like grey stuff pleated; and in the sand a hoop of ribs; a bullock maggot-eaten in the sun; and in the shadow of the rock, savages; and in his hand a gun" (17).

Bart's wife, in an earlier draft of the novel, died in India. In the published text, it is the mother of Isa, Bart's daughter-in-law, who dies there, generalizing the sense of maternal death in an arid land. At a particularly oppressive moment in the present when "[t]he heat had increased. . . . All was sun now," Isa craves "above all things . . . a beaker of cold water" and pictures as an inaccessible oasis "water surrounded by walls of shining glass" (65–67). During an interval of the pageant, she articulates a fantasy about a wishing well (played against the cup of rusty tea she is offered) in which the vehicle and object of desire are conflated: "'[W]hat wish should I drop into the well? . . . That the waters should cover me, . . . of the wishing well'" (103). The desire for dissolution incorporates a desire for a return to a female origin, for the imagined well is located under a "'tree that keeps all day murmuring of the sea, and hears the Rider gallop,'" rejoining Isa to the story of the rider that captures her aunt's imagination (104–5). The two generations of women are linked through the fiction of a maritime origin whose muted echoes sound in contemporary life only through (Lucy's) story, (Miss La Trobe's) pageant, and (Isa's) poetry.

It is Miss La Trobe's representation of "The Present Time. Ourselves" that most forcefully indicates water's ambiguous status in the present. Her "experiment"—to "try ten mins. of present time" by removing all vestiges of dramatic illusion from the outdoor stage—is the most daring moment in the pageant, a moment that unsettles the audience, "suspended, without being, in limbo," and imposes on the author, deprived of her audience's faith, "death, death, death, . . . when illusion fails" (178–80). Relief comes with a sudden providential shower that dissolves the boundaries between author and audience, restoring the human community in a moment of collective lament that both articulates and heals the pain of isolation. That this is a super-natural shower, "all people's tears," is suggested by its "sudden and universal" character. Less clear is that the shower gratifies a powerful unstated desire of La Trobe's, betrayed in the clashing metaphors with which she states her intention: "She wanted to expose them, as it were, to douche them, with present-time reality" (179). Reality in this text is dry, nothing to be douched with. La Trobe has wanted simultaneously to expose her spectators to reality and to restore to them the illusion of collectivity her play both requires and denies. Hence the startling reversal through which rain, rather than sunshine, elicits her conclusion that "nature once more had taken her part.

115

The risk she had run acting in the open air was justified" (181). Yet by positioning this scene immediately before its social correlate, the sketch of the League of Nations, a "flattering tribute to ourselves" that by 1939 had lost all credibility, the text also undermines the illusion of community the rain fleetingly bestows (182).[19] By insisting on fragmentation, the subsequent scene of "cackle" and "cacophony" completes the demolition (183). Even while it showers, the provisional status of the moment of reprieve is betrayed through Isa's choice of the subjunctive: "'O that our human pain could here have ending!' . . . 'O that my life could here have ending'" (180–81).

Between the Acts repeats the question that dominates part 1 of To the Lighthouse: "'And which will it be'?" Lucy Swithin asks, "'Wet or fine'?" (22). Isa's irony deflates the question's former metaphysics—"Every year they said, would it be wet or fine; and every year it was—one or the other" (22)—but it *does* matter that this year it rains. However, the value of the weather has been reversed. What the earlier text represented as disaster, a wedge niched into the fabric of human relations, has here become a desired dissolution, a fleeting moment of maternal return, as nature, assuming Mary's guise, weeps the world's "[t]ears. Tears. Tears" and with them figuratively washes away the "[b]lood [that] seemed to pour" from Miss La Trobe's shoes when her audience withdrew its faith (180). Only through tears that gratify desire briefly and deceptively can the mother manifest herself in an England parched by her loss.

The "present-time reality" of Between the Acts consolidates a profoundly patriarchal past. The novel's plural subject is Pointz Hall, a country home passed from father to son.[20] As daughter, Lucy is dispossessed, a guest in the home her brother has inherited, and though "[s]he always meant to set up a house of her own," she never succeeds in establishing this autonomy (8). The maternal bedroom in which she was born is now a spare room, "tidy as a pin, not slept in for months," a perfectly preserved and marginalized relic of the past, a point of origin now external to the home and to the social group from which Lucy suddenly and inexplicably departs, driven by some strong and unstated motivation whose destination is precise: "'Here'," she declares to William Dodge, who follows her, "'I was born. In this bed'" (70). With its mid-Victorian furniture, its purple-dotted rug, and the circle the slop pail has left by the washstand, the room records history meticulously, except for the birth and the matrilineage erased by the bed's straight counterpane.

Nowhere is the asymmetrical heritage of Pointz Hall and the society it stages more pronounced then in the twinned portraits that hang in the dining room, presiding over the home as progenitors. Yet only the portrait of the man depicts an ancestor; the place of the ancestress is empty, held by an image with no historical referent: "The lady was a picture, bought by Oliver because he liked the picture; the man was an ancestor. He had a name" (36). The "lady" has an exclusively imaginary status: rather than being represented *as* a picture, she *is* a picture. Existing only as image, she has no name. The imaginary space created by her portrait, moreover, empties out life from the dining room, puncturing a hole in the heart of Pointz Hall.

> In her yellow robe, . . . she led the eye up, down, from the curve to the straight, through glades of greenery and shades of silver, dun and rose into silence. The room was empty.
>
> Empty, empty, empty; silent, silent, silent. The room was a shell, singing of what was before time was; a vase stood in the heart of the house, alabaster, smooth, cold, holding the still, distilled essence of emptiness, silence. (36–37)

Instead of representing a historical figure, the portrait of the lady makes space sing about prehistory, the canonical locus for the absent mother, rendered now as a mortuary image of an alabaster vase whose hollow shape commemorates the reproductive body that has always already disappeared.[21]

The ancestor, by contrast, is a "talk producer" whose portrait generates history, as well as recording it, by representing a moment recalled as anecdote. "'I always feel,' Lucy broke the silence, 'he's saying: "Paint my dog"'" (49). Though the dog (like the historical ancestress) is unrepresented, the ancestor's authority transforms this visual absence into a narrative presence. "It was, he seemed to say, addressing the company not the painter, a damned shame to leave out Colin whom he wished buried at his feet, in the same grave, about 1750; but that skunk the Reverend Whatshisname wouldn't allow it" (36). Nor will the artist. Yet the ancestor triumphs, and the unrepresented and speechless dog "has his place in history" and takes, as the ancestor's shadowy partner, the place of the ancestress (48). Within the history the painting represents, the dog replaces the wife; her absence from her husband's portrait, his discourse, and the adjacent portrait eludes the novel's commentary.

This silence at the heart of the patriarchal home is repeated in the structure of social relations. No one mentions Bart's wife, whose absence even from memory is disguised by a series of quiet substitutions. Bart's constant companion, his "familiar spirit" (116), is, like his predecessor's, a dog, an Afghan hound who sucks his "hairy flanks . . . in and out" in a monstrous parody of a womb, terrifying Bart's grandson George (13). With his "long nose resting on his paws, a fleck of foam on the nostril," the dog who takes the place of (grand)mother phallicizes the maternal (116). That Woolf names him Sohrab (changed from the more neutral "Captain" in the earlier typescript) suggests, through the allusion to Matthew Arnold, the dog's role as a son that has assimilated and dispensed with the mother who produced him.[22] Bart's other enduring companion is a sister who has no claim to be the "lady" of Pointz Hall and no status as matriarch within the Oliver family. By quietly substituting sister for wife, Woolf writes into the text a silence that, in the language of her narrator, "add[s] its unmistakable contribution to talk" by gesturing, beyond absence, toward unrepresentability (39).

A conceptual as well as actual void haunts *Between the Acts,* a new inability to think or write the mother, who is always already absent or subsumed (like Sohrab) to patriarchy. Woolf reveals this void through Bart, whose position as patriarch, rather than his personality, casts him as an apologist for norms from which he, unlike Giles, derives little personal gratification. Bart is as central to the novel's ideology as his son is to its action. Woolf not only gives him substitutes for the mother, she also assigns him criteria with which to disqualify mothers. For Lucy in reality *is* a mother, although Bart disparages her in that role; at the same time, he succumbs to the textual illusion that she fills the place of Giles's absent mother. By repeatedly citing to Lucy the opening lines from Swinburne's "Itylus"—"'Swallow, my sister, O sister swallow'"—Bart casts his sister, who perches "on the edge of a chair like a bird on a telegraph wire before starting for Africa," in the role of Philomela's sister Procne, who murdered her own son (116).[23] More directly, Bart criticizes Lucy for inadequately mothering *his* son, and his language suggests, bizarrely, that her failure is biological. "Was it that she had no body? Up in the clouds, like an air ball, her mind touched ground now and then with a shock of surprise. There was nothing in her to weight a man like Giles to the earth" (116). Never remembering Giles's actual mother, Bart faults Lucy for not fulfilling a function not properly hers. The terms of the critique, especially when yoked to the Procne allusion, are unjust. Yet neither Lucy nor the text counters the attack, for Lucy apparently neither visits nor mentions her two grown sons and, through her chosen identification with the swallows, with air and spirit rather than earth, evades the conditions of motherhood rather than posing an alternative account of it. Isa responds similarly to a version of the same critique, extended to the next generation through Bart's complaint that his daughter-in-law fails to nurture his grandson appropriately. "'Your little boy's a cry-baby,' he said scornfully" (18). Isa's response pits the pleasures of free flight against the ties of domesticity. "'Oh,' she sighed, pegged down on a chair arm [on which Lucy will subsequently perch?], like a captive balloon, by a myriad of hair-thin ties into domesticity. . . . And she loathed the domestic, the possessive; the maternal. And he knew it and did it on purpose to tease her, the old brute, her father-in-law" (19). Isa, like Lucy, imagines evasion as the only alternative to Bart's construction of motherhood.

The only exception is one brief moment in which Lucy and Isa ally in an alternative maternal stance toward the children. After being insulted by her brother, Lucy suddenly notices George and Caro crossing the lawn: "'Oh there they are—the darlings!'"—an exclamation Isa understands as a pact of faith in the children rather than the father. "What an angel she was—the old woman! . . . How courageous to defy Bart" (24). Yet the moment works a return that pivots with perverse fatality on the text's sole exchange about Isa's daughter, a dialogue that gestures toward the possibility of stitching aunt to niece (in law) and daughter in a patchwork matrilineage. "'And baby? Any sign of measles?'" Lucy asks. "Isa shook her head. 'Touch wood,' she added, tapping the table. 'Tell me, Bart,' said Mrs. Swithin, turning to her brother, 'what's the origin of that? Touch wood . . . Antaeus, didn't he touch earth?'" (24). Language itself turns the tables as maternal love spontaneously and colloquially expressed inaugurates a search for origins that returns to the father: to Bart as paternal authority and, through the reference to Antaeus, to the authority of patriarchal norms of motherhood as embodiment in the service of the father. For Lemprière, one of the sources Bart suggests would "settle" the question of Antaeus, describes the mythic figure as a giant, son of earth and sea, who "received new strength from his mother as often as he touched the ground" and who was consequently such an indomitable wrestler that "he boasted that he would erect a temple to his father with the skulls of his conquered antagonists." Antaeus was defeated only when Hercules, recognizing the source of his opponent's strength, "lifted him up in the air, and squeezed him to death in his arms."[24] The mother of Antaeus—mother as earth dedicated to restoring her son and nurturing his affiliation with his father—personifies the norm to which Bart struggles to "peg down" Lucy and Isa, the norm they flee through a figurative flight into the element in which Antaeus is destroyed.

This norm, to which language converts matrilineage, finds "present-day" incarnation in a more perfect rendition of motherhood, unimpeded by progeny—in a woman who, not biologically a mother, nevertheless offers her ample body for the rejuvenation of men. Committed to the commonality of "flesh and blood," though "she preferred men—obviously" (39), the "bouyant, abundant" Mrs. Manresa (119) "made old Bart feel young" (43); she becomes the standard by which he measures the efficacy of actual mothers. After condemning Lucy for failing "to weight a man like Giles to the earth," Bart spies his son with the "goddess-like" Manresa and blesses "the power of the human body to make the earth fruitful. Giles would keep his orbit so long as she weighted him to the earth" (119). Succeeding where Lucy and Isa both fail—since Giles's apparent unhappiness (like George's alleged inadequacy) is presumably due to Isa's defective nurture of masculinity—Mrs. Manresa is, like Antaeus's mother, a figure of Mother Earth whose regenerative body anchors and restores both son and father, providing a conduit for patrilineage.

119

Mrs. Manresa exploits her chosen role as body and nature, as source of the nurturant sensuality a desiccated culture needs. The text partially supports this posture. Breezing into and out of the society gathered at Pointz Hall, Mrs. Manresa demonstrates her independence, which her uncertain past, her marriage to a Jew, and her appearance, uninvited, with a homosexual companion, reinforce. She is, as she claims, an outsider to society, which is fertilized by her intrusion. Her vulgarity productively punctures convention, enabling those around her to "take advantage of the breach of decorum, of the fresh air that blew in, to follow like leaping dophins in the wake of an ice-breaking vessel" (41). A certain plausibility coats her self-representation as a "wild child of nature" who rejects re-straints on appetite, removes her stays and rolls in the grass, lets cream "curl luxuriously into her coffee, to which she added a shovel full of brown sugar candy," and retires with Giles to the greenhouse, the appropriate site for the sexual union Bart interprets as rebirth (41, 55). Yet the text also unmasks her pose, while retaining some lingering nostalgia for what she inadequately represents. If Mrs. Manresa promotes her image as nature's wild, impulsive child, "nothing like so grown up as you are," her ample age and body insure that she will be perceived instead as Mother Nature, "her cornucopia running over," a figure comfortable to culture (45, 110). The natural image, moreover, is constructed. Mrs. Manresa may remove her stays, but she paints her nails and powders her nose so heavily that even Bart, by the novel's end, detects the artifice: "plated," her make-up seems to him, "not deeply interfused" (202). Mrs. Manresa grooms her limited resources (for she is middle-aged, overweight, and ignorant) to reflect the shapes of male desire; she plays on, profits from, and ultimately (through Woolf's manipulation) parodies fantasies of woman as nature. Despite her minor infractions of social codes, she plays out the equation "nature = woman = mother" that, as fascism insisted, is axiomatic to patriarchy. The alliance of the natural and the maternal represented by the young Sally Seton, whose female-identified eroticism opposes both nature and nur-ture to patriarchy, has yielded to an identification contained by patriarchy and embodied in a woman who constitutes herself in the image of male desire.[25] Though Mrs. Manresa's language and behavior work to position her on the side of a nature exterior to culture, the text relentlessly de-constructs this opposition, revealing her incarnation of nature to be profoundly interior to culture. If Manresa counters the "scent" of culture, emitted by Lucy Swithin's description of classical French and Chinese drama, with the claims of the "jolly human heart," Woolf conflates culture and the human heart by making "heart" a metaphor for the location of Pointz Hall, a microcosm of British culture, and for the library ("'the heart of the house'") that is its collective text (142, 16). There is no maternal realm of nature exterior to culture in this text, whose bleakness derives in part from the collapse of this distinction, central to *Mrs. Dalloway* and *To the Lighthouse*. The earlier novels assert the possibility of some position "before" or "outside" culture and construct creativity as dependent on relatedness to this originary source. In *Between the Acts* cultural law achieves new sovereignty.

This sovereignty, exposed by the irony of Isa's maternal prayer for her daughter ("Touch wood"), assimilates to culture's boundaries any potentially feminine exterior. Even the one spot topographically defined as the outside and inverse of Pointz Hall slides across the fictive divide. The text's sole enduring source of water, that elusive object of female memory and desire, is a lily pond where "[w]ater, for hundreds of years, had silted down into the hollow, and lay there four or five feet deep over a black cushion of mud" (43). Here the women in the Oliver household, from the scullery maid to Lucy Swithin, retire for repose. Unlike the shower whose sudden descent into the dry world of the present betokens a moment of amazing grace, the lily pool collects the drops of water deposited through history. Dark and deep, where Pointz Hall is high and architecturally defined, the pool inscribes the boundlessness counterposed by the home's precise articulation of spatial, and social, relations. Described as a "deep center," a "black heart," the womblike pool of water opposes the patriarchal home that rises over England's dry interior (44).

Yet this dark maternal heart, seemingly beneath and outside patriarchy, is a highly ambiguous feminine locus, for "it was in that deep centre, in that black heart, that the lady had drowned herself" (44). The lily pond is a treacherous mother, more black hole than womb, since into it the generic "lady" vanishes in a mocking erasure of female history. Returning no sign of her existence, the pool collaborates with Pointz Hall's suppression of female genealogy. "Ten years since the pool had been dredged and a thigh bone recovered. Alas, it was a sheep's not a lady's" (44). As the heroine of servants' tales, the lady's historicity is in doubt; the lily pool strengthens Bart's case for her fictiveness. Like the portrait of the similarly (un)named "lady" who displaces the ancestress in the maternal heart within the home, substituting the seductive space of the imaginary for some record of the real, the lily pool consumes life rather than preserving it. Outside Pointz Hall, the lily pool operates, like Mother Earth, according to the laws that govern the interior.[26]

III

These laws also shape the pageant that dominates the novel. By recapitulating "our island's history" from the rupture of birth through "The Present Time. Ourselves," the pageant offers a painful version of the separation narrative whose positive articulation emerged through Lily Briscoe (86, 178). In the pageant, Miss La Trobe adapts the plot of separation to the history of England, represented through the Age of

Reason by and as women (a female child, a young girl, Queen Elizabeth, Reason herself), allegorized next as a Victorian constable directing the traffic of empire (a deliberate choice of gender to represent an age traditionally personified by its queen), and finally incarnate in the "scraps, orts, and fragments" that constitute the present day (188).[27] History, like maturation, proceeds as separation, from birth through the delineated boundaries that characterize masculinity (as the "separatist" Bart demonstrates) to fragmentation. It is a process that posits a maternal origin and moment of mother-infant unity; but there is no longer any possibility of recovering them, for the mother of infancy is always already incorporated by the father. The pageant dramatizes the futility of further enactments of this matricentric plot and points toward the father-daughter plot that Miss La Trobe embraces as the subject of her next play.

The separation narrative receives its first and most explicit formulation in the prologue to the pageant. Spoken by Phyllis Jones, "a small girl, like a rosebud in pink," the prologue announces the historical framework of the pageant, "This is a pageant, all may see / Drawn from our island history," and the historical myth that informs it:

England am I. . . .

A child new born, . . .
Sprung from the sea
Whose billows blown by mighty storm
Cut off from France and Germany
    This isle

(76, 77)

The myth accords England a prehistory of fusion with her parent nations, France and Germany. National birth is figured as a moment of separation graphically rendered in the dangling final line. The newly born land is appropriately personified by a child who forgets her lines, who has not quite mastered the skills of speech and memory. England is granted a violent birth by this fictive genealogy, but the narrative present—with France poised precariously before an expansionist Germany—forbids nostalgia for these lost parental origins.[28] Germany's hegemony is given literary form by the prologue's governing rhyme scheme (see, history, sea, Germany). The mother is already in the father's power—as Isa is in Giles's, beyond the reach of her infant son. International and domestic politics mirror one another: when George crosses the "channel" that divides him from his mother by "swimming blindly" toward her, the reunion that is enabled by the change in Isa—"as if she had got out of one dress and put on another"—is revoked by the appearance of George's father. "Then again she changed her dress. This time, from the expression in her eyes it was apparently something in the nature of a strait waistcoat. Hirsute, handsome, virile, the young man . . . was her husband. And she his wife" (105–6). The altered origin, prohibiting even the desire for return, disturbs the flow of history.

The developmental narrative that informs La Trobe's pageant is significantly, and problematically, bolstered by the official history cited in the novel: the *Outline of History* that Lucy Swithin reads and renames "*her* Outline of History*" (217; emphasis added). Lucy interprets Trevelyan to offer an account of England's prehistory, "[b]efore there was a channel" (108), "when the entire continent, not then, she understood, divided by a channel, was all one" (8).[29] Read just before dawn of the day that contains the novel's action, the historical narrative authorizes Miss La Trobe's fiction, as Lucy echoes—from the other end of the age spectrum—the story told by Phyllis Jones: the old lady dwells, appropriately, on the primal unity; the young girl, on the "child new born." The authority, however, is partially self-cancelling, for the anachronistic Lucy's investment in this story dates it. Yet within this last rehearsal of the separation story, Lucy highlights the problem of origins by imagining the inhabitants of the undivided continent as "elephant-bodied, seal-necked, heaving, surging, slowly writhing, and, she supposed, barking monsters; the iguanodon, the mammoth, and the mastodon; from whom presumably, she thought, jerking the window open, we descend" (8–9). These fantasied ancestors are rendered monstrous by their agglomerated parts; those who populate the predivided land are themselves undifferentiated. Like Sohrab in George's fantasy, these monstrous parents defy the rules of difference, blurring mother with other, dispersing her.

The pageant articulates the consequences of this troubled origin. Historicizing them, it offers a dual starting point: counterposing the patterns of individual growth presented through Phyllis Jones's "child new born" is a collective story of birth and death changed by a chorus of identically dressed villagers. As the point of view shifts from the individual to the collective, cycles replace development. "Cutting the roads . . . up to the hill top . . . we climbed. . . . Ground roots between stones . . . Ground corn . . . till we too . . . lay under g-r-o-u-n-d . . . " (78). "Ground" is the chant's key word, a pun, yet unproblematic as the name of a communal point of origin and return carried as verb into the work of civilization. Prior to a notion of individuality, boundaries pose no problem. However, the pageant authorizes this account of history only until the Renaissance. With the advent of the Elizabethan theater, and a new conception of history, the chorus withdraws to become an audience.

With the Elizabethan Age begin the parodic theater pieces that together compose an individuation story, the pattern for the separate scenes as well. Despite the different period conventions they spoof, the first two playlets, renditions of a Shakespearean romance and a Restoration comedy, are subtly paralleled. Set in enclosed spaces designed to resemble stage sets, they are presented as self-conscious parodies of intricately plotted comic plays. Beneath the surface complexity, moreover, they share certain features of a common story: severed from its mother, a baby in a basket is placed in a woman's custody. In the first play, the child is a persecuted prince who will win his claim to be the "rightful heir"; in the second, the child is a daughter who will be disinherited; both are groomed for their destinies by women not their mothers. Contemporary with modern understandings of history are male and female variants of a story that begins with the assumption of an unrecoverable mother.

According to the program, a romantic plot governs the action of the first play, but a different tale emerges through the aged crone's soliloquy, an Elizabethan medley of our culture's central hero myths. The old beldam has saved the rightful heir by hiding in the rushes "the babe in the basket" that a "man with a hood on his face, and the bloody hands" had ordered her to slay (89). Twenty years later the prince returns and claims the "sweet Carinthia" as his love. "'My child! My child!'" the old crone cries when a mole on the prince's arm reveals his true identity; her task performed, the old lady dies (91–92). If the setting of her tale suggests the Moses story, with the crone in the role of the Egyptian princess; if her language in her description of her own disobedience alludes to the story of Christ—"'Yet the cock did crow ere he left me'"; if the recognition scene reminds us of the *Odyssey;* the structure of the tale suggests a comedic Oedipus, with the crone in the role of the shepherd who saves the endangered baby and the narrative revised to allow a happy ending. Given the implicit Oedipal framework, the silence surrounding the mother is especially striking. For though the child appears in a basket, parentless, we distinctly sense a hostile father in the workings of the plot and in the action of characters— such as the hooded man and the three thugs—who appear to be his agents. In contrast, the mother's place is only briefly and incompletely held—by a surrogate, who dies when the son reaches maturity.

The mother's absence is more conspicuous and problematic in the pageant's second act, whose paradigmatic character is not immediately apparent, because we lack a tradition of daughter narratives. The Restoration comedy dramatizes a developmental matrix in which the mother is both absent and unmentioned, the father successfully exerts control even from beyond the grave, and the mother substitute (here, the father's sister) speaks in the name of the father. The maternal ingenuity that may save sons from fathers is not available to daughters: hence the basket in which the old crone hides the prince evolves into the cradle in which Flavinda floats from the shipwreck (in which her father drowns) to the aunt who welcomes both her niece and, "'[w]hat's more to the point,'" the paternal will that arrives neatly packaged in the cradle (130). Executrice of her brother's will—of the father's desire and of his text—Lady Harpy Harraden also strives to become its beneficiary by plotting to marry Flavinda to Sir Spaniel Lilyliver in exchange for half of her dead brother's fortune, willed to Flavinda if she marries according to her aunt's decree. Father and aunt concur that the daughter's body should comply with the father's will. The identification of paternal desire with writing is crucial here, and Flavinda's escape from paternal control, her reading and enactment of her own desire, is comically condemned by Lady Harraden as a violation of patriarchal textuality: "O! Didn't the Horn book teach you Honour thy Great Aunt? How have you misread it and misspelt it, learnt thieving and cheating and reading of wills in old boxes" (143). In freeing her own will from her father's, Flavinda wrests the title of the play away from Sir Spaniel and Lady Harraden; *"Where there's a Will there's a Way"* ultimately celebrates the daughter's rebellious and victorious desire. Although this desire culminates in a romantic elopement, as the conventions of comedy dictate, Miss La Trobe appends another ending that crosses class boundaries to include another "daughter," Lady Harpy's maid, who follows in Flavinda's footsteps by fleeing her mistress's service, leaving behind a text that announces she is "'off with the raggle-taggle gipsies, O!'" (148). The daughter's story pivots on co-optation and rebellion. The mother's death and absence are axiomatic, her place completely vacant except for a surrogate, who is the father's spokesman.

The last two acts of the pageant, which represent a period continuous with the present and within the memory of many in the audience, form a unit comparable to the Renaissance and Restoration pair. Rather than burlesquing literary conventions, however, these plays parody the conventions of social texts; and rather than contrasting son and daughter stories, they historicize the question of the mother by charting a progression from the Victorian matriarch, a powerful servant of patriarchy, to the void at the heart of the present day.

Woolf assimilates the Victorian age to the present by interweaving the audience's comments, drawn from their personal memories, with the language of the pageant and by integrating the actual setting with the stage props of the play: hence real swallows dart across the sheet that represents a lake, and Pointz Hall at sunset, its windows blazing, emblematizes the Victorian home. The doxa of Victorian social and political life, the creeds of "'Er Majesty's Empire,'" are the "text" the pageant parodies (161). The constable who personifies the era holds sway over the domestic, as well as the public, spaces of empire: "'Over thought and religion; drink; dress; manners; marriage too, I wield my truncheon. Prosperity and respectability always go, as we know, 'and in 'and'" (162). Accordingly, within the domestic arena that constitutes the second scene of this act, the role of policeman passes easily to the Victorian mother, who supervises family manners and morals. Mrs. Hardcastle divides her allegiance between family and church; her overriding project is to marry off her daughters, preferably to clergymen. Eleanor happily complies, plighting her troth to Edgar, whom she will join in converting the African heathen. Mother and daughter are equally wedded to the interests of society. Imperialism and domestic ideology are blended in the performances that conclude this scene at Mrs. Hardcastle's command. Directed by their mother, Eleanor and Mildred dutifully sing "I'd be a butterfly," a fitting expression of feminine inconsequentiality; Edgar and Arthur sing "Rule Britannia"; and Mr. Hardcastle leads the group in prayer. After the constable has evoked the pleasures of the Victorian home and merged with the figure of the father as the "'bread-winner, home from the city,'" the drama concludes with the memories of Mrs. Lynn Jones, a member of the audience, which condense the family to its gendered roles and texts, the "yards and yards of Papa's beard, of Mama's knitting" an unchanged Victorian culture would produce (172, 174). Cut from a single fabric, maternal and paternal texts afford no loophole to the daughter who would seek a different past.

This lack becomes dramatic in the pageant's final scene, when the community's children prance onto the stage holding mirrors that transform the disconcerted audience into the subject of the play. Like the aggressively unsocialized children at the end of *The Years*, these "imps—elves—demons" reverse familial as well as dramatic roles (183). Marking an absent maternal function (the one Mrs. Ramsay, for example, performs for Lily Briscoe), the children hold up the mirror to their parents, aggressively exposing in "the present moment[,] . . . now" a lack quiescently accepted in the pageant (186). As the dancing, flashing mirrors finally come to rest, the image they reflect is the face of the Manresa, the novel's reconstruction of the fascist mother, and the sole intact identity amidst the fragments of the present. The only member of the audience unembarrassed by her own reflection, she uses the mirror nonchalantly as a looking glass, powders her nose, and arranges her hair. The drama of the present concludes with Bart's tribute to the nonmother who embodies his ideal of maternity. "'Magnificent!' cried old Bartholomew. Alone she preserved unashamed her identity, and faced without blinking herself" (186).

In this icon of Manresa, the novel and the pageant intersect. The children, at La Trobe's instruction, enact an anger, pervasive but suppressed, that discloses the face of the Manresa. Miss La Trobe is the repository of anger in the text, anger at failed attention, at imperfect mirroring—the anger of the unrecognized child whose perspective, seemingly absent from this novel, is present, but submerged, in the figure of the artist cut off from her audience.[30] Her rage is most forcibly provoked by the interruptions ("'O,' Miss La Trobe growled behind her tree, 'the torture of these interruptions!'") which fracture her fragile connection with her audience (79). And her production is plagued by interruptions, mechanical, social, and natural: the gramophone doesn't work, the audience demands its tea, and the wind blows the words away in an echo of the "mighty storm" that severed England from the continent. A channel divides the author from the audience. Raging from the place of the "child new born" whose history she dramatizes, she works to heal the separation she recounts, to undo the process she shows to be inexorable, to repossess through the audience the mother that has disappeared.

Hence her art must be theater. It is the relation to her audience that energizes Miss La Trobe, both in her most inventive moments, such as her use of mirrors and an empty stage, and in her furious asides ("'Blast 'em!' cursed Miss La Trobe, hidden behind the tree" [77]). Her goal is the creation of "illusion"—whose opposite is "death"—and this project is of necessity a shared and urgent one. Miss La Trobe is both radically dependent on her audience as a source of imaginative life and furious at this dependency: "O to write a play without an audience—*the* play," she sighs, though she deliberately chooses a genre (whose name also designates the child's activity) which entails a relation to an audience (180). She is not interested in constructing autotelic texts that would demonstrate the author's autonomy. Despite her name, etymologically linked with "trope," her skills are less verbal than visual. The language of the pageant is not original but imitative, a tissue of near citations. Miss La Trobe's gift is in "getting things up," in making the most of minimal costumes, staging, and props; and despite her sense of prophetic mission, her metaphors for her desired effect stress seeing rather than hearing. This lack of discursive content is what makes the Reverend Streatfield's concluding paraphrase so inadequate. La Trobe's text in itself is minimal: what she seeks is a direct play, an immediate bond, with her audience—hence, the significantly named Bond, the cowman, who looks "like a withered willow, bent over a stream, . . . in his eyes the whimsical flow of the waters," is the only member of the unresponding audience to look "fluid and natural" when the play begins (28, 77). As in the contemporaneous essay "Anon," Woolf locates the origins of art in an intimate author-audience connection that reconstitutes the interplay of mother and child.[31] In seeking to recreate this bond, La Trobe embraces contradictory imperatives.

La Trobe wants to demonstrate that the bond she struggles to create is impossible in a present whose truth is fragmentation and whose history is the corruption of any principle of unity. She can seduce her audience easily through patriotic songs and sentimentality, but this would be merger with the mother celebrated by fascist ideology, the mother at whom she directs her greatest rage. La Trobe wants to generate a shared aesthetic illusion, but she also wants to dispel the illusions of community (elicited by music and language, then disrupted by rapid shifts of tone) and art (called into question by the minimalism of her stage effects, which allow real people and places to show through). She insistently presents the discontinuity of experience, salutary in contrast to demands for uniformity.[32] Trying both to proclaim and to mend fragmentation, the pageant fractures into contradictory parts: scraps, orts, fragments, and harmony.

IV

With its final rehearsal in the pageant, the matricentric narrative is played out. For her next play, Miss La Trobe abandons her plan to reproduce, in idealized form, the plot of mothers and children: "For another play always lay behind the play she had just written. Shading her eyes, she looked. The butterflies circling; the light changing; the children leaping; the mothers laughing—'No, I don't get it,' she muttered and resumed her pacing" (63). Instead, her inspiration, figured as emerging from the mud of the lily pond in which the "lady" vanishes, is drawn from the dance of love and hate performed by Isa and Giles.

Isa openly names this plot, but she sees herself as its victim rather than its author. "Love and hate—how they tore her asunder! Surely it was time someone invented a new plot, or that the author came out from the bushes" (215). Isa's love/hate plot, like her author's, is focused on the figure of the father, in Isa's case, "'The father of my children, whom I love and hate'" (215). Isa's choice of this "cliché conveniently provided by fiction" suggests that she invokes the Victorian epithet primarily to cover, and to indicate, an emotional absence and to foreclose the option of her own escape; but the phrase also signals her perception of her husband as a father (14). From the scene of their courtship through the domestic arrangements in which Giles dictates standards of morality ("It made no difference; his infidelity—but hers did" [110]), Isa submits in practice, if not in feeling, to her husband's authority. Their marital politics reproduce the father-daughter relationship Woolf analyzes in *Three Guineas:* Isa lives in Giles's family home, and her sexuality and creativity are accountable to him. Giles never views her as the "mother of his children"; their roles as parents do not counterbalance the asymmetries of power. By repeatedly affixing the plot of love and hate to Giles in his capacity as father, Isa weaves together a heterosexual plot in which the original object of desire and his surrogates are blurred.

This plot differs from its counterpart in *Three Guineas,* however, through its assumption of women's innate heterosexuality. The two-sentence paragraph describing the courtship of Isa and Giles encapsulates the new heterosexual economy. Having met as equals "fishing—she from one rock, he from another," Isa "give[s] over" as her line becomes tangled and as she becomes entangled by the sexual charisma of the man whose casting arm displays and displaces a kind of phallic power: "[S]he had given over, and had watched him with the stream rushing between his legs, casting, casting" (48). The catching of the fish becomes her own capture as she silently descends the spectrum from fisherwoman to fish, inserting herself as the final item in a sequence that simultaneously identifies her with the fish and asserts the fisherman's superiority: "[L]ike a thick ingot of silver bent in the middle, the salmon had leapt, had been caught, and she had loved him" (48). The mini-courtship narrative repeats that of Sir William and Lady Bradshaw in *Mrs. Dalloway,* but here there is no external coercion: Isa is ensnared by the force of her desire.

Like Miss La Trobe, Isa is a writer, but she never writes the story of her entangling and entangled love and hate. Although she "reads" this story rather compulsively, driven by her own ambivalence to find it everywhere ("The plot was only there to beget emotion. There were only two emotions: love; and hate," she muses during the first act of Miss La Trobe's pageant [90]), she writes a safer romantic poetry inspired by her fantasies about the gentleman-farmer Haines (whom she has seen twice). Actor and reader of the plot of love and hate, she lacks the courage to author it, producing instead a poetry of evasion and cliché.

It is the alienated and angry Miss La Trobe who writes Isa's story. Miss La Trobe's vision of her next play's setting—"It would be midnight; there would be two figures, half concealed by a rock. The curtain would rise"—predicts and assimilates Isa's final scene with Giles (210). At the end of the novel, night falls; Pointz Hall is swallowed up in darkness; history unwinds. The tone is set by Lucy's reading from the *Outline of History* about the time that "'Prehistoric man, . . . half-human, half-ape, roused himself from his semi-crouching position and raised great stones'" (218). The inhabitants of Pointz Hall retire to bed, leaving Isa and Giles alone together for the first time that day.

> Alone, enmity was bared; also love. Before they slept, they must fight; after they had fought, they would embrace. From that embrace another life might be born. But first they must fight, as the dog fox fights with the vixen, in the heart of darkness, in the fields of night.
> Isa let her sewing drop. The great hooded chairs had become enormous. And Giles too. And Isa too against the window. The window was all sky without colour. The house had lost its shelter. It was night before roads were made, or houses. It was the night that dwellers in caves had watched from some high place among rocks.
> Then the curtain rose. They spoke. (219)

The end of the novel marks a beginning that recasts origins. Woolf moves us, in the space of a single text, from dawn, when Lucy Swithin reads about fusion and separation, to night and warring copulation, a moment both prior and subsequent to birth. As dawn recedes to night, and separation yields to generation, the plot of object relations gives way to the plot of heterosexual love and hate. Woolf's final scene is a variation on Freud's primal scene: two outsized figures, woman and man, spread to the horizons, and our perspective shrinks to a child's. As history becomes theater, and Stonehenge the Freudian stage, the audience is transformed from viewers exhorted to see, to participate in the creation of illusion, to voyeurs of an erotic scene that launches a new text and a new cycle of history.

The space "between the acts," from this perspective, measures not only a historical era between two world wars but also the moment in Woolf's own history in which she refigures her relationship to psychoanalytic plots as the literary space of her final text. *Between the Acts* recalls and reverses the interplay of narratives in *To the Lighthouse;* juxtaposed, the two texts demonstrate both the continuities and the discontinuities between the two major decades of Woolf's career. Through the issue that *To the Lighthouse* submerges—that only the nonbiological mother (Lily's rather than Cam's) can constitute a narrative point of origin for her "daughter"—the earlier novel reaches forward to the denouement of *Between the Acts;* but the opposition between the two texts overshadows the connection. The mother-based plot toward which Woolf moved in the composition of *To the Lighthouse* calls into question and ultimately dwarfs the father-based plot(s) with which she began. In her final novel, Woolf dramatizes the opposite course as Miss La Trobe replaces a fully discredited matricentric narrative with the heterosexual plot that originates, for women, with the father.

NOTES

Preface

1. 28 November 1928, *The Diary of Virginia Woolf*, ed. Anne Olivier Bell, 5 vols. (New York: Harcourt Brace Jovanovich, 1977–84), 3:209.

2. In "Phases of Fiction," which she was composing when she made this diary entry, Woolf describes Proust's fusion of the poet and the thinker as a "dual vision" which makes his characters and fictional world "more like a globe, of which one side is always hidden, than a scene laid flat before us"; his work, she explains, is "so spherical, so comprehensive" (in *Granite and Rainbow* [New York: Harcourt, Brace & World, 1958], 126, 139). Gillian Beer argues that Woolf's commitment to circular forms reflects her rejection of plot. I see Woolf's creation of what Lily Briscoe calls "globed, compacted things" as a mode of plotting that incorporates the dimension of time as depth. See Beer, "Virginia Woolf and Pre-History," in *Virginia Woolf: A Centenary Perspective*, ed. Eric Warner (London: Macmillan, 1984), 99–123; and "Beyond Determinism: George Eliot and Virginia Woolf," in *Women Writing and Writing about Women*, ed. Mary Jacobus (London: Croom Helm, 1979), 80–99.

3. Woolf, "Modern Fiction," in *The Common Reader: First Series* (New York: Harcourt, Brace & World, 1925), 156–57.

4. Woolf, 15 October 1923 and 30 August 1923, *Diary* 2:272, 263.

5. My insistence on this disjunction fundamentally differentiates my argument from Ellen Bayuk Rosenman's sensitive reading of the mother's constant (if conflictual) presence in Woolf's life and work. See Rosenman, *The Invisible Presence: Virginia Woolf and the Mother-Daughter Relationship* (Baton Rouge: Louisiana State University Press, 1986).

Since I wish to foreground the ideological pressures on Woolf's career, I focus on *Three Guineas* rather than on its companion piece, *The Years* (1937), which dramatizes the changing social relations *Three Guineas* theorizes. I also omit *The Waves* (1931), whose experiment in dissolving identity sets it outside my concerns; the very disembodiment that characterizes the text, however, suggests a heightened ambivalence toward the body's origin. *The Waves* marks the terminus of Woolf's progression through the 1920s toward an ambivalent engagement with maternal origins.

6. The tradition of pairing Woolf and Freud reaches from Jan Ellen Goldstein's thorough study, "The Woolfs' Response to Freud: Water-spiders, Singing Canaries, and the Second Apple" (*Psychoanalytic Quarterly* 43, no. 3 [1974]:438–76), to Toril Moi's breezy assertion in *Sexual/Textual Politics: Feminist Literary Theory* (London: Methuen, 1985) that "Woolf undoubtedly knew . . . psychoanalytic theory," which Moi equates with Freud (9). The more recent project of reading Woolf through the lens of object relations theory, on the other hand, usually brackets Freud; see, for example, Rosenman, *The Invisible Presence;* Joan Lidoff, "Virginia Woolf's Feminine Sentence: The Mother-Daughter World of *To the Lighthouse," Literature and Psychology* 32, no. 3 (1986):43–59; and Susan Merrill Squier, *Virginia Woolf and London: The Sexual Politics of the City* (Chapel Hill: University of North Carolina Press, 1985), and "Mirroring and Mothering: Reflections on the Mirror Encounter Metaphor in Virginia Woolf's Works," *Twentieth Century Literature* 27, no. 3 (Fall 1981): 272–88. Woolf's juxtaposition of the two discourses has not been a subject of inquiry. The more general tendency to pair literature and psychoanalysis can be seen in the critical tradition launched by the special issue of *Yale French Studies* (55/56), *Literature and Psychoanalysis: The Question of Reading—Otherwise,* in which literary and psychoanalytic discourse exchange places but resist the mediation of a third term (such as history).

Chapter 1

1. Virginia Woolf, "A Sketch of the Past," in *Moments of Being: Unpublished Autobiographical Writings,* ed. Jeanne Schulkind (New York: Harcourt Brace Jovanovich, 1985), 122. Bernard uses a similar figure to "sum up" the collective life of the six characters in *The Waves* (New York: Harcourt, Brace & World, 1931): "Let us turn over these scenes as children turn over the pages of a picture-book and the nurse says, pointing: 'That's a cow. That's a boat'" (239).

2. Woolf, *To the Lighthouse* (New York: Harcourt, Brace & World, 1927), 254; hereafter cited in the text. Note the similarity to the language of Woolf's "rough visual description of childhood" in "A Sketch of the Past": "several violent moments of being, always including a circle of the scene which they cut out: and all surrounded by a vast space" (79).

3. Woolf, *A Room of One's Own* (New York: Harcourt, Brace & World, 1929), 3; hereafter cited in the text.

4. Woolf, "Jane Austen," in *The Common Reader: First Series* (New York: Harcourt, Brace & World, 1925), 142, 149.

5. Woolf, *The Voyage Out* (New York: Harcourt, Brace & World, 1920), 216; *Between the Acts* (1941; New York: Harcourt Brace Jovanovich, 1969), 39;

"The Anatomy of Fiction," in *Granite and Rainbow* (New York: Harcourt, Brace & World, 1958), 54.

6. I am following Joseph Frank's analysis of Proust in "Spatial Form in Modern Literature," in *The Widening Gyre: Crisis and Mastery in Modern Literature* (Bloomington: Indiana University Press, 1968), esp. 19–25. Woolf is absent from Frank's modernist lineup (Pound, Eliot, Joyce, Proust, and Djuna Barnes), I would argue, because she uses the modernists' spatializing strategies not to counteract narrative but to create an alternative form for it.

7. 22 December 1940, *The Diary of Virginia Woolf*, ed. Anne Olivier Bell, 5 vols. (New York: Harcourt Brace Jovanovich, 1977–84), 5:345.

8. Woolf, "A Sketch of the Past," 80, 108; 28 November 1928, *Diary* 3:208. For the biographical context of Woolf's representation of her origins, see Quentin Bell, *Virginia Woolf: A Biography* (New York: Harcourt Brace Jovanovich, 1972); Phyllis Rose, *Woman of Letters: A Life of Virginia Woolf* (New York: Oxford University Press, 1978); Ellen Bayuk Rosenman, *The Invisible Presence: Virginia Woolf and the Mother-Daughter Relationship* (Baton Rouge: Louisiana State University Press, 1986), pt. 1; and Shirley Panken, *Virginia Woolf and the "Lust of Creation": A Psychoanalytic Exploration* (Albany: State University of New York Press, 1987), chaps. 2 and 3.

9. The weight of Freudian orthodoxy slowed the pace of the revisions Klein initiated; Woolf's novels leap ahead to the position articulated by object relations theorists in the 1950s and 1970s. On the status of paternal genealogies in nineteenth-century fiction, see Peter Brooks, *Reading for the Plot: Design and Intention in Narrative* (New York: Alfred A. Knopf, 1984). Brooks discusses only male protagonists, but even for nineteenth-century female protagonists, as Margaret Homans has shown, the mother is rarely represented as other than an obstacle. See Homans, *Bearing the Word: Language and Female Experience in Nineteenth-Century Women's Writing* (Chicago: University of Chicago Press, 1986).

10. The publication in 1861 of Johann Jakob Bachofen's *Mutterrecht* and Henry Maine's *Ancient Law* installed gender at the center of the narrative of social evolution that dominated social anthropology from the mid–nineteenth century through the 1920s. For a thorough account of the emergence of this narrative, see Rosalind Coward, *Patriarchal Precedents: Sexuality and Social Relations* (London: Routledge & Kegan Paul, 1983); for a critique of the narrative, see Elizabeth Fee, "The Sexual Politics of Victorian Social Anthropology," in *Clio's Consciousness Raised: New Perspectives on the History of Women*, ed. Mary Hartman and Lois W. Banner (New York: Harper & Row, 1974), 86–102. By the late 1920s, the evolutionary genre was discredited and displaced by functionalism. But the cross-fertilization between psychoanalysis and anthropology persisted for a while in the anthropological adaptation of the developmental narrative as a device for organizing cultural comparisons. See, for example, Margaret Mead, *Coming of Age in Samoa: A Psychological Study of Primitive Youth* (1928; New York: Morrow Quill, 1961); Bronislaw Malinowski, *Sex and Repression in Savage Society* (1927; see n. 73 below); and Audrey I. Richards, *Hunger and Work in a Savage Tribe: A Functional Study of Nutrition among the Southern Bantu* (1932; see n. 111 below).

11. *Totem and Taboo* [1913–14], *The Standard Edition of the Complete Psy-*

chological Works of Sigmund Freud, trans. and ed. James Strachey, 24 vols. (London: Hogarth Press, 1953–66; New York: Macmillan, 1953–74), 13:145; hereafter the *Standard Edition* will be cited as *SE*.

12. Ernest Jones, "Mother-Right and the Sexual Ignorance of Savages" [1924], in *Essays in Applied Psycho-Analysis,* 2 vols. (London: Hogarth Press and the Institute of Psycho-Analysis, 1951), 2:148.

13. Freud to Wilhelm Fliess, 15 October 1897, *SE* 1:265.

14. Freud's letters to Fliess between 21 September and 15 October 1897 outline the rapid passage from the daughter's to the son's desire. In his next extended discussion of the Oedipal configuration, in *The Interpretation of Dreams* (*SE* 4:260–61), Freud insists on its universal validity.

15. Freud does not, of course, disavow the narrative of the *Three Essays,* but he shifts his attention away from it and makes no further revisions (although there are new editions) after 1924. Although the Oedipal narrative has no single textual locus comparable to the *Three Essays,* it assumed hegemony as *the* psychoanalytic narrative. For a repositioning of the *Three Essays* at the center of psychoanalysis, see Jean Laplanche, *Life and Death in Psychoanalysis,* trans. Jeffrey Mehlman (Baltimore: Johns Hopkins University Press, 1976), especially chap. 1.

16. Freud, *Three Essays on the Theory of Sexuality, SE* 7:226.

17. Freud, "The Dissolution of the Oedipus Complex," *SE* 19:173.

18. Freud, *The Ego and the Id, SE* 19:36.

19. Freud, "The Infantile Genital Organization (An Interpolation into the Theory of Sexuality)," *SE* 19:145.

20. Freud, "The Dissolution of the Oedipus Complex," *SE* 19:179.

21. Ibid., 176.

22. When he returns to the phylogenetic correlate of this narrative in *Moses and Monotheism,* Freud is explicit about the process of condensation: "The story is told in an enormously condensed form as though it happened on a single occasion, while in fact it covered thousands of years and was repeated countless times during that long period" (*SE* 23:81). In contrast to the plot Freud articulated in *Beyond the Pleasure Principle* (1920), in which the gap between plot and story is relatively small, the Oedipal plot has a classical, crystalline form. On the literary ramifications of what Peter Brooks calls Freud's "masterplot," or what we might call the plot of thanatos, see Brooks, *Reading for the Plot,* especially "Freud's Masterplot: A Model for Narrative," 90–112.

23. Freud, "The Infantile Genital Organization," *SE* 19:142–43; "The Dissolution of the Oedipus Complex," *SE* 19:177.

24. Freud, *The Ego and the Id, SE* 19:32.

25. Freud, "Some Psychical Consequences of the Anatomical Distinction between the Sexes," *SE* 19:252.

26. Freud, "Psychical Consequences," *SE* 19:258. In his later essay "Femininity" (1933), Freud differentiates the psychoanalytic commitment to narrative from any form of essentialism: "In conformity with its peculiar nature, psychoanalysis does not try to describe what a woman is—that would be a task it could scarcely perform—but sets about enquiring how she comes into being, how a woman develops out of a child with a bisexual disposition" (*SE* 22:116).

27. Freud, "Psychical Consequences," *SE* 19:256.

28. Quoted in Ernest Jones, *The Life and Work of Sigmund Freud,* ed. and abr. Lionel Trilling and Steven Marcus (New York: Basic Books, 1961), 377.

29. On the son's "first and most important identification" with his father, see *The Ego and the Id, SE* 19:31. Freud sometimes qualifies the rupture he posits between the girl's prehistory and history: a woman's relation to her husband, he claims, may replay that with her mother. In theory, however, there is a radical break, which object relations theorists subsequently called into question.

30. Freud, "Female Sexuality," *SE* 21:226.

31. Ibid., 234. Freud also cites other incentives to anger, most of which are consequences of the mother's supervision of the child's training and bodily care, but these essentially contingent factors are less important theoretically than the decisive perception of "castration."

32. On the distinguishing features of Klein's play therapy, see the first two chapters of her *Psycho-Analysis of Children* (London: Hogarth Press, 1932); "Personification in the Play of Children" [1929], in *Love, Guilt, and Reparation and Other Works, 1921–1945* (New York: Dell, 1975), 199–209; and "The Psycho-Analytic Play Technique: Its History and Significance," in *New Directions in Psycho-Analysis: The Significance of Infant Conflict in the Pattern of Adult Behavior,* ed. Melanie Klein, Paula Heimann, and R. E. Money-Kyrle (New York: Basic Books, 1955), 2–37. For her disagreements with Anna Freud, see "Symposium on Child Analysis" [1927], in *Love, Guilt, and Reparation,* 139–76. In *Melanie Klein: Her World and Her Work* (New York: Alfred A. Knopf, 1986), Phyllis Grosskurth provides a thorough and fascinating account of Klein's complex position in the psychoanalytic world.

33. Quoted in Riccardo Steiner, "Some Thoughts about Tradition and Change Arising from an Examination of the British Psycho-Analytical Society's Controversial Discussions (1943–1944)," *International Review of Psycho-Analysis* 12, no. 27 (1985): 30. Steiner also quotes Freud's ominous reply: "Melanie Klein's work has aroused considerable doubt and controversy here in Vienna."

34. James Strachey to Alix Strachey, 8 January 1925, 7 May 1925, *Bloomsbury/Freud: The Letters of James and Alix Strachey, 1924–1925,* ed. Perry Meisel and Walter Kendrick (New York: Basic Books, 1985), 175, 258. This collection establishes the Stracheys' absolute centrality in bringing Klein to England.

35. For Jones's letter to Freud explaining the background of the British Society's openness to Klein, see Steiner, "Some Thoughts about Tradition and Change," 33; for Glover's version of Klein's success, see Grosskurth, *Melanie Klein,* 154. Steiner and Grosskurth both detail Klein's complex role in the history of British psychoanalysis. See also Pearl H. M. King, "The Life and Work of Melanie Klein in the British Psycho-Analytical Society," *International Journal of Psycho-Analysis* 64 (1983): 251–60; and Hanna Segal, *Melanie Klein* (Harmondsworth, Middlesex: Penguin, 1979). Recent Lacanian feminist discussions of the Jones/ Freud debate on female sexuality, the focus of the first exchange lectures between the British Society and the Viennese Society, has obscured the more fundamental differences between Klein and Freud, the subject addressed by the second exchange lecture, given by Joan Riviere. On the Jones/Freud debate, see Jane Gallop, "Of Phallic Proportions: Lacanian Conceit," in *The Daughter's Seduc-*

tion: Feminism and Psychoanalysis (Ithaca, N.Y.: Cornell University Press, 1982), 15–32; and Juliet Mitchell, "Introduction—I" to *Feminine Sexuality: Jacques Lacan and the "école freudienne,"* ed. Juliet Mitchell and Jacqueline Rose, trans. Jacqueline Rose (New York: W. W. Norton, 1982), 1–26.

36. Quoted in Grosskurth, *Melanie Klein,* 194. In her preface to the third edition of *The Psycho-Analysis of Children* [London: Hogarth Press, 1948], Klein asserts: "[T]his book as it stands represents fundamentally the views I hold today. . . .[T]he more recent development of my work derives organically from the hypotheses here presented" (13). Since Klein's account of infantile subjectivity assumes a narrative form from the beginning, there is no need to chart the narrative's composition chronologically.

37. Klein, "The Oedipus Complex in the Light of Early Anxieties," in *Love, Guilt, and Reparation,* 412; "Weaning," in *Love, Guilt, and Reparation,* 291.

38. Klein, "A Contribution to the Psychogenesis of Manic-Depressive States," in *Love, Guilt, and Reparation,* 262.

39. Ibid., 268.

40. Ibid., 288. Although Klein does not explicitly compare the depressive position to the Oedipus complex, her repeated claims that this position constitutes the central developmental situation imply its comparable status. Her commentators reinforce this implication. For example, D. W. Winnicott claims that the depressive position is Klein's most important contribution and "ranks with Freud's concept of the Oedipus complex" ("A Personal View of the Kleinian Contribution," in *The Maturational Processes and the Facilitating Environment* [London: Hogarth Press, 1965], 176).

41. Klein, "Mourning and Its Relation to Manic-Depressive States," in *Love, Guilt, and Reparation,* 345.

42. Klein, "Weaning," 294.

43. For contrast, see Freud's 1908 essay "Creative Writers and Daydreaming," *SE* 9:143–53. The aesthetic dimension of Kleinian theory is emphasized in the essays collected as *New Directions in Psycho-Analysis;* see, especially, Marion Milner, "The Role of Illusion in Symbol Formation"; Adrian Stokes, "Form in Art"; and Joan Riviere, "The Unconscious Phantasy of an Inner World Reflected in Examples from English Literature." See also Hanna Segal, "A Psycho-Analytical Approach to Aesthetics," *International Journal of Psycho-Analysis* 33, no. 2 (1952): 196–207. For a different reading of the Kleinian aesthetic based on her early (and anomalous) paper "Early Analysis" (1923), see Leo Bersani, "'The Culture of Redemption': Marcel Proust and Melanie Klein," *Critical Inquiry* 12, no. 2 (Winter 1986): 399–421. Some of Woolf's descriptions of her own aesthetic process echo the Kleinian emphasis on mending fragmentation: see, for example, her claim in "A Sketch of the Past" that she responds to shock by "putting it into words. It is only by putting it into words that I make it whole; this wholeness means that it has lost its power to hurt me; it gives me . . . a great delight to put the severed parts together" (72). However, Woolf consistently represents herself as a victim, not an agent, of aggression.

44. Klein, "Early Stages of the Oedipus Conflict," in *Love, Guilt and Reparation,* 197.

45. Klein, "The Oedipus Complex in the Light of Early Anxieties," 412. Prior to 1935, when she clearly differentiated the depressive from the paranoid

position, Klein held that the Oedipus complex originated at the peak of oral sadism and that aggression toward the mother, rather than desire for her, was the instinct requiring repression.

46. Klein, *The Psycho-Analysis of Children*, 271.

47. Ibid., 270.

48. Klein, "The Oedipus Complex in the Light of Early Anxieties," 413.

49. Ibid., 419.

50. Klein, *The Psycho-Analysis of Children*, 157, 333; and "Some Theoretical Conclusions Regarding the Emotional Life of the Infant," in *Developments in Psycho-Analysis*, ed. Joan Riviere (London: Hogarth Press, 1952), 220.

51. The fullest account of the connections between Bloomsbury and British psychoanalysis is offered by *Bloomsbury/Freud* (see n. 34 above). In their introduction the book's editors, Meisel and Kendrick, underscore the threat James Strachey, a staunch member of Bloomsbury and Freud's official translator, posed to Ernest Jones: "Thanks only to James's absolute lack of administrative ambition, Jones continued to maintain the helm [of the British Society] until his death in 1958" (41). On the early history of psychoanalysis in England, see Victor Brome, *Ernest Jones: Freud's Alter Ego* (New York: W. W. Norton, 1983); Ernest Jones, *Free Associations: Memories of a Psycho-Analyst* (New York: Basic Books, 1959); Edward Glover, "Psychoanalysis in England," in *Psychoanalytic Pioneers*, ed. Franz Alexander, Samuel Eisenstein, and Martin Grotjahn (New York: Basic Books, 1966); and Claude Girard, "La psychanalyse en Grande-Bretagne," in *Histoire de la psychanalyse*, ed. Roland Jaccard (Paris: Hachette, 1982), 313–61.

52. See Woolf, 30 September 1925 and 27 June 1925, *Diary* 3:46, 34. In a diary entry from the period when her sister Vanessa was living with Adrian and Karin, Woolf gives a vivid sense of the proximity of her Bloomsbury friends and relatives: "I saw Nessa's new home, no. 50, inspected Pippa [Strachey]'s chaos at no. 51; & looked in upon Adrian & Karin doing biology in their dining room. Coming out we ran upon James [Strachey]—such is the rabbit warren nature of the place" (6 March 1920, *Diary* 2:23). For Woolf's distress at Adrian and Karin's separation, see 3 December 1923, *Diary* 2:277. The diaries and letters chronicle fairly frequent visits with the Stephens (individually and together) over the summer of 1925: the Woolfs spent a weekend at the Stephens' summer home in Essex in June (a few weeks before Klein's lectures), and all summer Woolf negotiated with Karin about an exchange of servants.

53. Woolf, 20 July 1925, *Diary* 3:36.

54. M. Masud R. Khan, Introduction to *Through Paediatrics to Psycho-Analysis*, by D. W. Winnicott, xiii. Khan may be deliberately echoing Ernest Jones's phrase hailing the publication of Klein's lectures. Khan's list of the significant analysts attending these lectures begins (in this order): Ernest Jones, the Stracheys, the Stephens.

55. See Woolf's letters to Harmon H. Goldstone, 19 March 1932 and 16 August 1932, *The Letters of Virginia Woolf*, ed. Nigel Nicolson and Joanne Trautman, 6 vols. (New York: Harcourt Brace Jovanovich, 1975–80), 5:36, 91. For some indications of Adrian's and Karin's informal discussions of psychoanalysis, see Woolf's notes on Adrian's account of her lack of emotion at Lady Strachey's death (9 December 1928, *Diary* 3:212); and her description of Karin's interpretation of the childhood sources of Adrian's unhappiness (24 May 1923, *Letters* 3:43;

and 12 May 1923, *Diary* 2:242). We must read between the lines of Woolf's letters to detect other informal conversations about psychoanalysis; see, for example, her remark in a letter to Roger Fry that Maynard Keynes agreed that Clive Bell's essay "Dr. Freud on Art" was cribbed from Fry's *The Artist and Psycho-Analysis* (22 September 1924, *Letters* 3:132).

56. James Strachey to Alix Strachey, 14 May 1925, *Bloomsbury/Freud,* 264.

57. Woolf, 14 May 1925, *Diary* 3:19, 21.

58. See Alix Strachey's contribution to *Recollections of Virginia Woolf,* ed. Joan Russell Noble (New York: William Morrow, 1972), 111–18. Strachey attributes this reasoning to Leonard Woolf, but presumably it was shared by Virginia.

59. The *Collected Papers* were eventually followed by the comprehensive twenty-four volumes of the *Standard Edition,* translated by James Strachey, between 1953 and 1966. For a list of the volumes of the International Psycho-Analytical Library published by the Hogarth Press, see J. Howard Woolmer, *A Checklist of the Hogarth Press, 1917–1938* (Andes, N.Y.: Woolmer and Brotherson, 1976). Brill's early translations include *Three Contributions to the Sexual Theory* (1910), *The Interpretation of Dreams* (1913), *The Psychopathology of Everyday Life* (1914), and *Totem and Taboo* (1918). For an account of the deficiencies of Brill's translations, see *Bloomsbury/Freud,* 315. The impact of the Hogarth Press edition can be gauged by the review of the first two volumes in the *Nation and Athenaeum* (17 January 1925): "It is a great satisfaction to have, for the first time, a really good translation of the long series of contributions in which Freud has gradually built up, during more than thirty years, the imposing structure of psychoanalytic theory. . . . This opportunity of closely following the historical development of Freud's experience and thought is the great service the present collection will render to serious students of psychoanalysis" (556).

60. Woolf to Marjorie Joad, 20[?] July 1924, *Letters* 3:119; see also Woolf to Vanessa Bell, 8 October 1931, *Letters* 4:387.

61. Woolf, 18 November 1924, *Diary* 2:322.

62. Woolf to Vanessa Bell, 22 May 1927, *Letters* 3:381.

63. The review, originally published in the *New English Weekly* (1914), is extensively quoted by Leonard Woolf in *Beginning Again: An Autobiography of the Years 1911 to 1918* (New York: Harcourt, Brace & World, 1963), 168.

64. *Nation and Athenaeum,* 24 October 1925, 145.

65. A. Wohlgemuth, *Nation and Athenaeum,* 22 August 1925, 619. See also the lengthy review of volumes 1 and 2 of the *Collected Papers* in the *Times Literary Supplement,* 5 February 1925, which compares Freud's mind to that which constructed the bestiaries of the Middle Ages: "It is the type of mind which, when not united with a strong critical faculty, is almost the exact opposite of the scientific mind[,] . . . an illogical, uncritical system maker" (82).

66. A. G. Tansley, *Nation and Athenaeum,* 17 January 1925, 556. That Tansley, analyst, botanist, friend of James Strachey, and author of *The New Psychology and Its Relation to Life* (London: George Allen & Unwin, 1920), was the probable source of the Tansley in *To the Lighthouse* suggests Woolf's familiarity with some of these debates.

67. Siela, *Nation and Athenaeum,* 29 August 1925, 644.

68. Philippe Mairet, "Psycho-Analysis or Psycho-Synthesis," *New Age* 38, n.s., 7–8 (5 November 1925): 7.

69. Ella Freeman Sharpe, "The Impatience of Hamlet" [1929], in *Collected Papers on Psycho-Analysis,* ed. Marjorie Brierly (New York: Brunner/Mazel, 1978), 213.

70. Glover, "Psychoanalysis in England," 535.

71. Leonard Woolf, *Downhill All the Way: An Autobiography of the Years 1919 to 1939* (New York: Harcourt Brace Jovanovich, 1967), 164. In her diary entry of 18 June 1919, Virginia Woolf describes Adrian's decision to become an analyst: "The more profound cause is, I suppose, the old question which used to weigh so heavy on Adrian, what to do?" (*Diary* 1:282).

72. Girard, "La psychanalyse en Grande-Bretagne," 333. The perspective of the British Psycho-Analytic Society is well summarized by Edward Glover: "Psycho-analysis, which seeks to penetrate the mysteries of cultural development, must become and remain a cultural as well as a therapeutic or professional pursuit" ("The Position of Psycho-Analysis in Great Britain," in *Selected Papers on Psycho-Analysis,* vol. 1 [New York: International Universities Press, 1956], 363).

73. Malinowski, *Sex and Repression in Savage Society* (1927; Chicago: University of Chicago Press, 1985), vii.

74. Girard, "La psychanalyse en Grande-Bretagne," 333.

75. Bryher [Winifred Ellerman] to Susan Stanford Friedman, 1 October 1971, quoted in Friedman, *Psyche Reborn: The Emergence of H.D.* (Bloomington: Indiana University Press, 1981), 18.

76. Woolf, "Freudian Fiction," in *Contemporary Writers* (London: Hogarth Press, 1965), 152–53, 154.

77. Freud's letter to Lytton Strachey (25 December 1928) is included as an appendix to *Bloomsbury/Freud,* 332–34.

78. Woolf, 28 November 1928, *Diary* 3:208–9. Although Woolf's criticism of *Elizabeth and Essex* was not limited to its psychoanalytic approach, I want to underscore the contrast between Freud's insistence on the text's profundity and her equally adamant insistence on its shallowness.

79. Leonard Woolf, *Downhill All the Way,* 164. Lytton Strachey's interest in Freud rivals Leonard Woolf's. The same year as Woolf's review of *The Psychopathology of Everyday Life,* and in response to same text, Strachey dramatized the operations of the Freudian unconscious in a skit he called "According to Freud" (in *The Really Interesting Question and Other Papers,* ed. Paul Levy [London: Weidenfeld & Nicholson, 1972]). Lytton was a member of the British Society for the Study of Sex Psychology, founded in 1914. In a diary entry of 21 January 1918, Virginia Woolf recounts his description of a meeting: "Incest between parent & child when they are both unconscious of it, was their main theme, derived from Freud. I think of becoming a member" (*Diary* 1:110).

80. Woolf to Roger Fry, 22 September 1924, *Letters* 3:132.

81. See Clive Bell, "Dr. Freud on Art," *Nation and Athenaeum,* 6 September 1924, 690–91; and the responses in the issues of 20 and 27 September. Herbert Read's review of Roger Fry's essay demonstrates the dismay that even Freudian art critics felt about Freud's conceptualization of art. See Read, review of *The Artist and Psycho-Analysis,* by Fry, *Criterion* 3, no. 11 (April 1925): 471–72.

82. Woolf to Molly McCarthy, 2 October 1924, *Letters* 3:134–35.

83. Freud, "The Sense of Symptoms," in *Introductory Lectures on Psycho-Analysis* [1916–17], *SE* 16:264. Woolf, or course, had personal reasons for feeling threatened by the disclosure of a sexless marriage and the story of an unsuccessful wedding night. "Why do you think people make such a fuss about marriage and copulation? . . . [C]ertainly I find the climax immensely exaggerated," she wrote to Ka Cox shortly after her own wedding night (4 September 1912, *Letters* 2:6). But protest against Freud's emphasis on sexuality was a pervasive feature of the British public's response to psychoanalysis. "Antipathy to the Freudian method has been largely roused by the exclusively sexual origin that he posits for neurosis," Woolf's friend Jane Harrison notes in a review in the *Nation and Athenaeum* (3 May 1924, 147).

84. Ella Freeman Sharpe, "Variations of Technique in Different Neuroses," in *Collected Essays*, 95; and see Joanna Field [Marion Milner], *A Life of One's Own* (London: Chatto & Windus, 1936; Los Angeles: J. P. Tarcher, 1981).

85. Woolf, 29 January 1939, *Diary* 5:202. It is, of course, important to take into account the difference in age between Klein (sixty-one) and Freud (eighty-three, and dying).

86. Woolf, 11 March 1939, *Diary* 5:208.

87. Woolf, 16 March 1939, *Diary* 5:209.

88. For accounts of the Controversial Discussions, which institutionalized the disagreements between the Kleinians and the (Anna) Freudians, see Phyllis Grosskurth, *Melanie Klein*, 281–362; Riccardo Steiner, "Some Thoughts about Tradition and Change Arising from an Examination of the British Psycho-Analytical Society's Controversial Discussions (1943–44)" (see n. 33 above); and Pearl H. M. King, "The Life and Work of Melanie Klein in the British Psycho-Analytical Society" (see n. 35 above).

89. See Ernest Jones, Preface to *Psychoanalysis and Medicine: A Study of the Wish to Fall Ill*, by Karin Stephen (Cambridge: Cambridge University Press, 1933).

90. Karin Stephen, "On Human Misery" (unpublished manuscript), 82, 96.

91. See n. 69 above.

92. Freud to Sándor Ferenczi, 30 November 1911, quoted in Ernest Jones, *The Life and Work of Sigmund Freud*, 3 vols. (New York: Basic Books, 1953–57), 2:352. There are, of course, manifold discrepancies between the orientation of anthropology and that of psychoanalysis. Even Jones concedes that "anthropologists united in discounting [Freud's] conclusions and in maintaining that he had misunderstood the evidence" (360). For some of the anthropological criticisms of *Totem and Taboo*, see A. L. Kroeber, "*Totem and Taboo:* An Ethnologic Psychoanalysis," *American Anthropologist*, n.s., 22 (1920): 48–55; and Clyde K. Kluckhohn, "The Impact of Freud on Anthropology," in *Freud and Contemporary Culture*, ed. Iago Galdston (New York: International Universities Press, 1957), 66–72.

93. Freud, *Totem and Taboo*, *SE* 13:156, 145; hereafter cited, by page number only, in the text.

94. The first three sections of the book, Freud wrote to Ferenczi on 8 May

1913, are "the thicket behind which the Princess sleeps. Later on you will get the interesting part, which is also a disturbing one" (quoted in Jones, *Life* 2:354).

95. The passage cited identically in *Primal Law* and *Totem and Taboo* is Freud's only reference to Darwin in *Totem and Taboo*. In *Freud, Biologist of the Mind: Beyond the Psychoanalytic Legacy* (New York: Basic Books, 1979), the most extensive analysis of Darwin's influence on Freud, Frank Sulloway agrees that Atkinson was Freud's primary source for the narrative of patricide in the primal horde.

96. Andrew Lang, *Social Origins* and J. J. Atkinson, *Primal Law* (London: Longmans, Green, and Co., 1903), 228, 231. Although Atkinson appears radical vis-à-vis Freud's erasure of the mother from the origins of morality, he clearly inherits the rhetoric of domestic ideology, contrasting the harmonious effects of maternal love to nature rather than to the marketplace and granting these effects a diachronic rather than synchronic role. Note, for example, the similarity between Atkinson's description of "the sons whose parricidal hands were so soon again clenched in fratridical strife" (228) and Sarah Stickney Ellis's account of the world of commerce: "[E]very man's hand against his brother, and each struggling to exalt himself, not merely by trampling upon his fallen foe, but by usurping the place of his weaker brother" (*Women of England*, quoted in Catherine Gallagher, *The Industrial Reformation of English Fiction, 1832–1867* [Chicago: University of Chicago Press, 1985], 116). The influence of domestic ideology on early twentieth-century social anthropology differentiates the anthropological representation of the mother from the far less sentimental image posited by Klein.

97. J. G. Frazer, *Totemism and Exogamy: A Treatise on Certain Early Forms of Superstition and Society*, 4 vols. (London: Macmillan, 1910) 4:57, 61. Freud dismisses the theory on the grounds that the Aruntas are too sophisticated to cast light on the origins of totemism. Frazer's final decision that totemism evolved independently of exogamy was also antithetical to Freud's project of integrating these phenomena.

98. Sándor Ferenczi, "A Little Chanticleer," in *Sex in Psychoanalysis*, trans. Ernest Jones (Boston: Richard G. Badger, 1916), 249. Ferenczi, Klein's first analyst, is more equivocal about his interpretation than is Freud; for example, he calls Arpad's desires "cannibalistic" and claims that their object is "probably" the father. My claims about the repression of eating in *Totem and Taboo* are deeply indebted to an unpublished paper by Kim Chernin.

99. William Robertson Smith, *Lectures on the Religion of the Semites*, ed. Stanley A. Cook (1889; New York: Macmillan, 1927), 274; emphasis added.

100. Malinowski, *Sex and Repression in Savage Society*, 9–10, 109–10. See also Malinowski, *The Father in Primitive Psychology* (New York: W. W. Norton, 1927); and his tribute to Frazer in his review of *Totemica: A Supplement to "Totemism and Exogamy,"* in *Nature* (19 March 1938), reprinted in Malinowski, *Sex, Culture, and Myth* (New York: Harcourt, Brace & World, 1962), 277–82. In *Primitive Paternity: The Myth of Supernatural Birth in Relation to the History of the Family* (London: David Nott, 1909), Edwin Sidney Hartland offers further examples of the pervasive belief in maternal procreation.

101. Robert Briffault, *The Mothers: The Matriarchal Theory of Social Origins* (1927; New York: Macmillan, 1931), 23. For a modern feminist account of evolution inspired primarily by Briffault, see Evelyn Reed, *Woman's Evolution* (New

York: Pathfinder Press, 1975). Briffault has little credibility within anthropology, however. "Yet another monument of brilliantly speculative erroneousness" is Malinowski's response to *The Mothers* in "Must Kinship Be Dehumanized?" *Man* 30, no.2 (February 1930): 19–29. Briffault, on the other hand, complains that Malinowski is too faithful to Freud.

102. Sandra M. Gilbert, "Potent Griselda: 'The Ladybird' and the Great Mother," in *D. H. Lawrence: A Centenary Consideration,* ed. Peter Balbert and Phillip L. Marcus (Ithaca, N.Y.: Cornell University Press, 1985), 132.

103. Ernest Jones, "Mother-Right and the Sexual Ignorance of Savages," 170 (see n. 12 above). After carefully distinguishing among matriarchy, matrilineage, and matrilocality—terms critically differentiated within anthropology—and arguing that evidence supports only the claims for matrilineage, Jones (as his title indicates) uses the terms interchangeably. James Strachey describes this meeting of the British Psycho-Analytical Society in his letter to Alix Strachey, 20 November 1924, in *Bloomsbury/Freud,* 121.

104. Jones, "Mother-Right and the Sexual Ignorance of Savages," 145. The reference to Bachofen is a symbolic concession, for Bachofen's theory of matriarchal social origins had little influence on the British anthropological tradition from which Freud and Jones both drew and which had its own proponents of matriarchy. Bachofen had a greater impact on literary figures than on social scientists. For his role in the "erotic movement" that included Frieda and D. H. Lawrence, see Martin Green, *The Von Richtofen Sisters: The Triumphant and the Tragic Modes of Life* (New York: Basic Books, 1974). Joseph Campbell's Introduction to *Myth, Religion, and Mother Right,* by J. J. Bachofen (trans. Ralph Manheim [1861; Princeton, N.J.: Princeton University Press, 1973], xxv–lvi), traces Bachofen's influence on matriarchalists on Germany.

105. Ernest Jones, "Psycho-Analysis and Anthropology," in *Essays in Applied Psycho-Analysis* 2:137; emphasis added.

106. Woolf, Holograph Reading Notes, vol. 21, Berg Collection, New York Public Library. In *Virginia Woolf's Reading Notebooks* ([Princeton, N.J.: Princeton University Press, 1983], 116), Brenda R. Silver reproduces the other notes on *Group Psychology* that indicate Woolf's interest in gender and mass psychology in the political movements of the twentieth century.

107. Jane Harrison's status as a representative "liberal-minded" reader of psychoanalysis is suggested by Alix Strachey's marginal note on the word *Bestatigung* in the proofs of Freud's case history of Little Hans (which the Stracheys were translating): "This 'confirmation' of the interpretation, it's too glaring. What on earth can the Prof. mean by it? It'll simply throw the liberalminded reader (Jane—Gilbert Murray, etc.)—into FITS" (*Bloomsbury/Freud,* 48). Woolf knew and admired Harrison for over a decade and had probably been acquainted with her anthropological work since the turn of the century. In "Apollo and the Erinyes in the *Electra* of Sophocles" (*Classical Review* 16 [May 1902]: 195–200) Janet Case, who became Woolf's Greek tutor (and lifelong friend) in 1901, draws heavily from Harrison's work on the evolution of religious cults at Delphi. For Harrison's enormous intellectual impact on Woolf, see Jane Marcus, *Virginia Woolf and the Languages of the Patriarchy* (Bloomington: Indiana University Press, 1987).

108. Jane Ellen Harrison, *Reminiscences of a Student's Life* (London: Hogarth Press, 1925), 81–82.

109. "And now you must pull yourself together, entertain the [Gilbert?] Murrays and bury Jane," Woolf wrote in October 1928 to Pernel Strachey, sister of James and Lytton, principal of Newnham College, and Woolf's hostess during the first of the lectures that would become *A Room of One's Own* (25 October 1928, *Letters* 3:551). Harrison presides over *Room's* pastoral vision of Fernham (Newnham), where the October day inexplicably gives way to a scene of springtime beauty that commemorates the moment before her death.

110. Woolf, 12 September 1921, *Diary* 2:136; Woolf to Janet Case, 2 September 1921, *Letters* 2:482.

111. Jane Harrison, *Epilegomena to the Study of Greek Religion* (1921; New York: University Books, 1962), xxv–xxvi.

112. Malinowski, *Sex and Repression in Savage Society,* 6. The second half of the text focuses on *Totem and Taboo,* which Malinowski dismisses primarily for its logical inconsistencies. The most disturbing aspect of Malinowski's argument, as Ernest Jones's critique of it in "Mother-Right and the Sexual Ignorance of Savages" reveals, was his representation of the father's contingency.

113. Malinowski, Preface to *Hunger and Work in a Savage Tribe: A Functional Study of Nutrition among the Southern Bantu,* by Audrey I. Richards (London: G. Routledge and Sons, 1932; Glencoe, Ill.: Free Press, 1948), xv, xi, x. Although I am concerned with the psychological arguments of these texts, it is important to note that these are embedded in the larger project of systematic synchronic interpretation endorsed by the functionalist school which Malinowski and Boas initiated.

114. Richards, *Hunger and Work,* 1.

115. Ibid., 189.

Chapter 2

1. Feminist literary criticism, Elaine Showalter claims in one of the founding essays in the field, presents us with a "radical alteration of our vision, a demand that we see meaning in what has previously been empty space. The orthodox plot recedes, and another plot, hitherto submerged in the anonymity of the background, stands out in bold relief like a thumbprint" ("Literary Criticism," *Signs* 1, no. 2 [Winter 1975]: 435). The authoritative discussion of the palimpsestic character of women's texts is Sandra M. Gilbert and Susan Gubar, *The Madwoman in the Attic: The Woman Writer and the Nineteenth-Century Literary Imagination* (New Haven, Conn.: Yale University Press, 1979). The tension between a dominant romantic plot and a submerged mother-daughter plot has become a recent focus of feminist criticism. See, for an outstanding example, Marianne Hirsch, "A Mother's Discourse: Incorporation and Repetition in *La Princesse de Cleves,*" *Yale French Studies* 62 (1981): 67–87.

2. Virginia Woolf, *Mrs. Dalloway* (New York: Harcourt, Brace & World, 1925), 51, 52–53; hereafter cited in the text. On the psychological continuity of lesbian love and the mother-daughter bond, see Adrienne Rich, *Of Woman Born: Motherhood as Experience and Institution* (New York: W. W. Norton, 1976); Ca-

tharine R. Stimpson, "Zero Degree Deviancy: The Lesbian Novel in English," *Critical Inquiry* 8, no. 2 (Winter 1981): 363–79; and Helene Deutsch, "Female Homosexuality," in *The Psycho-Analytic Reader: An Anthology of Essential Papers with Critical Introductions,* ed. Robert Fliess (New York: International Universities Press, 1948), 208–30.

3. "Female Sexuality," *The Standard Edition of the Complete Psychological Works of Sigmund Freud,* trans. and ed. James Strachey, 24 vols. (London: Hogarth Press, 1953–66; New York: Macmillan, 1953–74), 21:229; hereafter the *Standard Edition* will be cited as *SE.*

4. Woolf's subversive account of the force required to break the daughter's attachment to her mother anticipates Adrienne Rich's argument about the origins of female heterosexuality. See "Compulsory Heterosexuality and Lesbian Existence," *Signs* 5, no. 4 (Summer 1980): 631–60.

5. For a reading of this scene as part of a pattern of interruption in *Mrs. Dalloway,* see Emily Jensen, "Clarissa Dalloway's Respectable Suicide," in *Virginia Woolf: A Feminist Slant,* ed. Jane Marcus (Lincoln: University of Nebraska Press, 1983), 162–79. In "Something Central Which Permeated: Virginia Woolf and *Mrs. Dalloway*" in *The Fields of Light: An Experiment in Critical Reading* [New York: Oxford University Press, 1951], 123–37), Reuben Brower argues that the tension between interruption and continuity generates the metaphorical patterns that unify *Mrs. Dalloway,* but he does not find that these patterns have any particular psychological basis, for he excludes Sally Seton from his reading of the novel. For a reading of the positive force of interruption in Woolf's texts, see Lucio P. Ruotolo, *The Interrupted Moment: A View of Virginia Woolf's Novels* (Stanford, Calif.: Stanford University Press, 1986).

6. Peter's question—"Star-gazing?"—may reinforce his role in the implied sexual drama. According to W. H. Auden, "star-gazer" is a name for the male genitals (*A Certain World: A Commonplace Book* [New York: Viking Press, 1970], 269), an allusion underscored by Peter's own name. Peter's interruption echoes his earlier interruption of Clarissa's terrace reverie, his statement that he "prefer[s] men to cauliflowers," a comment which shifts in Clarissa's reverie to "a few sayings like this about cabbages" (3–4). Auden lists "cabbage" as a name for the female genitals. I am grateful to James Chandler for bringing Auden's text to my attention.

7. Woolf was reading *The Fox* in 1923 as she was beginning work on *Mrs. Dalloway.* For her reading notes on the story, see *Virginia Woolf's Reading Notebooks,* ed. Brenda R. Silver (Princeton, N.J.: Princeton University Press, 1983), chapter 25, B.11.

8. Woolf, "Mrs. Dalloway in Bond Street," in *Mrs. Dalloway's Party,* ed. Stella McNichol (New York: Harcourt Brace Jovanovich, 1975), 27.

9. Elizabeth Janeway suggests the resonance of this name in an essay entitled "Who Is Sylvia? On the Loss of Sexual Paradigms," *Signs* 5, no. 4 (Summer 1980): 573–89. She concludes the essay by asking, "Who is Sylvia, whose name carries an edge of wildness and a hint of unexplored memory? We do not know, but we will surely recognize her when she comes." In *Jacob's Room,* the novel immediately preceding *Mrs. Dalloway,* a character sings: "Who is Sylvia? what is she? / That all our swains commend her?" ([New York: Harcourt, Brace & World, 1922], 88).

10. The situations in these Shakespearean works are remarkably similar: in

both, men dispute each other's claims to possess the most chaste and beautiful of women, the dispute prompts one man to observe and/or test the virtue of the other's wife, and this encounter culminates in the real or pretended rape of the woman and eventually her actual or illusory death. Shakespeare himself calls attention to these parallels: Jachimo, the villain in *Cymbeline,* specifically compares himself to the rapist in *The Rape of Lucrece* (2.2.12–14) and notes that Imogen has been reading the story of Philomela's rape, the tale embroidered in the tapestry described in detail in *The Rape of Lucrece.* The allusions to Othello's passion for Desdemona reinforce the pattern of women sacrificed to male rivalry.

11. Freud, "Female Sexuality," *SE* 21:229–30; "Femininity," *SE* 22:118. Freud's account of female sexuality should be situated in the discussions pervading the psychoanalytic community. For a description of these controversies, see Zenia Odes Fliegel, "Feminine Psychosexual Development in Freudian Theory: A Historical Reconstruction," *Psychoanalytic Quarterly* 42, no. 3 (1973): 385–408.

12. Freud, "Femininity," *SE* 22:118.

13. Ibid., 117.

14. Ibid., 126; "Female Sexuality," *SE* 21:229–30.

15. Freud, "Female Sexuality," SE 21:229–30.

16. For other discussions of the conflation of these routes, see Elizabeth Janeway, "On 'Female Sexuality,'" in *Women and Analysis: Dialogues on Psychoanalytic Views of Femininity,* ed. Jean Strouse (New York: Grossman Publishers, 1974), 60; and Sarah Kofman, "The Narcissistic Woman: Freud and Girard," *Diacritics* 10, no. 3 (Fall 1980): 45.

17. Freud, "Femininity," *SE* 22:128.

18. Ibid., 134–35.

19. For a discussion of the role of the *Memoirs,* see Phyllis Rose, *Woman of Letters: A Life of Virginia Woolf* (New York: Oxford University Press, 1978), 144.

20. In her Introduction to the Modern Library edition of *Mrs. Dalloway* (New York: Random House, 1928), Woolf explicitly presents Septimus as Clarissa's double: "In the first version Septimus, who later is intended to be her double, had no existence. . . . Mrs. Dalloway was originally to kill herself or perhaps merely to die at the end of the party" (vi). Almost every critical study of *Mrs. Dalloway* discusses the relation of Clarissa and Septimus as doubles. For some examples, see Alex Page, "A Dangerous Day: Mrs. Dalloway Discovers Her Double," *Modern Fiction Studies* 7, no. 2 (Summer 1961): 115–24; Nancy Topping Bazin, *Virginia Woolf and the Androgynous Vision* (New Brunswick, N.J.: Rutgers University Press, 1973), 102–23; and Barbara Hill Rigney, *Madness and Sexual Politics in the Feminist Novel* (Madison: University of Wisconsin Press, 1978), 39–64.

21. See, for example, J. Hillis Miller, "Virginia Woolf's All Soul's Day: The Omniscient Narrator in *Mrs. Dalloway,*" in *The Shaken Realist: Essays in Modern Literature in Honor of Frederick J. Hoffman,* ed. Melvin J. Friedman and John Vickery (Baton Rouge: Louisiana State University Press, 1970), 100–127; and Maria DiBattista, *Virginia Woolf's Major Novels: The Fables of Anon* (New Haven, Conn.: Yale University Press, 1980), 22–63.

22. Brower, "Something Central Which Permeated," 135.

Chapter 3

1. Virginia Woolf, 18 June 1923, entry in holograph notebook dated variously from 9 November 1922 to 2 August 1923; quoted in Charles G. Hoffmann, "From Short Story to Novel: The Manuscript Revisions of Virginia Woolf's *Mrs. Dalloway*," *Modern Fiction Studies* 14, no. 2 (Summer 1968): 183.

2. 20 July 1925, *The Diary of Virginia Woolf,* ed. Anne Olivier Bell, 5 vols. (New York: Harcourt Brace Jovanovich, 1977–84), 3:36.

3. Woolf, "A Sketch of the Past," in *Moments of Being: Unpublished Autobiographical Writings,* ed. Jeanne Schulkind (New York: Harcourt Brace Jovanovich, 1985), 81.

4. *To the Lighthouse* is routinely represented as Woolf's most overtly psychoanalytic text, but critics have usually insisted on explicating specific psychoanalytic discourses rather than exploring the novel's psychoanalytic heterogeneity. See, for example, Helen Storm Corsa, "*To the Lighthouse:* Death, Mourning, and Transfiguration," *Literature and Psychology* 21 (November 1971): 115–32; Ernest S. Wolf and Ina Wolf, "'We Perished, Each Alone': A Psychoanalytic Commentary on Virginia Woolf's *To the Lighthouse*," *International Review of Psycho-Analysis* 6 (1979): 37–47; and Jane Lilienfeld, "'The Deceptiveness of Beauty': Mother Love and Mother Hate in *To the Lighthouse*," *Twentieth Century Literature* 23, no. 3 (October 1977): 345–76. For some readings that highlight the tensions between father-based and mother-based psychoanalytic discourses, see Marianne Hirsch's chapter on Woolf and Colette in *Unspeakable Plots: Mothers, Daughters, and Narrative* (Bloomington: Indiana University Press, 1989), and Mary Jacobus, "'The Third Stroke': Reading Woolf with Freud," in *Grafts: Feminist Cultural Criticism,* ed. Susan Sheridan (London: Verso, 1988), 93–110.

5. Woolf, *To the Lighthouse* (New York: Harcourt, Brace & World, 1927), 270, 278; hereafter cited in the text.

6. For some accounts of Lacan's reading of Freud, see Anika Lemaire, *Jacques Lacan,* trans. David Macey (London: Routledge & Kegan Paul, 1977); *Interpreting Lacan,* ed. Joseph H. Smith and William Kerrigan (New Haven, Conn.: Yale University Press, 1983); Jane Gallop, *Reading Lacan* (Ithaca, N.Y.: Cornell University Press, 1985); and Juliet Flower MacCannell, *Figuring Lacan: Criticism and the Cultural Unconscious* (Lincoln: University of Nebraska Press, 1986). As Margaret Homans points out, "Jacques Lacan's account of language . . . provides the most explicit and compelling contemporary formulation of a myth that was, in its largest outlines, already at the heart of nineteenth-century European literature culture. . . . The Lacanian view of language is not a universal truth, but the psycholinguistic retelling of a myth to which our culture has long subscribed" (*Bearing the Word: Language and Female Experience in Nineteenth-Century Women's Writing* [Chicago: University of Chicago Press, 1986], 5–6).

7. As the youngest daughter in the Ramsay family, Cam occupies the same position as Woolf in the Stephen family. Moreover, Cam's full name, Camilla, is the name of Virginia Woolf's counterpart in Leonard Woolf's novel, *The Wise Virgins: A Story of Words, Opinions, and a Few Emotions* (London: Edward Arnold, 1914). Camilla is also the name of a legendary maiden in the *Aeneid* (7.803; 11.539–828). A huntress brought up by her father—who, to protect her from their tribal

enemies, tied her to a javelin, dedicated her to Diana, and threw her across the Amasenus river—she has a clear affiliation with patrilineage. This affiliation, and its discontents, are also suggested by the nickname of Woolf's character, the name of the river identified with the university attended by generations of Stephen males. I am grateful to Jane Marcus for pointing these associations out to me. For a radically different reading of Cam as Woolf's vehicle for a presymbolic language "based as far as possible on the continued presence of the mother," see Homans, *Bearing the Word*, 16–20; I locate this "presymbolic language," by contrast, in Lily Briscoe's use of paint.

Lily's role as Woolf's aesthetic counterpart and as Mrs. Ramsay's "daughter" has become a critical commonplace; for some especially lucid accounts, see Lilienfeld, "'The Deceptiveness of Beauty'"; Phyllis Rose, *Woman of Letters: A Life of Virginia Woolf* (New York: Oxford University Press, 1978), 153–73; Joan Lidoff, "Virginia Woolf's Feminine Sentence: The Mother-Daughter World of *To the Lighthouse*," *Literature and Psychology* 32, no. 3 (1986): 43–59; and Ellen Bayuk Rosenman, *The Invisible Presence: Virginia Woolf and the Mother-Daughter Relationship* (Baton Rouge: Louisiana State University Press, 1986), 93–113.

8. See, for example, Maria DiBattista's claim that Mr. Ramsay is a "hero of thought" whose "necessary tyranny" enables a comic resolution to the novel by separating its "Oedipal origin from its psychological end" in "freedom and reality" *(Virginia Woolf's Major Novels: The Fables of Anon* [New Haven, Conn.: Yale University Press, 1980], 83–84, 88, 106). Avrom Fleishman argues that "there is a comic resolution to this [father-son] conflict: as the group finally reaches the Lighthouse, the father approves the son's coming of age . . . and the son comes to recognize the stark truths implicit in the more experienced generation's dour attitude to life" *(Virginia Woolf: A Critical Reading* [Baltimore: Johns Hopkins University Press, 1975], 121).

9. S. P. Rosenbaum analyzes Woolf's adaptation of G. E. Moore's philosophy in "The Philosophical Realism of Virginia Woolf," in *English Literature and British Philosophy*, ed. S. P. Rosenbaum (Chicago: University of Chicago Press, 1971), 316–56.

10. William Browne's "Siren Song" (quoted in DiBattista, *Virginia Woolf's Major Novels*, 82–83) in full is:

> Steer hither, steer your winged pines,
>   All beaten mariners!
> Here lie Love's undiscovered mines,
>   A prey to passengers;
> Perfumes far sweeter than the best
> Which makes the Phoenix's urn and nest.
>   Fear not your ships,
> Nor any to oppose you save our lips
>   But come on shore
> Where no joy dies till love hath gotten more.
> For swelling waves, our panting breasts
>   Where never storm arise,

Exchange; and be awhile our guests:
    For stars, gaze on our eyes.
The compass Love shall hourly sing,
As he goes about the ring,
    We will not miss
To tell each point he nameth with a kiss.
    Then come on shore,
Where no joy dies till love hath gotten more.

DiBattista reads the poem in relation to Mr. Ramsay rather than to James.

In "Conclusions: Masculinity in Men," the final chapter of *Sex and Gender,* vol. 2 (New York: Jason Aronson, 1976), Robert J. Stoller states: "Deep within, unless well protected by good parental care, the pull toward merging again into mother's femaleness terrifies and enthralls men: it is the Siren's Song" (296).

11. Fleishman argues that the sonnet derives "from the Neoplatonic *topos* of the natural object as a 'shadow' of the ideal and ultimately real" and plays into the novel's concern with "visible substitutes" for Mrs. Ramsay as the beloved (*Virginia Woolf,* 128). DiBattista similarly reads the sonnet as foretelling the death of Mrs. Ramsay as the novel's "original figure of delight" (*Virginia Woolf's Major Novels,* 93). Neither extends this presaging of Mrs. Ramsay's loss to the son who recalls it—not as death but as repression—at the moment he succumbs to the paternal prohibition that marks his accession to the symbolic.

12. The attitude of the male philosophers in Woolf's text is closely echoed by Freud, who argues in *Civilization and Its Discontents* that "love comes into opposition to the interests of civilization" and that "women soon come into opposition to civilization and display their retarding and restraining influence. . . . Women represent the interests of the family and of sexual life. The work of civilization has become increasingly the business of men" (*The Standard Edition of the Complete Psychological Works of Sigmund Freud,* trans. and ed. James Strachey, 24 vols. [London: Hogarth Press, 1953–66; New York: Macmillan, 1953–74], 21:103; hereafter the *Standard Edition* will be cited as *SE*).

13. For a similar, but far more extensive, analysis of the discourse of philosophy (and of Platonic philosophy in particular) as an expression of masculine subjectivity, see Jane Flax, "Political Philosophy and the Patriarchal Unconscious: A Psychoanalytic Perspective on Epistemology and Metaphysics," in *Discovering Reality: Feminist Perspectives on Epistemology, Metaphysics, Methodology, and the Philosophy of Science,* ed. Sandra Harding and Merrill B. Hintikka (Boston: D. Reidel Publishing Co., 1983), 245–81. In *Bearing the Word,* Margaret Homans sees Mr. Ramsay's quest as paradigmatic of Western metaphysics, which "requires that the mother remain perpetually out of reach in order for Mr. Ramsay and his kind to speculate forever on how to reach her, or to replace her with their own abstractions" (2).

14. We see these fish only through Cam's eyes. Even the bracketed section 6, which reports from an omniscient perspective the mutilation of a fish, interrupts her train of thought: "They have no suffering there, she thought" ends section 4; "They don't feel a thing there, Cam thought" opens section 8. The fact that in Woolf's original plan it is Mr. Ramsay who fishes underlines the helpless

daughter's identification with them. For a different reading of the mutilated fish, see John Burt, "Irreconcilable Habits of Thought in *A Room of One's Own* and *To the Lighthouse*," *ELH* 49, no. 3 (Fall 1982): 889–905.

15. On the distinctive problems of this (inevitable) collusion, generated by women's "(ambiguously) non-hegemonic" relation to the dominant discourse, see Margaret Homans, "'Her Very Own Howl': The Ambiguities of Representation in Recent Women's Fiction," *Signs* 9, no. 2 (Winter 1983): 186–205; and Rachel Blau DuPlessis and Members of Workshop 9, "For the Etruscans: Sexual Difference and Artistic Production—The Debate over a Female Aesthetic," in *The Future of Difference*, ed. Hester Eisenstein and Alice Jardine (Boston: G. K. Hall & Co., 1980), 128–156. On the question of Woolf's own evasion of anger in her literary theory and practice, see Elaine Showalter, "Virginia Woolf and the Flight into Androgyny," in *A Literature of Their Own: British Women Novelists from Brontë to Lessing* (Princeton, N.J.: Princeton University Press, 1977), 263–97. Woolf's account in "A Sketch of the Past" of her acquiescence to Thoby's aggressiveness provides an explicit autobiographical parallel to Cam's relationship to James (71).

16. Woolf's account of Cam's relationship to Mr. Ramsay has deeply autobiographical roots. In *Virginia Woolf: A Biography* (New York: Harcourt Brace Jovanovich, 1972), Quentin Bell recounts the famous anecdote about the young Virginia's alleged preference for her father (26). In "Virginia Woolf and Leslie Stephen: History and Literary Revolution" (*PMLA* 96, no. 3 [May 1981]: 351–62), Katherine C. Hill discusses Sir Leslie's appointment of Virginia as his literary heir and his recommendation that she study *history* and *biography*. Some direct lines of descent are apparent in Woolf's essay "Hours in a Library," titled after her father's book, and in "Leslie Stephen" (in *The Captain's Death Bed and Other Essays* [New York: Harcourt, Brace & World, 1950]), which recounts Sir Leslie's unusual decision to allow "a girl of fifteen the free run of a large and quite unexpurgated library" (74)—precisely Cam's experience. Cam's relationship to Mr. Ramsay also reveals the more oppressive side of Sir Leslie's relation to his daughter, the side commemorated in Woolf's famous diary entry: "Father's birthday. He would have been . . . 96, yes, today; & could have been 96, like other people one has known; but mercifully was not. His life would have entirely ended mine. What would have happened? No writing, no books;—inconceivable" (28 November 1928, *Diary* 3:208). For an illuminating account of the autobiographical sources of the father-daughter relationship in *To the Lighthouse*, see Louise A. DeSalvo, "1897: Virginia Woolf at Fifteen," in *Virginia Woolf: A Feminist Slant*, ed. Jane Marcus (Lincoln: University of Nebraska Press, 1983), 78–108.

17. In *A Room of One's Own*, Woolf explains that "mirrors are essential to all violent and heroic action. That is why Napoleon and Mussolini both insist so emphatically upon the inferiority of women, for if they were not inferior, they would cease to enlarge" [New York: Harcourt, Brace & World, 1929], 36). By *The Years*, "the character of Napoleon" has evolved into "the psychology of great men," exemplified explicitly by Napoleon, that obstructs the knowledge of "ourselves, ordinary people" (in this context, women, homosexuals, foreigners), which would enable us to make "laws and religions that fit"—in contrast, presumably, to such

NOTES • CHAPTER THREE

homogenizing codes as the tablets of eternal wisdom transmitted from father to son ([New York: Harcourt, Brace & World, 1937], 281–82).

18. In the holograph version of the novel, a Mrs. McLeod is visiting the cook when Cam brings Mrs. Ramsay's message to her. Cam describes Mrs. McLeod, who has come to get blankets for her dying mother, as "a very old woman . . . in the kitchen who wore bugles." That between the holograph and the printed versions of the text Woolf eliminated Mrs. McLeod's name and changed her characteristic traits from bugles and blankets to red cheeks and soup suggests an intention to point to her identity with Mrs. McNab (Woolf, *To the Lighthouse: The Original Holograph Draft,* transcribed and ed. Susan Dick [Toronto: University of Toronto Press, 1982; London: Hogarth Press, 1983], 94).

19. In both the holograph version of "Time Passes" and the French translation published in *Commerce* in the winter of 1926, Mrs. McNab clearly plays a heroic role as a primitive, enduring, female life force analogous to the rusty pump in *Mrs. Dalloway.* For a study of Woolf's "metaphor of the artist as charwoman to the world," see Jane Marcus, "*The Years* as Greek Drama, Domestic Novel, and Götterdämmerung," *Bulletin of the New York Public Library* 80, no. 2 (Winter 1977): 276–301.

20. "It is useless to go to the great men writers for help, however much one may go to them for pleasure," Woolf admonishes in *A Room of One's Own* (79).

21. Leon Edel, *Bloomsbury: A House of Lions* (New York: Avon Books, 1979), 90.

22. Cam's position as a fulcrum between two men is underscored by one resonance of her name: "a curved wedge movable about an axis and used for forcing or clamping two pieces together" (*Webster's Third New International Dictionary*). I am grateful to Judith Kegan Gardiner for bringing this definition to my attention. For theorizations of the cultural positioning of women "between men," see Luce Irigaray, *This Sex Which Is Not One,* trans. Catherine Porter with Carolyn Burke (Ithaca, N.Y.: Cornell University Press, 1985); and Eve Kosofsky Sedgwick, *Between Men: English Literature and Male Homosocial Desire* (New York: Columbia University Press, 1985).

23. As an account of women's silencing, the scene on the boat recurs in diverse guises throughout Woolf's corpus. For a reading of the Philomel and Procne myth as Woolf's primary vehicle for depicting the rape of the female tongue, see Jane Marcus, *Virginia Woolf and the Languages of Patriarchy* (Bloomington: Indiana University Press, 1987), chaps. 4 and 7; and Patricia Kleindienst Joplin, "The Voice of the Shuttle is Ours," *Stanford Literary Review* 1, no.1 (January 1984): 175–86.

24. Cam briefly revives her mother's voice in section 12 when, drifting off to sleep, she reproduces the images Mrs. Ramsay chanted when she put Cam to bed at the end of "The Window," the scene on which Margaret Homans bases her claim for Cam's presymbolic relation to her mother. But this momentary reversion to the language of the mother is dispelled by Mr. Ramsay's sudden exclamation: "Come now," which awakens Cam to a sense of "extraordinary adventure" under the leadership of her father (303).

25. This is the paradigmatic nineteenth-century story that Sandra M. Gilbert and Susan Gubar document in *The Madwoman in the Attic: The Woman*

Writer and the Nineteenth-Century Literary Imagination (New Haven, Conn.: Yale University Press, 1979).

Chapter 4

1. 30 July 1925, *The Diary of Virginia Woolf,* ed. Anne Olivier Bell, 5 vols. (New York: Harcourt Brace Jovanovich, 1977–84), 3:37.

2. Virginia Woolf, *To the Lighthouse: The Original Holograph Draft,* transcribed and ed. Susan Dick (Toronto: University of Toronto Press, 1982; London: Hogarth Press, 1983), 26. The holograph manuscript offers an illuminating insight into Woolf's transformation of the artist figure from Sophie Briscoe, a fifty-five-year-old landscape painter who has no particular relation to Mrs. Ramsay (who is her junior), into the thirty-three-year-old Lily, whose task of representing Mrs. Ramsay parallels Woolf's and reaches completion when Lily and Woolf are the same age. Absent from the early plans for the novel, Lily gains definition in conjunction with Woolf's shift of focus from the father to the mother.

3. Woolf, *To the Lighthouse* (New York: Harcourt, Brace & World, 1927), 266; hereafter cited in the text.

4. "A Sketch of the Past" makes clear the autobiographical basis for Woolf's portrayal of Mrs. Ramsay's unavailability; see especially Woolf's question: "Can I remember ever being alone with her [Julia Stephen] for more than a few minutes? Someone was always interrupting" (*Moments of Being: Unpublished Autobiographical Writings,* ed. Jeanne Schulkind [New York: Harcourt Brace Jovanovich, 1985], 83). See Ellen Bayuk Rosenman, *The Invisible Presence: Virginia Woolf and the Mother-Daughter Relationship* (Baton Rouge: Louisiana State University Press, 1986); and Shirley Panken, *Virginia Woolf and the "Lust of Creation": A Psychoanalytic Exploration* (Albany: State University of New York Press, 1987) for accounts of Woolf's thwarted longing for maternal nurture.

5. For an elegant reading of the use of spatial relations to represent early memories in "A Sketch of the Past," see Susan Merrill Squier, *Virginia Woolf and London: The Sexual Politics of the City* (Chapel Hill: University of North Carolina Press, 1985), chap. 2.

6. Literature, Woolf claimed in 1925, is "now undoubtedly . . . under the dominion of painting" (quoted in J. K. H. Johnstone, *The Bloomsbury Group: A Study of E. M. Forster, Lytton Strachey, Virginia Woolf, and Their Circle* [New York: Noonday Press, 1963], 82). Throughout her life Woolf envied and competed with the power of this sister (and sister's) art. See, for example, her Foreword to *Recent Paintings by Vanessa Bell* (London: Favil Press, 1930). On Lily's resemblance to Vanessa Bell, see Gayatri Chakravorty Spivak, "Unmaking and Making in *To the Lighthouse,*" in *Woman and Language in Literature and Society,* ed. Sally McConnell-Ginet, Ruth Borker, and Nelly Furman (New York: Praeger, 1980), 320–21; on Woolf's recurrent figuration of her relation to Vanessa as the difference between the verbal artist and the visual artist, see Jane Marcus, *Virginia Woolf and the Languages of Patriarchy* (Bloomington: Indiana University Press, 1987), chap. 7. By making the artist in *To the Lighthouse* a painter, Woolf simultaneously valorizes and appropriates the distinctive powers she attributed to painting.

7. On the special status of visual representation in Kleinian theory, see *The Image in Form: Selected Writings of Adrian Stokes,* ed. Richard Wollheim (New York: Harper & Row, 1972); "Concerning the Social Basis of Art: Donald Meltzer in a Dialogue with Adrian Stokes," in *The Critical Writings of Adrian Stokes,* vol. 3, *1955–1967* (London: Thames and Hudson, 1978), 219–35; and Joan Riviere, "The Inner World in Ibsen's Master-Builder," in *New Directions in Psycho-Analysis: The Significance of Infant Conflict in the Pattern of Adult Behavior,* ed. Melanie Klein, Paula Heimann, and R. E. Money-Kyrle (New York: Basic Books, 1955), 173–80.

8. Melanie Klein, "Infantile Anxiety-Situations Reflected in a Work of Art and in the Creative Impulse," in *Love, Guilt, and Reparation and Other Works, 1921–1945* (New York: Dell, 1975), 215–16. In view of the biographical link between Lily Briscoe and Vanessa Bell, it is interesting to note Frances Spalding's claim in *Vanessa Bell* (New York: Ticknor and Fields, 1983) that "Kleinian analysts would discover a cause for this [Vanessa's deep-rooted love of painting] in her relationship with her mother. If, as the facts of Julia's life suggest, she was obliged to curtail her intimacy with her children after the first few months of their life, then Vanessa's subsequent turning to art may have grown out of a need to repair a sense of loss, to reconstruct that sense of oneness with the world experienced by infants at the breast" (19).

9. On the evolution of object relations theory out of Klein's revision of Freud, see Harry Guntrip, *Personality Structure and Human Interaction* (New York: International Universities Press, 1961); Jay R. Greenberg and Stephen A. Mitchell, *Object Relations in Psychoanalytic Theory* (Cambridge, Mass.: Harvard University Press, 1983); Judith M. Hughes, *Reshaping the Psychoanalytic Domain: The Work of Melanie Klein, W. R. D. Fairbairn, and D. W. Winnicott* (Berkeley and Los Angeles: University of California Press, 1989); and D. W. Winnicott, "A Personal View of the Kleinian Contribution," in *The Maturational Processes and the Facilitating Environment* (London: Hogarth Press, 1965), 171–78.

10. D. W. Winnicott, "Transitional Objects and Transitional Phenomena," in *Playing and Reality* (Harmondsworth, Middlesex: Penguin Books, 1971), 6. See also "The Location of Cultural Experience," in *Playing and Reality,* 112–21.

11. Winnicott, "The Place Where We Live," in *Playing and Reality,* 124.

12. Winnicott, "The Location of Cultural Experience," 112.

13. Joanna Field [Marion Milner], *On Not Being Able to Paint* (New York: International Universities Press, 1957), 11, 14. For a study of the privileging of space in object relations, see Jessica Benjamin, "A Desire of One's Own: Psycho-analytic Feminism and Intersubjective Space," in *Feminist Studies/Critical Studies,* ed. Teresa de Lauretis (Bloomington: Indiana University Press, 1986), 78–101; on the contribution of object relations theory to visual aesthetics, see Peter Fuller, *Art and Psychoanalysis* (London: Writers and Readers, 1980), especially the Preface and "The Rise of Modernism and the Infant-Mother Relationship."

14. Field [Milner], *On Not Being Able to Paint,* 13, 24.

15. Nancy Chodorow, *The Reproduction of Mothering: Psychoanalysis and the Sociology of Gender* (Berkeley and Los Angeles: University of California Press, 1978), 110. For different accounts of the impact of the mother-daughter sym-biosis, see Jane Flax, "The Conflict between Nurturance and Autonomy in

Mother-Daughter Relationships and within Feminism," *Feminist Studies* 4, no. 2 (1978): 171–89; Dorothy Dinnerstein, *The Mermaid and the Minotaur: Sexual Arrangements and Human Malaise* (New York: Harper & Row, 1977); and Carol Gilligan, *In a Different Voice: Psychological Theory and Women's Development* (Cambridge, Mass.: Harvard University Press, 1982). In direct opposition to Chodorow, Robert J. Stoller uses object relations theory to argue that the problems of separation and "dis-identification" from the mother belong distinctively to the son. See *Sex and Gender,* vol. 2 (New York: Jason Aronson, 1976).

16. On twentieth-century feminist revisions of the *Künstlerroman,* see Susan Gubar, "The Birth of the Artist as Heroine: (Re)production, the *Künstlerroman* Tradition, and the Fiction of Katherine Mansfield," in *The Representation of Women in Fiction,* ed. Carolyn G. Heilbrun and Margaret R. Higgonet (Baltimore: Johns Hopkins University Press, 1983), 19–59.

17. Roger Fry, "Some Questions in Aesthetics," *Transformations* (New York: Brentano's, 1926), 19–20. On the relation between Woolf's aesthetic and Fry's, see John Hawley Roberts, "'Vision and Design' in Virginia Woolf," *PMLA* 61, no. 3 (September 1946): 835–47; Thomas B. Matro, "Only Relations: Vision and Achievement in *To the Lighthouse,*" *PMLA* 99, no. 2 (March 1984): 212–24; and Rosenman, *The Invisible Presence,* chap. 5. Matro points out that it would be a mistake to overstate the distinction between formal relations and human relations in Fry's theory, since Fry intermittently voices expressionist as well as formalist criteria of art. Nevertheless, Fry dismisses the role of infantile experience in art, even in his posthumously published *Last Lectures* (1939), where he first expresses some interest in a psychoanalytic theory of art. The notion that the spatial arena of painting reproduces early experiences of separation would have been anathema to him.

18. Roger Fry, *Cézanne* (New York: Macmillan, 1927), 37–38.

19. Fry, "Some Questions in Aesthetics," 3, 8.

20. Although it seems contradictory for Woolf to use Freud to criticize Fry, since she also uses Fry to criticize Freud, her alliance with Fry always left room for disagreements about form. In the same letter to Fry in which she expresses her enthusiasm about his critique of Freud, she explains that "form in fiction . . . is emotion put into the right relations; and has nothing to do with form as used of painting" (22 September 1924, *The Letters of Virginia Woolf,* ed. Nigel Nicolson and Joanne Trautman, 6 vols. [New York: Harcourt Brace Jovanovich, 1975–80], 3:133).

21. "In a world ordered by sexual imbalance," Laura Mulvey explains, "pleasure in looking has been split between active/male and passive/female" ("Visual Pleasure and Narrative Cinema," *Screen* 16, no. 3 [Autumn 1975]: 7). Mulvey analyzes what she calls the "fetishistic scopophilia" of the male gaze in film, which "builds up the physical beauty of the object [woman], transforming it into something satisfying in itself" as a way of neutralizing the anxiety produced by the image of woman, reminder of castration (14). Mrs. Ramsay, dyadically fused with James, would be a particularly reassuring image to the chaste and cautious Mr. Bankes.

22. The reference to the tombs of kings is qualified by a pervasive pattern associating textuality with maternal death. For example, the poetry of the self-

contained Augustus Carmichael, which Lily imagines "said something about death; . . . very little about love," flourishes during the First World War, whose devastations are rendered synechdocally by Mrs. Ramsay's death (290).

23. In "Mirror-role of Mother and Family in Child Development" (*Playing and Reality*), Winnicott insists on the importance of seeing oneself mirrored in the mother's face. Seeing is constitutive of subjectivity in object relations theory (as language is constitutive of a different subjectivity in Lacan). Winnicott does not gender the relation to the mother's face (although all the examples in the essay concern women); Woolf, however, suggests that the daughter's creativity is enduringly embedded in the mother's (recollected) gaze.

24. Woolf, "A Sketch of the Past," 81.

25. In "'The Deceptiveness of Beauty': Mother Love and Mother Hate in *To the Lighthouse*" (*Twentieth-Century Literature* 23, no. 3 [October 1977]: 345–76), Jane Lilienfield details the stages of mourning Lily works through in her painting. For other accounts of the novel's elegiac features, see Gillian Beer, "Hume, Stephen, and Elegy in *To the Lighthouse*," *Essays in Criticism* 34, no. 1 (January 1984): 33–55; and Joan Lidoff, "Virginia Woolf's Feminine Sentence: The Mother-Daughter World of *To the Lighthouse*," *Literature and Psychology* 32, no. 3 (1986): 43–59.

26. In his Oedipal reconstruction of the past in "The Lighthouse," James literally elides this scene by imagining that Mrs. Ramsay, in response to her husband's demand, had "gone away and left him [James] there, impotent, ridiculous, sitting on the floor grasping a pair of scissors" (278). In "The Window," however, Mrs. Ramsay does not leave James for her husband; James is taken to bed by a nurse and Mrs. Ramsay enjoys her orgasmic communion with the lighthouse beam before she joins her husband. Although James does not himself observe his mother's solitary scene, its omission from his narrative is not innocent, for it reiterates Freud's erasure of maternal subjectivity from the Oedipal exchanges between father and son.

27. On the relation between Lily's brushstrokes and Mrs. Ramsay's solitary scene, see Gubar, "The Birth of the Artist as Heroine," 47–48.

28. For some representative readings of Lily's painting as an androgynous work of art, see Ralph Freedman, *The Lyrical Novel: Studies in Hermann Hesse, André Gide, and Virginia Woolf* (Princeton, N.J.: Princeton University Press, 1963), 226–43; Alice van Buren Kelley, *The Novels of Virginia Woolf: Fact and Vision* (Chicago: University of Chicago Press, 1973), 114–43; and Nancy Topping Bazin, *Virginia Woolf and the Androgynous Vision* (New Brunswick, N.J.: Rutgers University Press, 1973), especially 45–46. For a contrary reading that instead sees men as Lily's instruments, see Spivak, "Unmaking and Making in *To the Lighthouse*," 323–24.

29. Winnicott, "The Location of Cultural Experience," 115.

30. Ibid., 119.

Chapter 5

1. Virginia Woolf, *A Room of One's Own* (New York: Harcourt, Brace & World, 1929), 83; hereafter cited in the text.

2. Woolf, *To the Lighthouse* (New York: Harcourt, Brace & World, 1927), 60, 297.

3. Critics have almost uniformly followed Woolf's account of her career: "What has happened of course is that after abstaining from the novel of fact all these years—since 1919—& N[ight]. & D[ay]. indeed, I find myself infinitely delighting in facts for a change, & in possession of quantities beyond counting: though I feel now & then the tug to vision, but resist it. This is the true line, I am sure, after The Waves" (2 November 1932, *The Diary of Virginia Woolf,* ed. Anne Olivier Bell, 5 vols. [New York: Harcourt Brace Jovanovich, 1977–84], 4:129). For a comprehensive study of the historical issues structuring Woolf's career in general, and the discursive texts in particular, see Alex Zwerdling, *Virginia Woolf and the Real World* (Berkeley and Los Angeles: University of California Press, 1986), especially chaps. 8 and 9. Rachel Blau DuPlessis offers a different interpretation of the shape of Woolf's career as a shift from the critique of the romantic plot in the novels of the 1920s to the exploration of "postromantic relations" through multiple protagonists in the fiction beginning with *The Waves* (see *Writing Beyond the Ending: Narrative Strategies of Twentieth Century Women Writers* [Bloomington: Indiana University Press, 1986], chaps. 4 and 10).

4. Woolf frequently associates the ego with the phallus, for example, in this comment to Ethel Smyth: "[T]he state of reading consists in the complete elimination of the *ego;* and it's the ego that erects itself like another part of the body I dont dare to name" (Woolf to Smyth, 29 July 1934, *The Letters of Virginia Woolf,* ed. Nigel Nicolson and Joanne Trautman, 6 vols. [New York: Harcourt Brace Jovanovich, 1975–80], 5:319). Nelly Furman distinguishes between Mr. A's "I"—which represents "an individual psychological and historical being" that, in the context of *Room,* is "a specifically gender-marked male subject," an ego—and the explicitly fictive and depersonalized female "I" that the narrator assumes and that designates "a convenient term for somebody who has no real being" ("Textual Feminism," in *Women and Language in Literature and Society,* ed. Sally McConnell-Ginet, Ruth Borker, and Nelly Furman [New York: Praeger, 1980], 50–51; and see "*A Room of One's Own:* Reading Absence," in *Women's Language and Style,* ed. Douglas Butturff and Edmund L. Epstein [Akron, Ohio: University of Akron Press, 1978], especially 99–105). In her chapter on Woolf in *Crossing the Double-Cross: The Practice of Feminist Criticism* ([Chapel Hill: University of North Carolina Press, 1986], 89–114), Elizabeth A. Meese elaborates on Furman's comments to outline a theory of the fictive "I" in Woolf's feminist discourse. In *Virginia Woolf and the Problem of the Subject* (New Brunswick, N.J.: Rutgers University Press, 1987), Makiko Minow-Pinkney argues that Woolf's feminism anticipates a postmodern deconstruction of the subject.

5. Woolf anticipates (and corrobates) the argument first put forth by Kate Millett in *Sexual Politics* (Garden City, N.Y.: Doubleday, 1970), and elaborated by Sandra M. Gilbert and Susan Gubar in *No Man's Land: The Place of the Woman Writer in the Twentieth Century,* vol. 1, *The War of the Words* (New Haven, Conn.: Yale University Press, 1988), about the impact of the suffrage movement on masculine discourse in the early twentieth century. For a broader argument about the impact of egalitarian political discourse on the theorization of gender and sexuality, see Thomas Laqueur, "Orgasm, Generation, and the Politics of Reproductive Biology," *Representations* 14 (Spring 1986): 1–41.

6. J. J. Bachofen, *Myth, Religion, and Mother Right,* trans. Ralph Manheim (1861; Princeton, N.J.: Princeton University Press, 1973), 56; and see Freud, "Femininity," *The Standard Edition of the Complete Psychological Works of Sigmund Freud,* trans. and ed. James Strachey, 24 vols. (London: Hogarth Press, 1953–66; New York: Macmillan; 1953–74), 22:133; hereafter the *Standard Edition* will be cited as *SE.* In a text contemporary with "Femininity" and indebted to Bachofen, Helen Diner explains: "All mother goddesses spin and weave. In their concealed workshops, they weave veins, fibers, and nerve strands into the miraculous substance of the live body. Everything that is comes out of them" (*Mothers and Amazons: The First Feminine History of Culture,* ed. and trans. John Philip Lundin [New York: Julian Press, 1965], 22). In "Unmaking and Making in *To the Lighthouse*" (in *Women and Language in Literature and Society*), Gayatri Chakravorty Spivak argues that Woolf's novel reverses the values Freud assigns the phallus and (in Spivak's words) "the workshop of the womb" (324). For a brilliant reading of Arachne as a figure of the woman writer, see Nancy K. Miller, "Arachnologies: The Woman, the Text, and the Critic," in *The Poetics of Gender,* ed. Nancy K. Miller (New York: Columbia University Press, 1986), 270–95. Woolf's preoccupation with weaving and knitting as feminine figures of textuality (Mrs. Ramsay's knitting is an outstanding example) is reflected in the titles of some germinal essays on her poetics: for example, Erich Auerbach, "The Brown Stocking," in *Mimesis: The Representation of Reality in Western Literature,* trans. Willard R. Trask (Princeton, N.J.: Princeton University Press, 1953), 525–53; and Geoffrey Hartman, "Virginia's Web," in *Beyond Formalism: Literary Essays, 1958–1970* (New Haven, Conn.: Yale University Press, 1970), 71–84.

7. As a text that theorizes the practice of many of her contemporaries, *Room* is a central document in the shift that Sandra M. Gilbert and Susan Gubar disclose from phallic to maternal metaphors of literary creativity in the early twentieth century. See Gubar, "The Birth of the Artist as Heroine: (Re)production, the *Künstlerroman* Tradition, and the Fiction of Katherine Mansfield," in *The Representation of Women in Fiction,* ed. Carolyn G. Heilbrun and Margaret R. Higgonet (Baltimore: Johns Hopkins University Press, 1983), 25–26; and Gilbert, "Potent Griselda: 'The Ladybird' and the Great Mother," in *D.H. Lawrence: A Centenary Consideration,* ed. Peter Balbert and Phillip L. Marcus (Ithaca, N.Y.: Cornell University Press, 1985), 130–61. For a comprehensive account of the differences between male and female uses of the childbirth metaphor, see Susan Stanford Friedman, "Creativity and the Childbirth Metaphor: Gender Difference in Literary Discourse," *Feminist Studies* 13, no. 1 (Spring 1987): 49–82. In *Virginia Woolf and the "Lust of Creation": A Psychological Exploration* (Albany: State University of New York Press, 1987), Shirley Panken traces the childbirth metaphor through Woolf's autobiographical texts.

8. The tension between the discourses of androgyny and maternity, both active discourses in the 1920s, is a much-debated feature of *Room.* Claims for androgyny have recently been revived by feminist scholars in American studies and French literary theory. For example, Carroll Smith-Rosenberg, in "The New Woman as Androgyne: Social Disorder and Gender Crisis, 1870–1936" (in *Disorderly Conduct: Visions of Gender in Victorian America* [Oxford: Oxford University Press, 1985], 245–96), distinguishes between the maternal discourse appropriated by the first generation of New Women and the androgynous ideal of

Woolf and her female contemporaries. *Room* suggests, however, that Woolf conflates the mother and the androgyne in ways that privilege the maternal. In *Sexual/Textual Politics: Feminist Literary Theory* ([London: Methuen, 1985], 1–18), Toril Moi endorses Woolf's concept of androgyny by reading it (incorrectly, I believe) through the lens of Julia Kristeva. For early arguments pro and con androgyny in Woolf, see Carolyn G. Heilbrun, "The Bloomsbury Group," in *Toward a Recognition of Androgyny* (New York: Harper & Row, 1973); and Elaine Showalter, "Virginia Woolf and the Flight into Androgyny," in *A Literature of Their Own: British Women Novelists from Brontë to Lessing* (Princeton, N.J.: Princeton University Press, 1977), 263–97.

9. See Harvena Richter, "Virginia Woolf and Mary Hamilton," *Virginia Woolf Miscellany* 24 (Spring 1985): 1; and Alice Fox, "Literary Allusion as Feminist Criticism in *A Room of One's Own,*" *Philological Quarterly* 63, no. 2 (Spring 1984): 145–61.

10. In "The Birth of the Artist as Heroine," Susan Gubar notes Marie Stopes's pseudonym and argues for a pervasive connection between the birth control movement and female modernism. However, Gubar paints a broad picture of changing attitudes toward women's role in reproduction (beginning in the middle of the eighteenth century in Germany and gathering momentum in England and America toward the end of the nineteenth century), whereas I wish to emphasize the politics of birth control in England in the 1920s, and the relation of these politics to a new emphasis within British feminism. On the intensification of the birth control movement in the 1920s, and on Marie Stopes's problematic role in this evolution, see Robert E. Dowse and John Peel, "The Politics of Birth Control," *Political Studies* 13, no. 2 (June 1965): 179–97; Jane Lewis, "The Ideology and Politics of Birth Control in Inter-War England," *Women's Studies International Quarterly* 2, no. 1 (1979): 33–48; and Richard Allen Soloway, *Birth Control and the Population Question in England, 1877–1930* (Chapel Hill: University of North Carolina Press, 1982).

11. On the new feminism, see Jane Lewis, "Beyond Suffrage: English Feminism in the 1920s," *Maryland Historian* 6, no. 1 (Spring 1975): 1–17; and Sheila Rowbotham, *A New World for Women* (London: Pluto Press, 1977).

12. "Certainly it was a shock (to women in particular with their illusions about education, and so on) to see the faces of our rulers in the light of the shell-fire. So ugly they looked—German, English, French—so stupid" (15). For a different interpretation of the effects of the First World War on women's attitudes toward masculinity, see Sandra M. Gilbert, "Soldier's Heart: Literary Men, Literary Women, and the Great War," *Signs* 8, no. 3 (Spring 1983): 422–50.

Woolf's willingness to consider female bonding as a legitimate response to the postwar masculinization of culture had changed dramatically in the four years since the publication of *Mrs. Dalloway.* The obvious cause was Woolf's relationship with Vita Sackville-West, which had begun in 1925, after the completion of *Mrs. Dalloway,* and lasted through 1929. For Woolf's representation of this relationship in *Orlando,* published the year before *Room,* see Sherron E. Knopp, "'If I Saw You Would You Kiss Me?' Sapphism and the Subversiveness of Virginia Woolf's *Orlando,*" *PMLA* 103, no. 1 (January 1988): 24–34. For the broader context of the lesbian culture and literature that flourished in London and Paris in the 1920s, see Blanche Wiesen Cook, "'Women Alone Stir My Imagination': Lesbianism and the Cultural Tradition," *Signs* 4, no. 4 (Summer 1979): 718–39; Susan Gubar, "Sapphistries," *Signs* 10, no. 1 (Autumn 1984): 43–62; Esther Newton, "The Mythic Mannish Lesbian: Radclyffe Hall and the New Woman," *Signs* 9, no. 4 (Summer 1984): 557–75; Lilian Faderman, "Internalization and Rebellion" and "Writing Lesbian," in *Surpassing the Love of Men: Romantic Friendship and Love between Women from the Renaissance to the Present* (New York: William Morrow, 1981); Shari Benstock, *Women of the Left Bank* (Austin: University of Texas Press, 1986); and Ellen Bayuk Rosenman, "Sexual Identity and *A Room of One's Own:* 'Secret Economies' in Virginia Woolf's Feminist Discourse," *Signs* 14, no. 3 (Spring 1989): 634–50.

13. See Jane Marcus, "Sapphistry: Narration as Lesbian Seduction in *A Room of One's Own,*" in *Virginia Woolf and the Languages of Patriarchy* (Bloomington: Indiana University Press, 1987), 163–88. Marcus gives a thorough and illuminating account of Woolf's reaction to *The Well of Loneliness,* her role in the obscenity trial the novel provoked, and the reverberations of this trial in *Room.* The passage from *Well* (1928; New York: Simon and Schuster, 1974) to which the Fernham scene alludes occurs in a love scene between Mary and Stephen: "A star fell[,] . . . and something in the quality of Mary's youth, something terrible and ruthless as an unsheathed sword would leap out at such moments and stand between them" (308). Woolf's anxieties about *Room*'s lesbian innuendoes are suggested in her concern that she would be "attacked for a feminist and hinted at for a Sapphist" (23 October 1929, *Diary* 3:262). For Woolf's description of the obscenity trial and its presiding magistrate, see her diary entry of 10 November 1928, *Diary* 3:206–7. For an account of the role of homoerotic friendships among college women, see Martha Vicinus, "Women's Colleges: An Independent Intellectual Life," in *Independent Women: Work and Community for Single Women, 1850–1920* (Chicago: University of Chicago Press, 1985).

14. Parthenogenesis was a trope of feminist discourse in the 1920s and 1930s. In *Mothers and Amazons: The First Feminine History of Culture,* for example, Helen Diner reverses classical theories of embryology: "In the beginning, there was woman. She parthenogenetically severed activity from herself and made it into flagellum cilium: the male" (110; see n. 6 above). In *Herland* (1915; New York: Pantheon, 1979) Charlotte Perkins Gilman describes a utopian feminine community in which women reproduce parthenogenetically. In *Independent Women,* Martha Vicinus quotes Jane Harrison's description of her collaboration with Gilbert Murray: "Thoughts are self-begotten by some process of parthenogenesis, but there comes a moment when alone I cannot bring them to birth. . . . then, you want the mind of a man with its greater power of insulation" (153).

15. Woolf, *Three Guineas* (New York: Harcourt, Brace & World, 1938), 142; hereafter cited in the text.

16. Woolf's next sentence cites the phrase "natural and eternal law" (186n. 48). See also the description within the text of *Three Guineas* of the male need for replenishment, "or, as Herr Hitler puts it, the hero requiring recreation, or, as Signor Mussolini puts it, the wounded warrior requiring female dependents to bandage his wounds" (111). In her note to this description Woolf claims: "This particular definition of woman's task comes not from an Italian but from a German source. There are so many versions and all are so much alike that it seems unnecessary to verify each separately" (178n. 18). One source, however, is Hilary Newitt,

Women Must Choose: The Position of Women in Europe To-day (London: Victor Gollancz, 1937), who quotes an official Nazi propagandist, the president of the Catholic National Women's Council: "The life of man is based on struggle[;] . . . woman's task must be to heal his wounds" (130). Woolf copied this sentence into her reading notes on Newitt's text (Holograph Reading Notes, vol. 26, Berg Collection, New York Public Library).

17. These volumes of clippings form part of the twelve volumes of notes Woolf produced between these years from her reading of newspapers, magazines, biographies, and histories. For a thorough catalog and analysis of Woolf's reading notes, see *Virginia Woolf's Reading Notebooks,* ed. Brenda Silver (Princeton, N.J.: Princeton University Press, 1983). Silver notes that Woolf had to become "a systematic reader of her culture" to produce her sequel to *Room* (22).

18. *Times* (London), 16 December 1937, cited in *Reading Notebooks,* 299. Woerman's recourse to natural and eternal law typifies Nazi pronouncements on sexual difference. In his address to women at the Nuremberg Parteitag on 8 September 1934, for example, Hitler declares: "Man and woman must therefore mutually value and respect each other when they see that each performs the task which Nature and Providence have ordained." The speech is quoted extensively by Newitt in *Women Must Choose,* 40–41. Woolf insisted that "the woman question" was of central importance to the fascists. When Princess Bibesco, who solicited Woolf's support for an antifascist exhibition initiated by the Cambridge Anti-War Council, challenged this centrality by commenting sarcastically, "I am afraid that it had not occurred to me that in matters of ultimate importance even feminists cd. wish to segregate & label the sexes," Woolf replied, "What about Hitler?" (6 January 1935, *Diary* 4:273).

19. Paula Siber, *Die Frauenfrage und ihre Losung durch den Nazional-socialismus,* quoted (along with a score of quotations from official Nazi propaganda pamphlets written by women recruited to the cause between 1933 and 1934), in Newitt, *Women Must Choose,* 42. Hitler describes this "one single point[,] . . . the Child" in his speech at Nuremberg on 8 September 1934, also quoted in Newitt, *Women Must Choose,* 40. For similar claims, see Hitler's speech to Die Frauenschaft on 13 September 1936, quoted in George L. Mosse, *Nazi Culture: Intellectual, Cultural, and Social Life in the Third Reich* (New York: Grosset and Dunlap, 1966), 39. For a thorough account of the Nazi co-optation of the German women's movement, see Claudia Koonz, *Mothers in the Fatherland: Women, the Family, and Nazi Politics* (New York: St. Martin's Press, 1987), and the essays collected in *When Biology Became Destiny: Women in Weimar and Nazi Germany,* ed. Renate Bridenthal, Atina Grossmann, and Marion Kaplan (New York: Monthly Review Press, 1984).

20. Speech of Reich physician leader Dr. Wagner, announcing the award, quoted in Mosse, *Nazi Culture,* 45–46; trans. Salvator Attanasio. See also Tim Mason, "Women in Germany, 1925–40: Family, Welfare, and Work," *History Workshop* 1, no. 2 (Spring–Autumn, 1976): 74–113, 5–32. Joined to a program of marriage loans whose principal was reduced by 25 percent for each child born (contingent on the wife's withdrawal from the workplace and on neither partner being a Jew), to the closing of birth control centers, and to an increase in legal penalties for abortion, the ideology of motherhood had for the Nazi regime the multiple benefits of opening jobs for men in a severely depressed economy, pro-

moting racial purity, and insuring a large future generation of Nazis loyal to the Third Reich. Despite obvious political differences between England and Germany, certain common demographic and economic problems fostered a British version of maternal ideology. In *The Twilight of Parenthood* (London: Watts & Co., 1934), Enid Charles notes that the advances of birth control in England through the 1920s were slowed in the 1930s by concern over the declining birthrate.

21. *Times* (London), 12 August 1935, 9; and see *Three Guineas,* 186n. 48.

22. Hitler's speech is quoted in the *Sunday Times* (London), 13 September 1936. Woolf doesn't identify the quotation, presumably to emphasize its generic status. For similar claims see Hitler's speech at the Nuremberg Parteitag on 8 September 1934, in Newitt, *Women Must Choose.* Explaining that he has translated "very few extracts from the speeches made to women by Hitler: all such speeches run on the same lines and each adds little to those which have preceded it," Norman H. Baynes offers several more examples of this claim in *The Speeches of Adolf Hitler: April 1922–August 1939,* ed. and trans. Norman H. Baynes (London: Oxford University Press, 1942), 527–33. For a broader spectrum of Nazi pronouncements on sexual difference, see the documents collected under "The Ideal of Womanhood" in Mosse, *Nazi Culture,* 39–47. For the effects of Nazi ideology on British economic policy, see Winifred Holtby, *Women and a Changing Civilization* ([London: Bodley Head, 1934], 151–69), a text Woolf very likely had read.

23. Oswald Mosley, *The Greater Britain* (London: British Union of Fascists, 1931), 42. In a letter to Quentin Bell, 24 January 1934, Woolf writes: "They [the Labour party] think Mosley is getting supporters. If so, I shall emigrate" (*Letters* 5:273). Woolf's understanding of the mother's contamination by fascism divides her from the contemporaneous perspective of the Frankfurt school, which shares her identification of fascism and patriarchy but which tends to represent the mother as a positive site of alterity. See, for example, Max Horkheimer, "Authoritarianism and the Family," in *The Family: Its Function and Destiny,* ed. Ruth Nanda Anshen (New York: Harper & Brothers, 1949); and Erich Fromm, "The Significance of the Theory of Mother Right for Today," in *The Crisis of Psychoanalysis* (New York: Holt Rinehart Winston, 1970), 79–109, and "The Oedipus Complex and the Oedipus Myth," in *The Family.*

24. Louise Bernikow discusses the impact of fascism on the lesbian culture of the 1920s in *Among Women* (New York: Harmony Books, 1980), chap. 5.

25. The egg was a trope of the fascist discourse on gender roles. For example, Joseph Goebbels, the Nazi minister of propaganda, explains: "The mission of woman is to be beautiful and to bring children into the world. This is not at all as rude and unmodern as it sounds. The female bird pretties herself for her mate and hatches the eggs for him" (*Michael: Ein deutsches Schicksal in Tagebuchblattern* [1929]; quoted in Mosse, *Nazi Culture,* 41; trans. Salvator Attanasio). Hatching (as opposed to laying) the eggs characterizes the female role as auxiliary. Note also Hitler's rhetoric in his speech of 8 September 1934, which Woolf would have read in Newitt: "That which man sacrifices in the struggles of his people, woman sacrifices in the struggle to preserve the single cells of this people" (*Women Must Choose,* 40). The discussion of the breakfast egg in *Three Guineas* (140) offers a parable of the circumscription of maternity in the 1930s.

26. For a different evaluation of the prostitute as a metaphor of the woman writer's definition through the marketplace, see Catherine Gallagher, "George

Eliot and *Daniel Deronda:* The Prostitute and the Jewish Question," in *Sex, Politics, and Science in the Nineteenth-Century Novel,* ed. Ruth Bernard Yeazell (Baltimore: Johns Hopkins University Press, 1986), 39–62.

27. For the antithetical equation of maternity and chastity in fascist ideology, see Maria-Antoinetta Macciocchi, "Female Sexuality in Fascist Ideology," *Feminist Review* 1 (1979): 67–82. Macciocchi's analysis and its precursor, Wilhelm Reich's *The Mass Psychology of Fascism* (1933), provide an interesting comparison to *Three Guineas* by advocating the fulfillment of sexual desire (in contrast to the strict identification of sex and reproductive roles) as an antifascist, antipatriarchal act. *Three Guineas* envisages *no* form of heterosexuality as free from complicity with patriarchy.

28. The word "rank," which the *Oxford English Dictionary* defines as "grossly rich, heavy, or fertile," "having an offensively strong smell," and "lustful, licentious, in heat," emphasizes the association between the sexual female body and the garden. For the psychoanalytic association of the olfactory sense with female sexuality, see Jane Gallop's reading, in *The Daughter's Seduction: Feminism and Psychoanalysis* ([Ithaca, N.Y.: Cornell University Press, 1982], 27–30), of two footnotes in Freud's *Civilization and Its Discontents.* On the immediacy of the "odor di femina," the anxiety it produces, and the function of representation in stabilizing this anxiety, see Michèle Montrelay, "Inquiry into Femininity" (*m/f* 1 [1978]: 83–101); and the commentary on it by Gallop in *The Daughter's Seduction,* 27–30, and by Mary Jacobus in *Reading Woman: Essays in Feminist Criticism* (New York: Columbia University Press, 1986), 241–45.

29. See Janet Adelman, "'Man and Wife Is One Flesh': *Hamlet* and the Confrontation with Maternal Sexuality," in *Suffocating Mothers: Some Consequences of the Female Site of Origin* (forthcoming from Routledge). It is likely that Woolf would have had *Hamlet* on her mind while working on *Three Guineas.* John Gielgud's *Hamlet* played in London for 155 performances between 14 November 1934 and 23 March 1935. Woolf saw it on 23 January 1935. For her awareness of the extraordinary success the play was having, see her entry for 19 January 1935 in *Diary* 4:275. In her entry of 1 January 1935, Woolf notes the resurgence of her desire to write "On Being Despised," the current title for *Three Guineas* (see *Diary* 4:271).

30. Fascism confirmed an anxiety visible in Woolf's novels from the mid-1920s. Sally Seton's evolution into the complacent mother of "five great boys" and Mrs. Ramsay's dual role as her husband's antithesis and his agent suggest a latent recognition that the mother ultimately sustains, and is contained by, patriarchy, but in the 1920s Woolf highlights the moments of erotic and emotional autonomy.

31. Martha Vicinus's chapter in *Independent Women* on the suffrage movement offers a powerful and thorough account of the metaphorics and staging of hunger as spiritual resistance by the suffragettes. Vicinus also comments on the literalization of the body in the postsuffrage generation; although Woolf confines her discussion to attitudes toward sexuality, an analogous literalization of appetite is suggested by *Room.* Woolf's familiarity with the emancipation discourse on hunger is obvious in her extensive discussion, in the University of Sussex Library typescript draft of *Room,* of Florence Nightingale's *Cassandra,* first published in 1928 as an appendix to Ray Strachey's *The Cause: A Short History of the Women's*

Movement in Great Britain (1928; London: Virago, 1978). The following passage of Nightingale's text typifies this discourse: "To have no food for our heads, no food for our hearts, no food for our activity, is that nothing? If we have no food for the body, how we do cry out, how all the world hears of it, how all the newspapers talk of it, with a paragraph headed in great capital letters, DEATH FROM STARVATION! But suppose we were to put a paragraph in the 'Times,' *Death of Thought from Starvation,* or *Death of Moral Activity from Starvation,* how people would stare, how they would laugh and wonder! One would think we had no heads or hearts, by the indifference of the public towards them. Our bodies are the only things of any consequence" (407–8). In *The Female Malady: Women, Madness, and English Culture, 1830–1980* (New York: Pantheon, 1985), Elaine Showalter interprets the upsurge of anorexia nervosa among women in the late nineteenth century (the illness was named in 1873) as a form of cultural protest. See also Joan Jacobs Brumberg, *Fasting Girls: A Social and Cultural History of Anorexia Nervosa* (Cambridge, Mass.: Harvard University Press, 1987).

32. In *Literary Women* (Garden City, N.Y.: Doubleday, 1977), Ellen Moers describes as a defining feature of female modernism the shift from the courtship narrative to the mother-daughter narrative produced by Woolf, Cather, Stein, Colette, and Mansfield. For an account of the historical pressures shaping the emergence of the mother-daughter narrative in the early twentieth century, see Marianne Hirsch, *Unspeakable Plots* (Bloomington: Indiana University Press, 1989). In "The Domestic Politics of *To the Lighthouse*," in *Virginia Woolf and the Real World,* Zwerdling describes the evolution among women in the postwar decade of nostalgia for the Victorian past that feminism had contributed to bringing to a close. See also Jane Lilienfeld, "Reentering Paradise: Cather, Colette, Woolf, and Their Mothers," in *The Lost Tradition: Mothers and Daughters in Literature,* ed. Cathy N. Davidson and E. M. Broner (New York: Frederick Ungar, 1980), 160–75. The emergence of the mother-daughter plot in the 1920s suggests links between narrative and history analogous to those which shaped the Oedipal plot of nineteenth-century fiction by men.

33. In "'Forward into the Past': The Complex Female Affiliation Complex" (in *Historical Studies and Literary Criticism,* ed. Jerome J. McGann [Madison: University of Wisconsin Press, 1985], 240–65), Sandra M. Gilbert and Susan Gubar argue persuasively, through readings of several of Woolf's essays on women writers, that Woolf *was* ambivalent toward her female precursors and that this ambivalence typifies the dilemma of the twentieth-century woman writer, who for the first time encounters an established literary matrilineage. However, I see in the various repressions and displacements of *Room* an attempt to protect the "complex female affiliation complex" from the more explosive narrative of hunger. Gilbert and Gubar record a culturally erased etymological source of the word "affiliation" given by the *American Heritage Dictionary:* the Indo-European *dhei,* "to suck." Woolf is complicit in this erasure. If Jane Marcus is correct that the source for Woolf's theoretical claim that "we think back through our mothers if we are women" is Colette's image in *My Mother's House* of a "chain of mutually sucking cats" (*Virginia Woolf and the Languages of Patriarchy,* 7), this transformation of nurture into literary geneology is simply a dramatic instance of the repression generally at work in Woolf's discourse on matrilineage. For a contemporaneous

interpretation of reading as eating, see James Strachey, "Some Unconscious Factors in Reading," *International Journal of Psycho-Analysis* 11 (July 1930): 322–30.

34. There is, of course, an objective basis for the sense of starvation at Fernham. "Starved but valiant young women" is Woolf's description of the Girton students to whom she delivered one of the papers on "Women and Fiction" that were published as *Room* (27 October 1928, *Diary* 3:200). Martha Vicinus claims that "Reminiscences from all of the colleges echo Virginia Woolf's comments about the appalling food at Newnham in the 1920s" (*Independent Women*, 130). It is revealing to compare the imagery in one of these reminiscences with that of *Room*, however. Joan Evans recalls: "Never in my life have I eaten so much reasty ham and over-salt salt beef, more wooden carrots and more tasteless milk puddings[,] . . . and there was a mysterious sweet that appeared on Sunday evenings, apparently made from the remains of other puddings stuck together with custard, that the whole College knew as the Ancient of Days" (quoted in Vicinus, *Independent Women*, 130–31). Woolf's imagination translates poor cooking into a distinctively maternal stinginess.

35. Woolf, *To the Lighthouse*, 79.

36. Defining patriarchal power in economic rather than erotic terms, *Room* anticipates recent feminist historians and anthropologists who find in the sexual division of labor, deepened in western Europe by the development of industrial capitalism, the primary source of women's devaluation. In *Room* Woolf uses the separation of spheres to explain women's inability to produce and to reproduce at the same time. In *Three Guineas* she challenges the need for that division, revising the amount of time required for exclusive mothering from five years per child in *Room* to "a fraction" of a lifetime, approximately two months per child, in *Three Guineas*. She also dares, in a footnote to *Three Guineas*, to report the "bold suggestion . . . that the occupation is not necessarily maternal, but should be shared by both parents" (186n. 47). For some overviews of recent feminist arguments about the separation of spheres and the contraction of feminine power and authority, see Michelle Zimbalist Rosaldo, "Woman, Culture, and Society: A Theoretical Overview," in *Woman, Culture, and Society*, ed. Michelle Zimbalist Rosaldo and Louise Lamphere (Stanford, Calif.: Stanford University Press, 1974), 17–42; Nancy Chodorow, "Mothering, Male Dominance, and Capitalism," in *Capitalist Patriarchy and the Case for Socialist Feminism*, ed. Zillah R. Eisenstein (New York: Monthly Review Press, 1979), 83–106; and Elizabeth Fox-Genovese, "Placing Women's History in History," *New Left Review* 133 (May–June 1982): 5–29.

37. See Robert Briffault, *The Mothers: The Matriarchal Theory of Social Origins* (1927; New York: Macmillan, 1931) which makes "mothercare" the focus of nostalgia for a matriarchal past.

38. The biographical background here is the legacy of twenty-five hundred pounds left to Virginia by her father's unmarried sister, Aunt Caroline Emelia Stephen (the "Nun"), who cared for Virginia in the critical period after her father's death and whose special bond with Virginia is evidenced by the contrast between this legacy and the one hundred pounds she left both Vanessa and Adrian. Woolf's letter to Clive Bell, 13 April 1909, suggests that she felt considerable guilt over this preferential treatment (*Letters* 1:391). In *Room*, however, she reconstructs

these facts as a fantasy solution to the economic constraints on motherhood. For Caroline Emelia's spiritual influence on her niece, see Jane Marcus, "The Niece of a Nun: Virginia Woolf, Caroline Stephen, and the Cloistered Imagination," in *Virginia Woolf: A Feminist Slant,* ed. Jane Marcus (Lincoln: University of Nebraska Press, 1983), 7–36.

39. For the importance of an independent income in freeing the writer from the need to cater to publishers and popular taste, see the chapters on "Class and Money" and "Virginia Woolf's Feminism in Historical Perspective" in Zwerdling, *Virginia Woolf and the Real World.* While in no way disputing Woolf's sense of the aesthetic benefits of economic autonomy, I want to foreground the context in which she dramatizes the inheritance in *Room.*

40. By "unconscious" I mean that rather than theorizing this fear, the text acts it out by repressing or magically assuaging a hunger that threatens to generate both rage and guilt. It would be easy to make a biographical argument about Woolf's own relationship to hunger. According to Leonard Woolf, "There was always something strange, something slightly irrational in [Virginia's] attitude toward food. It was extraordinarily difficult ever to get her to eat enough to keep her strong and well. . . . [T]here was . . . at the back of her mind or in the pit of her stomach a taboo against eating. Pervading her insanity generally there was always a sense of some guilt, the origin and exact nature of which I could never discover; but it was attached in some peculiar way particularly to food and eating" (*Beginning Again: An Autobiography of the Years 1911 to 1918* [New York: Harcourt, Brace & World, 1963], 162–63). Virginia's refusal to eat during her breakdowns, her conviction that the punitive voices she heard came from overeating (see, for example, her letter to Violet Dickinson, 22[?] September 1904, *Letters* 1:142–43), testify abundantly to her association of appetite and guilt. Although Leonard refrains from interpreting the "taboo" and guilt he repeatedly notes in Virginia's relationship to food, it seems plausible to connect them to an unconscious equation of hunger and oral rage. For evidence of Woolf's pervasive association of aggression and orality, see Panken, *Virginia Woolf and the "Lust of Creation."* In *All That Summer She Was Mad: Virginia Woolf, Female Victim of Male Medicine* (New York: Continuum, 1982), Stephen Trombley reports that Dr. Miyeko Kamiya, a Japanese psychiatrist planning a psychoanalytic study of Virginia Woolf, diagnosed Virginia as anorexic. Trombley interprets the anorexia as "a rejection of male sexuality" (63). *Room,* however, strongly suggests that Woolf located the question of hunger in the context of mothering. For a theorization of hunger's vicissitudes within this context, see Kim Chernin, *The Obsession: Reflections on the Tyranny of Slenderness* (New York: Harper & Row, 1981) and *The Hungry Self: Women, Eating, and Identity* (New York: Random House, 1985). Chernin's claim that eating disorders erupt among women most powerfully in periods of rapid cultural change, when the sense of the mother's inability to nurture is especially acute, helps contextualize the generational issues Woolf dramatizes in *Room.*

41. Woolf, 2, 8, and 9 December 1939, *Diary* 5:248–50. See also the entries for 17 December 1939, 9 February 1940, and 27 June 1940 (*Diary* 5:251–52, 265–66, 299). For a thorough analysis of Bloomsbury's pessimism in the 1930s as a critical factor in determining Woolf's response to Freud, see Alex

Zwerdling's chapter "Pacifism without Hope," in *Virginia Woolf and the Real World*.

42. Woolf, 11 November 1936, *Diary* 5:32. On 24 November, she notes: "Began 3Gs. yesterday. & liked it" (35). Although she had been preparing to write *Three Guineas* for years, she did not begin composing it until November 1936.

43. Albert Einstein and Sigmund Freud, *Why War?* (Paris: International Institute of Intellectual Cooperation, 1933), 11, 23.

44. Woolf writes gender similarly into a masculine exchange in a sentence she adapts from an earlier Freudian text on war, "Thoughts for the Times on War and Death" (1915), which was collected with *Why War?* and selections from *Civilisation and Its Discontents* (1929) in *Civilisation, War, and Death,* published by the Hogarth Press in 1939, and edited by John Rickman, one of the analysts Woolf met at Adrian's and Karin's dinner party. Freud writes in "Thoughts for the Times on War and Death": "Science herself has lost her passionless impartiality and makes weapons. . . . The anthropologist is driven to declare the opponent inferior and degenerate" (1). *Three Guineas* declares: "Science, it would seem, is not sexless; she is a man, a father, and infected too. Science, thus infected, produced measurements to order: the [female] brain was too small to be examined" (139). The echoes between these texts suggest Woolf had read the essays Rickman collected before the volume's publication. Leonard Woolf's involvement with the League of Nations makes it especially likely that she had seen *Why War?* by 1935, the date she assigns the fictive letter that elicits *Three Guineas,* and the year she devised the text's epistolary form and shifted its focus from misogyny to war. For Bloomsbury's investment in the League of Nations, see Alex Zwerdling, "Pacifism without Hope," *Virginia Woolf and the Real World,* especially 292–95; for the evolution of the form and focus of *Three Guineas,* see especially Woolf's diary entries from 15 October 1935 and 30 December 1935 (*Diary* 4:346–47, 361), and 3 January 1936 (*Diary* 5:3).

45. For a similar argument that "the father needs the daughter because she is a suitably diminished 'milk giver,' a miniaturized version of the mother whom patriarchal culture absolutely forbids him to desire," see Sandra M. Gilbert, "Life's Empty Pack: Notes toward a Literary Daughteronomy," *Critical Inquiry* 11, no. 3 (March 1985): 355–84.

46. Freud presents his fullest discussion of his shift from the seduction theory to a theory of infantile desire in *An Autobiographical Study* (1925). The Hogarth Press published James Strachey's translation of this text in 1935, the critical year in Woolf's formulation of the focus of *Three Guineas. An Autobiographical Study* offers the following account, particularly resonant in light of Woolf's own experiences of seduction: "[T]he majority of my patients reproduced from their childhood scenes in which they were sexually seduced by some grown-up person. With female patients the part of seducer was almost always assigned to their father. I believed these stories. . . . My confidence was strengthened by a few cases in which relations of this kind with a father, uncle, or older brother had continued up to an age at which memory was to be trusted. . . . When I had pulled myself together, I was able to draw the right conclusions from my discovery: namely, that the neurotic symptoms were not related directly to actual events but to wishful phantasies, and that as far as the neurosis was concerned psychical reality

was of more importance than material reality. . . . I had in fact stumbled for the first time upon the *Oedipus complex,* which was later to assume such an overwhelming importance." Seduction retained a minor role in the evolution of neurosis, Freud continues, "But the seducers turned out as a rule to have been older children" (*SE* 20:33–34).

For some reports of the controversies surrounding this altered explanation of paternal seduction, see Jeffrey Moussaieff Masson, *The Assault on Truth: Freud's Suppression of the Seduction Theory* (New York: Farrar, Strauss & Giroux, 1984); Judith Lewis Herman, with Lisa Hirschman, *Father-Daughter Incest* (Cambridge, Mass.: Harvard University Press, 1981); Christine Froula, "The Daughter's Seduction: Sexual Violence and Literary History," *Signs* 11, no. 4 (Summer 1986): 621–44; David Willbern, *"Filia Oedipi:* Father and Daughter in Freudian Theory," in *Daughters and Fathers,* ed. Linda Boose and Betty Sue Flowers (Baltimore: Johns Hopkins University Press, 1989), 75–96; and Sandra Gilbert, "Life's Empty Pack: Notes toward a Literary Daughteronomy." For the biographical context of Woolf's own experience(s) of seduction, see Louise A. DeSalvo, *Virginia Woolf: The Impact of Childhood Sexual Abuse on her Life and Work* (Boston: Beacon Press, 1989).

47. The context of French feminism, Jane Gallup argues in *The Daughter's Seduction,* enables us to see how desire drives a wedge between the father's penis and the phallus, disempowering the father as fully as the daughter; desire thus poses few theoretical or practical problems for the daughter. The Anglo-American tendency (apparent in Woolf) to censor or disavow female heterosexual desire appears puritanical from this perspective; from the Anglo-American perspective, the French disembedding of paternal desire from its economic and political supports appears naive. Woolf's anxiety about the daughter's desire should be seen in the larger cultural context of Freud's reception by British feminists in the 1930s. For example, Winifred Holtby in *Women and a Changing Civilization* (New York: Longmans, Green, 1935) holds "the whole force of the Freudian revelation" responsible for making women slaves of sexual desire, and therefore of men (161).

Chapter 6

1. Virginia Woolf, *Between the Acts* (1941; New York: Harcourt Brace Jovanovich, 1969), 199; hereafter cited in the text.

2. Freud introduces the concept of the death instinct (thanatos), which can be turned outward as aggression, in *Beyond the Pleasure Principle* [1920] (*The Standard Edition of the Complete Psychological Works of Sigmund Freud,* trans. and ed. James Strachey, 24 vols. [London: Hogarth Press, 1954–66; New York: Macmillan, 1953–74], 18:3–64; hereafter the *Standard Edition* will be cited as *SE*); his fullest discussion of the son's conflicting love for and rivalry with his father occurs in *Totem and Taboo* (*SE,* vol. 13); for the daughter's ambivalence toward the mother, see "Female Sexuality" (*SE,* vol. 21) and "Femininity" (*SE,* vol. 22).

3. Woolf, "A Sketch of the Past," in *Moments of Being: Unpublished Autobiographical Writings,* ed. Jeanne Schulkind (New York: Harcourt Brace Jovanovich, 1985), 108. The text is part of the seventy-seven-page typescript (dated 19 June 1941) discovered in 1980, which links the typescript and the

manuscript portions of "A Sketch of the Past"; it is included in the "Sketch" in the second edition of *Moments of Being,* 107–24.

4. In "Theater of War: Virginia Woolf's *Between the Acts,*" (in *Virginia Woolf: A Feminist Slant,* ed. Jane Marcus [Lincoln: University of Nebraska Press, 1983]), Sally Sears provides a particularly compelling account of this world's emptiness (although she explains it differently): "When the characters are not spectral they are mechanical, false, lifeless. . . . Silence, distance, isolation, remoteness, vacancy, incoherence, absence; 'disembodied voices,' 'bodiless eyes'; inaudible, broken, 'abortive' communications; pursuits of persons pursuing others (all in vain); ritualized gestures and unconsummated desires: these are the qualities, attributes, and activities that 'fill' the characters' world, shape their experience, reflect their spiritual state" (222).

5. Alex Zwerdling, *Virginia Woolf and the Real World* (Berkeley and Los Angeles: University of California Press, 1986), 308.

6. *The Letters of Virginia Woolf,* ed. Nigel Nicolson and Joanne Trautman, 6 vols. (New York: Harcourt Brace Jovanovich, 1975–80), 6:346. I am grateful to Gillian Beer for bringing this letter to my attention.

7. Paul Ricoeur offers the best summary of the "impressive number of hazardous hypotheses" in *Moses and Monotheism;* see *Freud and Philosophy: An Essay on Interpretation,* trans. Denis Savage (New Haven, Conn.: Yale University Press, 1970), 245–47. See also Marthe Robert, *From Oedipus to Moses: Freud's Jewish Identity,* trans. Ralph Manheim (Garden City, N.Y.: Anchor Press/Doubleday, 1976), chap. 5. For Freud's own doubts about the historical accuracy of his argument, see his letter to Arnold Zweig, November 1934, and his letter to Lou Salome, January 1935, cited in Ernest Jones, *The Life and Work of Sigmund Freud,* ed. and abr. Lionel Trilling and Steven Marcus (New York: Basic Books, 1961), 504–5.

8. Freud, *Totem and Taboo, SE* 13:149.

9. On the contest between the Mosaic father God and the goddesses worshipped among the Canaanites, see Raphael Patai, *The Hebrew Goddess* (New York: Ktav Publishing House, 1967); Steve Davies, "The Canaanite-Hebrew Goddess," in *The Book of the Goddess, Past and Present: An Introduction to Her Religion,* ed. Carl Olson (New York: Crossroad Press, 1983), 68–79; Bruno Bettelheim, *Symbolic Wounds: Puberty Rites and the Envious Male* (New York: Collier Books, 1962), 158–59; and Julia Kristeva, *Powers of Horror: An Essay on Abjection,* trans. Leon S. Roudiez (New York: Columbia University Press, 1982), chap. 4. In "The Meaning of Anxiety in Rabbinic Judaism" (in *Judaism and Psychoanalysis,* ed. Mortimer Ostow [New York: Ktav Publishing House, 1982], 77–109), Richard Rubenstein interprets the Jewish father God as a defense against the terrifying mother goddesses who threatened to return cosmos into chaos.

10. First presented by Anna Freud on her father's behalf at the Paris International Psycho-Analytical Congress, August 1938, "The Advance in Intellectuality" was subsequently published in the *Int. Z. Psychoan. Imago* 24, nos. 1–2 (1939): 6–9. It is to this section of *Moses and Monotheism* that most general psychoanalytic commentary refers. See, for example, Jonathan Culler, *On Deconstruction: Theory and Criticism after Structuralism* (Ithaca, N.Y.: Cornell University Press, 1982), 59.

11. Freud, *Moses and Monotheism: Three Essays, SE* 23:103; hereafter cited,

by page number only, in the text. On Freud's complex relationship to Judaism, see Robert, *From Oedipus to Moses;* Carl Schorske, "Politics and Patricide in Freud's Interpretation of Dreams," in *Fin-de-Siècle Vienna: Politics and Culture* (New York: Knopf, 1980); John Murray Cuddihy, *The Ordeal of Civility: Freud, Marx, Lévi-Strauss, and the Jewish Struggle with Modernity* (New York: Basic Books, 1974); Michael Rogin, "On the Jewish Question," *democracy* 3 (Spring 1983): 101–14; and *Judaism and Psychoanalysis,* ed. Ostow.

12. In his Introduction to *Myth, Religion, and Mother Right* (trans. Ralph Manheim [1861; Princeton, N.J.: Princeton University Press, 1973]), Bachofen declares: "The progress from the maternal to the paternal conception of man forms the most important turning point in the history of the relations between the sexes. . . . The mother's connection with the child is based on a material relationship, it is accessible to sense perception and remains always a natural truth. But the father as begetter presents an entirely different aspect. Standing in no visible relation to the child, he can never, even in the marital relation, cast off a certain fictive character" (109). Bachofen goes on, as does Freud, to discuss the depiction of the shift from maternal to paternal conceptions in the *Oresteia.* Bachofen, however, represents this shift as a far more ethically ambiguous progression.

13. In *Freud on Femininity and Faith* (Berkeley and Los Angeles: University of California Press, 1982), Judith van Herik argues persuasively that in Freud's oeuvre faith in a benign parental deity is associated with the psychic stance of femininity.

14. For a fuller account of Mary's inheritance from the cult of the mother goddess, see Freud, "Great Is Diana of the Ephesians" [1911], *SE,* vol. 12. In "Héréthique de l'amour" (1977; reprinted as "Stabat Mater," trans. Arthur Goldhammer, in *The Female Body in Western Culture: Contemporary Perspectives,* ed. Susan Rubin Suleiman [Cambridge, Mass.: Harvard University Press, 1986]), Julia Kristeva extends Freud's analysis of Mary's matriarchal lineage.

15. For an overview of the Frankfurt school's association of patriarchy and fascism in the 1930's, see Martin Jay, *The Dialectical Imagination: A History of the Frankfurt School and the Institute of Social Research, 1923–1950* (Boston: Little, Brown & Co., 1973). Erich Fromm recapitulates his own position in "The Significance of the Theory of Mother Right for Today" in *The Crisis of Psychoanalysis* (New York: Holt Rinehart Winston, 1970), 79–109. Freud's stance toward this perspective is revealed in his approval of the International Psychoanalytic Association's expulsion of Wilhelm Reich in 1934; in *The Mass Psychology of Fascism* (1933; trans. Theodore P. Wolfe [New York: Orgone Institute, 1946]) Reich had linked fascism with patriarchy.

16. Freud's reading of fascism is grounded in certain historical realities. In *The Von Richtofen Sisters: The Triumphant and the Tragic Modes of Life* (New York: Basic Books, 1974), Martin Green identifies Munich-Schwabing, the home of the matriarchalist group the Cosmic Circle, which took *"Mutterrecht"* as its ideological slogan, as the birthplace of Nazism, in its way "an anti-Apollonian and anti-patriarchal party" (374). In Green's account, the anti-Semitism of the Cosmic Circle was (as Freud asserts about the Nazis generally) an endorsement of paganism over Judeo-Christian monotheism. In *Powers of Horror,* Kristeva also reads fascism as a return of the repressed maternal body; see also Juliet Flower MacCannell, "Kristeva's Horror," *Semiotica* 62, nos. 3–4 (1986): 325–55; and

Alice Jardine, "Opaque Texts and Transparent Contexts: The Political Difference of Julia Kristeva," in *The Poetics of Gender,* ed. Nancy K. Miller (New York: Columbia University Press, 1986), 96–116. The opposite claim, powerfully argued by Klaus Theweleit in *Male Fantasies,* vol. 1, *Women, Floods, Bodies, History* (Minneapolis: University of Minnesota Press, 1987), is that fascism emerges from the fear of engulfment by the pre-Oedipal mother's body. According to Theweleit's reading, which parallels Rubenstein's interpretation of Judaism in "The Meaning of Anxiety in Rabbinic Judaism," Freud's response to fascism would be itself a symptom of fascism.

17. Evelyn Haller's argument in "Isis Unveiled: Virginia Woolf's Use of Egyptian Myth" (in *Virginia Woolf: A Feminist Slant*) reinforces the contrast I draw between Woolf and Freud. Haller does not discuss *Moses and Monotheism,* but one could easily add Judaism to her list of the unifying ideologies Woolf opposed: "Not only did Woolf side with Egypt against imperialism, Christianity, and patriarchy, but she conveyed this preference through her use of Egyptian myth—especially the figure of the subversive and triumphant Isis, about whom the final phase of paganism crystallized" (110). Although I am not always persuaded by Haller's evidence of Woolf's allusions to Isis, I find her general claims about the function of Egyptian mythology compelling.

18. Woolf's "most important" memory in "A Sketch of the Past" (1939–40), the memory which contains "the purest ecstasy" she "can conceive," is "of lying half asleep, half awake, in bed in the nursery at St Ives[,] . . . of hearing the waves breaking, one, two, one, two, and sending a splash of water over the beach; and then breaking, one, two, one, two, behind a yellow blind. . . . The feeling, as I describe it sometimes to myself, of lying in a grape and seeing through a film of semi-transparent yellow" (64–65). The womblike ambiance of this scene is repeated in her other primal memory "of red and purple flowers on a black ground—my mother's dress. . . . I was on her lap" (64). Contemporary with this reconstruction of the maternal past are entries in Woolf's diary about the experience of being "marooned" in the present, and about the ecstasy she felt when the river Ouse (in which she would drown herself five months later) burst its banks. See, for example, the entry for 5 November 1940, in which, echoing Genesis, she imagines a world returned blissfully to its uterine origins: "The haystack in the floods is of such incredible beauty. . . . When I look up I see all the marsh water. . . . Oh may the flood last for ever—a virgin lip; no bungalows; as it was in the beginning" (*The Diary of Virginia Woolf,* ed. Anne Olivier Bell, 5 vols. [New York: Harcourt Brace Jovanovich, 1977–84], 5:336). Woolf's diaries repeatedly associate water with mothering, as in the entry for 20 June 1928, which anticipates the language of *Between the Acts:* "Nessa is back. My earth is watered again. I go back to words of one syllable" (*Diary* 3:186).

19. For a thorough account of Bloomsbury's loss of faith in the League of Nations, see "Pacifism without Hope" in Zwerdling, *Virginia Woolf and the Real World.*

20. One of Woolf's earliest diary references to the novel reads: "[W]hy not Poyntzet Hall: a centre: all lit. discussed in connection with real little incongruous living humour; & anything that comes into my head; but 'I' rejected: 'We' substituted: to whom at the end there shall be an invocation?" (26 April 1938, *Diary* 5:135).

21. See Ellen Bayuk Rosenman, *The Invisible Presence: Virginia Woolf and the Mother-Daughter Relationship* (Baton Rouge: Louisiana State University Press, 1986) for a different reading of the empty feminine center as the "arena for a potentially renewing experience" (116). Despite our differing assessments of the novel's construction of the feminine past, Rosenman and I ultimately agree about the daughter's fragile access to that past.

22. Sohrab is Rustum's son in Arnold's *Sohrab and Rustum*. For a different reading of this allusion, see Judith L. Johnston, "The Remediable Flaw: Revisioning Cultural History in *Between the Acts*," in *Virginia Woolf and Bloomsbury: A Centenary Celebration*, ed. Jane Marcus (London: Macmillan, 1987; Bloomington: Indiana University Press, 1987), 253–77.

23. Critics have variously interpreted the Philomela and Procne allusions in the novel. In "Liberty, Sorority, Misogyny" (in *The Representation of Women in Fiction*, ed. Carolyn G. Heilbrun and Margaret R. Higgonet [Baltimore: Johns Hopkins University Press, 1983]), Jane Marcus argues that *Between the Acts* is "the modern version of a lost Greek play—Sophocles' play on the myth of Procne and Philomela" (67). She finds the myth's focus in the text, however, in Isa's failure to assume Procne's role in relation to the rape reported in the newspaper. Judith Johnston also sees Isa as a failed Procne and reads Bart's citation of Swinburne as a transfer of "his own feelings of guilt onto his sister, as if he is rebuking her for forgetting the sons lost in the First World War ("The Remediable Flaw," 271). In his notes to his edition of *Pointz Hall: The Earlier and Later Typescripts of "Between the Acts"* (New York: University Publications, 1983), Mitchell A. Leaska argues, as part of his interest in brother-sister incest in *Between the Acts*, that Bart's citation of Swinburne evokes not only Tereus but "the affectionate sibling in Philomela whose words to Procne he addresses to Lucy" (220). My own interpretation emphasizes Bart's critique of Lucy as mother.

24. J. Lemprière, *A Classical Dictionary*, 12th ed. (London: T. Cadell, 1823), 62. In "Liberty, Sorority, Misogyny," Marcus also describes the significance of Lemprière's account of Antaeus, but without commenting on the irony of its emergence at the moment—the only moment—Isa expresses concern about her daughter.

25. Although one critical line on the novel acclaims Mrs. Manresa as Woolf's first powerful representation of female heterosexuality, I see Manresa's parade of femininity as closer to the notion of masquerade presented by Joan Riviere in "Womanliness as a Masquerade" (*International Journal of Psycho-Analysis* 10 [1929]: 303–11) and elaborated by Jacques Lacan and Luce Irigaray. The notes to Luce Irigaray's *This Sex Which Is Not One* (trans. Catherine Porter with Carolyn Burke [Ithaca, N.Y.: Cornell University Press, 1985]) define masquerade as follows: "An alienated or false version of femininity arising from the woman's awareness of the man's desire for her to be his other, the masquerade permits woman to experience desire not in her own right but as the man's desire situates her" (220).

26. Maria DiBattista, in *Virginia Woolf's Major Novels: The Fables of Anon* ([New Haven, Conn.: Yale University Press, 1980], 231–34), and J. Hillis Miller, in *Fiction and Repetition: Seven English Novelists* ([Cambridge, Mass.: Harvard University Press, 1982], 224–28), also connect the lily pool to the portrait of the "lady," but they invoke a Nietzschean perspective to valorize these feminine imagi-

native loci and oppose them to the masculine realm of history, language, and truth. I see more complicity between the two domains.

27. I am grateful to Janet Adelman for pointing out to me that Woolf's "scraps, orts, and fragments" allude to Troilus's lament over Cressida's infidelity: "The bonds of heaven are slipped, dissolved, and loosed, / And with another knot, five-finger-tied, / The fractions of her faith, orts of her love, / The fragments, scraps, the bits, and greasy relics / Of her o'ereaten faith, are given to Diomed" (*Troilus and Cressida*, 5.2.153–57). As Adelman argues in "'This Is and Is Not Cressid': The Characterization of Cressida" (in *The (M)other Tongue: Essays in Feminist Psychoanalytic Interpretation,* ed. Shirley Nelson Garner, Claire Kahane, Madelon Sprengnether [Ithaca, N.Y.: Cornell University Press, 1985]), "Insofar as his [Troilus's] union with Cressida is an attempt to recapture the infantile fusion with a maternal figure, the rupture of the union threatens to soil the idea of the mother herself. And insofar as the mother is the source both of wholeness and of nourishment, her soilure threatens to dissolve a universe felt as coherent into fragmented bits of spoiled food" (132). By referring us to Shakespeare's passage, Woolf writes into her account of the fragmented present a notion of the faithless, and consequently spoiled, maternal body.

28. France fell to Germany June 1940, during the composition of Woolf's text and exactly a year after the fictional date she gives it. In her diary entry of 9 June 1940, Woolf writes: "What we dread (its no exaggeration) is the news that the French Govt. have left Paris" (*Diary* 5:293). The role of France as lost maternal origin is implied in the novel by the exiled Miss La Trobe, whose name suggests a French origin of feminine gender. In the historical context of the pageant, France replaces the sea as a figure of the mother, and Germany becomes a figure of the overriding father.

29. The actual source is Trevelyan's *History of England;* for the evolution of this reference within Woolf's manuscript, see Mitchell Leaska's notes to Lucy's comments in his edition of *Pointz Hall.* The account of prehistory is not in fact part of Trevelyan's text, but is Lucy's—that is, Woolf's—invention.

30. Woolf's diary entries during her work on the novel emphasize her own distress over the loss of an audience. "No audience. No echo. That's part of one's death" (9 June 1940, *Diary* 5:293). "No echo comes back. I have no surroundings. I have so little sense of a public that I forget about Roger coming or not coming out. Those familiar circumvolutions—those standards—which have for so many years given back an echo and so thickened my identity are all wide and wild as the desert now" (27 June 1940, *Diary* 5:299). In addition to her audience, Miss La Trobe has lost a more personal mirror: her actress-lover. The broken homosexual relationship in the background of this text both echoes and, through its offhand treatment, contrasts with *Mrs. Dalloway,* where Clarissa loses with Sally Seton a whole maternal universe.

31. "Thus the singer had his audience, but the audience was so little interested in his name that he never thought to give it. The audience was itself the singer; 'Terly, terlow' they sang; and 'By, by lullay' filling in the pauses, helping out with a chorus," Woolf writes in "Anon" about the earliest stirrings of human song, which she contrasts with the printed text that severs author from audience (*Twentieth-Century Literature* 25, nos. 3–4 [Fall/Winter 1979]: 380–420). Woolf's essay "The Narrow Bridge of Art" (1927) anticipates her final privileging of

drama as the most appropriate form of modern art (*Granite and Rainbow* [New York: Harcourt Brace Jovanovich, 1958], 11–23). In "Some Sources for *Between the Acts*" (*Virginia Woolf Miscellany*, no. 6 [Winter 1977]: 1–3), Jane Marcus discusses Woolf's interest in women's theater, pointing out that Miss La Trobe is modeled on Edith Craig, the daughter of Ellen Terry. Woolf's interest in the relational character of drama differentiates her from the mainstream of literary modernism.

32. In "The Loudspeaker and the Human Voice: Politics and the Form of *The Years*" (*Bulletin of the New York Public Library* 80, no. 2 [Winter 1977]: 252–75), Margaret Comstock argues persuasively that the decentered form of *The Years*, the novel which immediately precedes *Between the Acts*, derives from "aesthetic principles which are the opposite of fascist" (254). Through Miss La Trobe, Woolf explores the tension between the desire for aesthetic and social unity and the need for an aesthetic of disruption to counter fascistic demands for uniformity.

INDEX

Abraham, Karl, 9
Adelman, Janet, 94
Akhenaten, 111
Androgyny: in *A Room of One's Own*,
 87, 89, 156n. 8; in *Three Guineas*,
 92, 94; and *To the Lighthouse*,
 154n. 28
Anthropology: British, 4, 20, 25;
 cultural, 27; and domestic
 ideology, 141n. 96; exogamy, 21–
 22, 141n. 97; figured as female,
 21; and Freud, 20–29; and food
 taboos, 23–24, 29; Frazer on, 28;
 and gender, xvi, 4, 25, 29;
 Harrison on, 27–28, 142n. 107;
 and history, 4, 29; Jones on, 16,
 140n. 92; and kinship, 28;
 Malinowski on, 16, 26, 28–29;
 and matrilineage, 25–29; and
 psychoanalysis, 4, 20, 23, 25,
 133n. 10, 140n. 92; Richards on,
 28–29; social, 20, 133n. 10, 141
 n. 96; W. R. Smith on, 24–25,
 28–29; and totemism, 21–26;
 and V. Woolf, 4, 29

Arnold, Matthew, 117–18
Art: and Bloomsbury, 72; and ego
 boundaries, 75; Freud on, 18, 21;
 Fry on, 17–18, 27, 72–73, 153n.
 17; Harrison on, 27; and object
 relations, 72; as painting, xvii,
 16, 47, 58, 69–83, 154nn. 27–
 28; and psychoanalysis, 139n. 81;
 as therapy, 11. *See also* Object
 relations, and *To the Lighthouse*
Aruntas, 22, 24, 141n. 97
Atkinson, J. J., 22, 26, 28–29, 141n. 96
Austen, Jane, 2–3, 84–85, 96

Bachofen, Johann, 26, 86, 106, 112,
 142n. 104
Bell, Clive, 17–18
Beresford, J. D., 17, 19
Bildungsroman, xvi
Birth Control Movement, 88, 101,
 157n. 10
Bloomsbury: and aesthetics, 72;
 and psychoanalysis, 13, 15–17,
 137n. 51
Briffault, Robert, 26, 141–42n. 101

INDEX

Psychoanalysis (*cont.*)
13, 15–17, 137n. 51; British, xvi,
10, 13–14, 16–17; and
Cambridge University, 16, 20;
critics of, 15–16; cultural
emphasis of, 16; and fiction, xvi–
xviii, 15–16; and gender, 4, 20,
85; and history, xvi, xviii;
humanistic cast of, 16; and
imagination, 15; and literature,
15–17, 132n. 6; Malinowski on,
16; and myth, 6; narratives of, 3–
4; popularity of, 16. *See also under*
V. Woolf

Richards, Audrey I., 28–29
Rylands, George, 14

Scene making: in *Mrs. Dalloway,*
45; in *To the Lighthouse,* 2, 79;
and V. Woolf, 1–3
Seligman, Charles, 26
Sellin, Ernst, 111
Shakespearean allusions: in *Between
the Acts,* 171n. 27; in *Mrs.
Dalloway,* 31, 34, 39, 43, 144–
45n. 10; in *A Room of One's Own,*
94; in *To the Lighthouse,* 53–54;
in *Three Guineas,* 94
Sharpe, Ella Freeman, 16, 19
Silence: in *Between the Acts,* 2,
117–18; in *Mrs. Dalloway,* 31,
43; in *To the Lighthouse,* 58, 60,
66, 150n. 23; in *Three Guineas,*
104; in V. Woolf, 2, 13–14
Smith, Elliot, 26
Smith, William Robertson, 24–25,
28–29
Stephen, Adrian, 13, 16, 19–20,
68, 103
Stephen, Karin, 13, 16, 20, 103
Stephen, Leslie, 65
Strachey, Alix, 9, 14, 16–17
Strachey, James, 9, 13–17, 26–27
Strachey, Lytton, 13, 17, 27
Stopes, Marie, 88
Suffrage movement, 95–96, 155n.
5, 161–62n. 31

Tagore, Rabindranath, 70
Tansley, A. G., 15
Totemism: Frazer on, 23, 26, 141n.
97; Freud on, 21–25, 141n. 97;
W. R. Smith on, 24. See also
Totem and Taboo, 4, 21–29, 111–
12; and *Totemism and Exogamy,*
22–23
Trevelyan, George Otto, 123

Vaihinger, Hans, 15
Virgin Mary, 112–13, 168n. 14
Visual, the: in *Between the Acts,*
127; in Freud, 5, 7, 12; in Klein,
69, 152n. 7; and object relations,
152n. 13; and painting, xvii, 47,
58, 69–83; in *A Room of One's
Own,* 86; in *To the Lighthouse,* 47,
69, 71, 73, 75–77, 80–82

War: Freud on, 103; and marriage,
41; and masculinity, 41; in *Mrs.
Dalloway,* 34, 41–42; in *Three
Guineas,* 89, 91, 103–4; V. Woolf
on, 103, 165n. 44
Weaving: in Freud, 86–87, 106; in
V. Woolf, 156n. 6
Winnicott, D. W.: and object
relations, 70, 83; and visual
representation, 71
Woerman, Dr., 90
Woolf, Leonard, 14–17, 20, 110
Woolf, Virginia: alliance with art
critics, 17; and anthropology, 4,
29; and art, 127, 136n. 43, 151n.
6; and Clive Bell, 17–18;
biographical sources, 3, 14–15,
65, 133n. 8, 146–47n. 7, 149n.
15, 149n. 16, 151n. 4, 164n. 40,
169n. 18; career of, 155n. 3;
daughter's creativity in, 154n. 23;
and Edwardian precursors, xv;
evasion of anger in, 149n. 15;
and fascism, 90, 161n. 30; female
desire in, 166n. 47; as feminist
theorist, 19; and fiction, xv–xvi,
1–3, 17, 20; and Roger Fry, 17–
18, 72, 139n. 78, 153n. 17,

178

patriarchy in, 92, 94, 104, 106; private/public spheres in, 92–93; psychoanalysis in, 103–7; reproductive imagery in, 85, 92–93; and *A Room of One's Own,* 90–92, 106; seduction theory in, 106; Shakespearean allusions in, 94; silence in, 104; Society of Outsiders in, 104; the unconscious in, 103; and war, 89, 91, 103–4, 165n. 44;
—*To the Lighthouse:* and aesthetics, 82; and androgyny, 154n. 28; artist in, 57, 68–69, 75–76, 82; autobiographical sources in, 13, 45–46, 65, 78, 152n. 8; birth metaphor in, 76–77; culture in, 60–62, 72–73, 76; daughter's role in, 46–47, 57–67, 71, 73–75, 83; and eating, 85; ego boundaries in, xvii, 47, 68–71, 74–83; as elegy, 154n. 25; as family romance, xvii, 44; father-son conflict in, 46, 48, 50–51, 53, 62, 65–66, 147n. 8; female body imagery in, 61, 64; feminine gaze in, 80; infantile desire, 74–75, 81; interruption in, 50, 52–53; Kleinian challenge in, 47; language in, 57–58, 61, 63, 66, 69, 71, 73–78, 80; lighthouse in, 45, 47, 49, 50, 52, 54–55, 58–62; masculine gaze in, 73–74, 153n. 21; masculine identity in, 56–57; the maternal

in, 47, 49, 53–54, 56, 62–63, 65, 68; maternal loss in, 57, 64, 68–69, 75–78, 83; maternal memory in, 2, 46–47, 50–53, 60–61, 63, 66–67, 69, 73–75, 77–83, 85, 87; maternal sympathy in, 56–57; memory in, 1–2, 59, 61, 64; nature in, 60–62;
and *Mrs. Dalloway,* 45–46, 48, 50, 52–53, 60, 67; and object relations, 84; Oedipal narrative in, 20, 46, 48–49, 50–53, 58, 74–75, 82, 154n. 26; painting in, xvii, 47, 58, 69–83, 154nn. 27–28; paternal authority in, 48–49, 58–60, 62–67, 75, 80; paternal censorship in, 48, 50–52; paternal idealization in, 59, 64–65; phallic imagery in, 48, 73; philosophy in, 55–57, 148n. 13; and psychoanalysis, 47, 71–72, 75–76, 82, 146n. 4; repression in, 48, 50–52, 54–55, 59–60; scene making in, 2, 79; sensuality in, 82; sex roles in, 59; Shakespearean allusions in, 53–54; silence in, 58, 60, 66, 150n. 23; son's desire in, 49, 51; the visual in, 47, 69, 71, 73, 75–77, 80–82; water imagery in, 19;
—*The Voyage Out,* xvi, 2;
—*The Years,* 43, 126, 171n. 32

Zwerdling, Alex, 109